Broken Pieces and the God Who Mends Them is the poignant story of a mother's emotional and spiritual journey alongside her son as he battles with cannabis abuse and schizophrenia. Simonetta Carr writes powerfully and movingly as she chronicles her son's decline into mental illness, his change of character, her daily anxiety and guilt, and the effects of his illn⸺ f the family. The book is not onl⸺ rridors of doctors, psychiatrists, a ⸺ grimage through the Gospels. W ⸺ hristian friends, the author leads ⸺ path of how to come to terms with men ⸺ on many levels. This book is an essential resource and guide for anyone living with or around schizophrenia.

—**Jonathan Aitken**, Former UK Cabinet Minister; Author, *John Newton: From Disgrace to Amazing Grace*

The most honest and deeply moving Christian book I've read in a long time. Simonetta opens up her broken heart to show us the painful darkness and agonizing tragedy of serious mental illness. But she also opens the door of hope and help for other families by sharing the hard-won knowledge and resources she discovered both in the common grace of God and in the church of God. May this book transform her beloved son Jonathan's death into life for many others.

—**David Murray**, Professor of Old Testament and Practical Theology, Puritan Reformed Theological Seminary, Grand Rapids; Author, *Christians Get Depressed Too*

In *Broken Pieces and the God Who Mends Them*, Simonetta vulnerably lays open her heart and shares a story of love and loss, of suffering and redemption. She masterfully explores the brokenness of the mental health care system, the imperfections of our churches, the confusion of those who live in the grip of mental illness, and the shattered hearts of those who love them. Yet in the midst of the pain and brokenness, Simonetta keeps drawing us back to the God who mends—the God of grace. *Broken Pieces* is a definite must-read for those who love someone living with a serious mental illness.

> —**Bev Roozeboom**, Author, *A Day in the Life: A Glimpse into the Chaos—and Hope—of Families with Children Living in the Grip of Chronic Mental Health Disorders*; Class Instructor, National Alliance on Mental Illness

Simonetta Carr describes a painful journey that no parent ever wishes or expects to travel: the two years lasting from her son Jonathan's diagnosis of schizophrenia to his death. She tells the story with vulnerability, expressing the pain that she, her husband, her son Jonathan, and their other children experienced, as well as their fear, frustration, helplessness, lament, and desperate seeking after God. By beginning many chapters with entries from Jonathan's journal, she invites him to speak into the story as well. In this raw and emotional story, many parents who are on unexpected and unwanted journeys with their own children's mental illnesses will find a fellow traveler who tells her story and provides wisdom and even hope that God is faithful in the darkest circumstances.

> —**Mark Stephenson**, Director of Disability Concerns, Christian Reformed Church in North America

The church has historically not understood mental illness well or handled those who have mental illness with appropriate care and compassion. That is thankfully changing, but many Christians still suffer from common illnesses such as depression and from even rarer ones such as psychosis and schizophrenia. To that we can add the countless family members who suffer because of the havoc they see these things wreaking on the lives of those they love. Simonetta Carr is one such person, and here is a heartfelt and heartbreaking account of how her own family has been been affected by such and how she still found hope, even in the darkest hour, in the God who saves.

—**Carl Trueman**, Christian Theologian and Church Historian; Professor at Grove City College

The most inspiring story I've ever read. Here is a woman who has suffered the greatest pain a woman can be said to suffer—the loss of her child. And yet that loss has refined and beautified her in a way that leaves the beholder awestruck at the mercy and goodness of God. This is a story of how God's grace and love really can and do sustain his people through even the most agonizing times—even redeeming them to sanctify and glorify.

—**Brooke Ventura**, Assistant Editor, *Modern Reformation*

A Christian mother's moving, practical, courageous, and eloquent reflections on the emotional turmoil involved in caring for a son with schizophrenia. She takes the reader deep into wrestling with all the emotions and questions that are raised by such a devastating illness. This is by far the best book I have encountered that combines wise personal, medical, psychological, historical, and deeply theological insights on a controversial topic. A great resource for families, students, and professionals.

—**Richard Winter**, Psychotherapist; Professor Emeritus of Applied Theology and Counseling, Covenant Theological Seminary, St. Louis, Missouri

BROKEN PIECES

AND THE GOD
WHO MENDS THEM

BROKEN
PIECES

AND THE GOD
WHO MENDS THEM

SCHIZOPHRENIA
THROUGH A MOTHER'S EYES

SIMONETTA CARR

P&R
PUBLISHING
P.O. BOX 817 • PHILLIPSBURG • NEW JERSEY 08865-0817

To find resources, articles, and discussions related to this book, visit the author's website, www.cbfyr.com, and click on Other Works.

This book reflects the personal experience and research of its author. Any idea, suggestion, or advice contained here is not intended to replace the service of a qualified professional. The description of the personal experience that the author or the persons she has interviewed have encountered with any specific program or facility is purely informational and is not meant as a sanction, recommendation, or denunciation. The author and publisher disclaim responsibility for any liability, loss, or adverse effects, personal or otherwise, resulting directly or indirectly from the information contained in this book.

Scripture quotations are from the ESV® Bible (The Holy Bible, English Standard Version®), copyright © 2001 by Crossway, a publishing ministry of Good News Publishers. Used by permission. All rights reserved.

Quotations from *The Center Cannot Hold: My Journey Through Madness* by Elyn R. Saks are copyright © 2007 by Elyn R. Saks. Used by permission of Hachette Books.

Printed in the United States of America

Library of Congress Cataloging-in-Publication Data

Names: Carr, Simonetta, author.
Title: Broken pieces and the God who mends them : schizophrenia through a mother's eyes / Simonetta Carr.
Description: Phillipsburg : P&R Publishing, 2019.
Identifiers: LCCN 2018041740| ISBN 9781629953960 (pbk.) | ISBN 9781629953977 (epub) | ISBN 9781629953984 (mobi)
Subjects: LCSH: Caring--Religious aspects--Christianity. | Schizophrenics.
Classification: LCC BV4910.9 .C375 2019 | DDC 248.8/626--dc23
LC record available at https://lccn.loc.gov/2018041740

In memory of Jonathan Branch Carr

"He picks up my broken pieces."

Jonathan Carr

Contents

Foreword

For several years, my children had a Sunday school teacher who not only taught them Scripture and the Heidelberg Catechism but also wrote books on the lives of great Christians throughout history. Clear, always informed, and yet humble, Simonetta Carr is a gift to the broader church of Christ and to the particular church of which we were members. Our families became friends, and we enjoyed her generous Italian hospitality in her home.

But Simonetta's life was shattered. She will tell her own story in these pages. We have all suffered in various ways—yet there is nothing more disorienting and despairing than being totally helpless as you watch your own child suffer and go to his grave before you. Simonetta experienced a depth of horror—it cannot be put more delicately—that my wife and I struggled to imagine. Through it all, Simonetta clung tenaciously to God's promises, but it was—and is—a kind of brokenness that makes us uncomfortable. It brings us face-to-face with our own mortality and the reality that this is not the way things were meant to be. Her story gently directs us to that fork in the road where we either find our only rest in Christ and his redeeming love or turn our back on the promise in sheer desperation and resentment. We need stories like hers, in which the right path is taken—but only by God's gracious grip.

This is a story about a mother's fierce love for a son—which I have seen firsthand. It is also a story about a subject that churches, even still, are often ill-prepared to handle: mental illness—in this case, schizophrenia. It is amazing that in an age of medical advancement, when we do not hesitate to rush to the doctor for symptoms of cancer or respiratory illness, so many Christians treat mental diseases as spiritual problems that can be solved with more prayer, Bible reading, and imperatives to be more content. A big part of the problem, I think, is that we imbibe a modern dualism (one that's associated especially with the philosopher Descartes) between mind and body, and then confuse the mind with the soul. But the mind is not the soul. It is the brain, and the brain is an organ—like the lungs and liver. Mental illness is a medical problem, a physical ailment, that requires professional treatment. Like all illnesses, it certainly involves the soul and requires the spiritual remedies of preaching, sacrament, prayer, pastoral care, and fellowship of the saints. But we need to think of mental illness like cancer.

My wife and I saw the huge emotional, physical, and spiritual toll that this illness took on each member of Simonetta's family. Simonetta holds nothing back as she describes fighting against the bureaucracy of hospitals and insurance companies, bringing hope to her other children when she herself felt weary and weak, and loving someone who often pushed her away because of a wretched disease. Yet what comes through so clearly is God's sovereignty and the comfort of the gospel.

Because of these experiences, as well as the depth of her knowledge of God's Word, Simonetta is able to provide practical wisdom for our own daily struggles through life—including its crises. She teaches us how to become an advocate for those whom we love in a system that can seem cold and heartless at times. She also teaches us how a church can love and provide spiritual care to someone with schizophrenia (and, by extension, to those with other mental health disorders).

In all these ways, this book offers a treasure of truth, wisdom, and practical advice that is desperately needed by us all. Whether we are suffering ourselves, suffering because of a loved one, or just caring for brothers and sisters in crisis, Simonetta's hard-won insights will bring fresh perspective to the meaning of the apostle in 1 Corinthians 12:26: "If one member suffers, all suffer together; if one member is honored, all rejoice together." With Simonetta's help, we will learn better how to suffer and rejoice together.

Michael Horton

Introduction

This is not a "how-to" book. In fact, it might very well be a "how-not-to" book. Caring for someone with mental illness is always difficult. I venture to say this is particularly true when your loved one has schizophrenia, because the person you have known for so long is often gone, and you are left with a stranger no one has taught you how to understand and love.

Some have compared schizophrenia to Alzheimer's. In some ways, though, schizophrenia is more intense and devastating, because it doesn't just erase a personality—it substitutes it with another. This can be terrifying.

The first part of the book simply tells our experience, pieced together largely from emails and diaries that were written at the time of the events. It's the story of my slow attempts at discovering the new person my son had become and at finding a proper way to love him and guide him. It's written in first person and mostly in the present tense, as if I were reliving each event. The events are told in chronological order, and no dialogue is invented. I have, however, changed a few names in the text to protect the identity of people who have chosen to remain anonymous.

Most of the time, I didn't include my husband Tom's thoughts and feelings, because I can't speak for him. This doesn't mean he was absent. To the contrary, he suffered deeply and intensely at my side. Most decisions about the care of our son were made together, but I had to make many on the spur of the moment.

The second part of the book is based on important questions I have received in the few years after my son's death. I am not an expert in this field, and I have read only a few of the large number of books that are available on this subject. I am not endorsing every portion of the books that are quoted in this volume. Many of the suggestions in this second section are given by parents, psychiatrists, pastors, and people with schizophrenia who have come into my life at different times. I hope this book will be helpful in conjunction with other, similar books.

In addition, any suggestion I have included here should be adapted to the individual situation. One of the most important lessons that I learned through my experience is not to take any word of advice as a step-by-step guide—as tempting as that can be. Every case is unique, and what works in one instance may not work in another.

Our family is Christian, and our theology has played an essential part in this story, shaping our view of the events and informing our responses. With this book, I am hoping to encourage other parents and relatives of people living with schizophrenia and possibly with other mental illnesses—regardless of their religious convictions—as they keep reading, finding resources, and seeking help.

PART 1

THROUGH THE UNKNOWN

JONATHAN'S STORY

1

What's Happening?

I am a timid mere cat
always quick to flinch.
I am your first ever
eccentric snowflake.
(Jonathan Carr)

"Mom, is this a game?"

Jonathan is sitting at a computer in front of me. My husband Tom has gotten him out of bed early to work on college applications. His eyes are perplexed and searching.

"Do you want to play a game?" I ask, hoping it can be that simple.

"No. Is this a game?"

"Do you mean life?"

"Yes."

I muster up all the poise I can and give some theological explanation about how life can seem like a game but God is in perfect control. All the while, an ominous feeling grips my heart. He adds something, but it's hard to make sense of what he is saying.

"I don't understand this extension."

"What do you mean?"

"This extension of life."

I scramble to find another explanation. Life can be confusing at eighteen.

My heart is racing. Calmly, I go to another corner of the house, where I frantically phone my husband. Hearing the panic in my voice, he comes back from work.

"Your mother is worried. How can we help you?"

"I need help to understand this extension," he repeats.

It has been six months since Jonathan left for the University of California, Merced, with high hopes and aspirations—and only three months since he returned. In the past, he was always a top student. In high school he attended an internship program in a couple of hospitals and decided to study medicine. He won a small scholarship. His grades were good and his SAT scores high, especially in math. In spite of this, he didn't make it through the first semester. He failed two of his four courses and was asked to leave. At least, so he told us.

Naturally we were disappointed, but we encouraged him to try other avenues. At one point my husband spoke to him sternly, and Jonathan cried. It was disconcerting. None of our boys had ever cried at that age. If anything, they tried to act tough.

Is that the "extension" he is talking about? A new direction in life, new choices? His eyes look anguished and empty at the same time. What's happening?

Charming Boy

The fifth of eight children (seven boys and one girl), Jonathan has always been one of a kind. Right from his birth in Viterbo, Italy, he has impressed others with his alertness and cheerful disposition. His observant brown eyes, high-lighted by long eyelashes, have always seemed ready to take in the world—often sparkling with excitement or twinkling with perceptive humor.

Jonathan, at age 14, with three of his siblings at his oldest brother's wedding. From left to right: Angelo Kevin, Renaissance, Jonathan, and Raphael

The name Jonathan seemed only fitting for a boy who was born after our son David. We hoped they would become good friends, like David and Jonathan in the Bible. His middle name was Branch. We were into nature names at that time; we just didn't have the courage to use it as his first name.

As his brothers were, he was homeschooled from an early age. He could read and write at the age of four and grasped mathematical concepts before most children. He especially enjoyed converting years into days, hours, minutes, and seconds. His mind was always active—investigating, calculating, analyzing.

As he grew up, he started to challenge his friends with perplexing math problems, to write insightful poetry, to dispute scientific claims and social conventions, and to invent genial games. His brothers still remember his game of "Gabagoochee," which was set in medieval times and was, in their words, "the greatest game ever invented."

Analyzing sports was also a passion, and his predictions were usually correct. He chose to support the Detroit Lions, for no reason other than they were the underdogs. When it came to playing, he was not the best; but he refused to give up. His Little League team exploded into a roar of claps and cheers when he hit the ball for the first time after months of unsuccessful but determined attempts.

He was hopelessly forgetful, but we attributed it to his genius—he was our "absent-minded professor." Often quiet, he found his spark in social settings and charmed those around him with his irresistible smile.

He saw himself as very intelligent but meek. This he expressed, when he was thirteen, in a poem entitled "I Am."

I am a homing pigeon
always trying to get back home.
I am a luscious meatball
never biting back.
I am a wise old gramps
always wanting to give advice.
I am a sports fan's chair
always waiting for a score.

I am a slippery worm
never causing problems as I go down.
I am a timid mere cat
always quick to flinch.
I am your first ever
eccentric snowflake.

His depth of thought was evident in matters of religion. He was only six when we started to attend a small Reformed church. After years at a fairly typical evangelical megachurch, I found the level of quality and abundance of theological teachings refreshing. Still, I was not sure how the kids would react to this quiet atmosphere in which parents and children worshipped together and Sunday school lessons came from an unedited, unillustrated catechism written in the sixteenth century.

Jonathan told me immediately how much he liked it. "Finally I am learning something," he said. In the other church, as in various Vacation Bible Schools we had tried, the lessons for children revolved around the same Bible stories (Noah and the ark, David and Goliath, Joseph and his coat), without getting any further than the few superficial details that would keep the children's interest alive.

He took religion seriously. He studied the catechism and had a clear understanding of theology. When it was time to pray, while his brothers resorted to the usual "Dear Lord, thank you for this day, help us to have a good day," he developed a very methodical system of using the Lord's Prayer as a framework, expanding on the "give us this day our daily bread" clause.

At church, he liked to sit in the front pew, where he helped his younger siblings to find their place in the hymnal and sang along with them. At home, he was always ready to teach them.

He made a public profession of faith when he was twelve. At that time, he was probably the youngest child to do so at our church. When he told me that he wanted to do it, I spoke very soberly to him to make sure that he knew what he was doing.

At our church, as in most Reformed churches, new members take a public oath, stating their belief in the historical articles of the Christian faith and promising to uphold them, confessing Jesus Christ as their only Savior and their desire to live a godly life, and promising to submit to the correction of the church government (the pastors and elders) if they ever "become delinquent in doctrine or in life." It is, of course, a voluntary agreement. Jonathan assured me he was ready to do it. He was examined by the elders and demonstrated a deep understanding of Christian doctrines, even at his young age.

Signs of Change

Having brought up four boys before Jonathan, Tom and I were used to the turmoil of the teenage years, with their natural desire for independence that is often frustrated by fearful apprehensions. Our older sons were often more irritable and edgy. We thought it was the same for Jonathan, although we realized that he was much more sensitive than the others.

He seemed especially annoyed by anything that he couldn't consider fair or logical and had to reason things out within his mind. At sixteen, he wrote in a paper for his Sunday School class, "I can't understand why it is that important to make my bed—whether it is made or not, nothing will change. And for a while I just stopped unless it was convenient. However, I thought about things we have learned and finally I gave myself one good reason. My dad wants me to. God wants me to. God saved me from eternity in hell."

One sign of his independence was trying different things with his hair. The mohawk phase was the shortest, as it was almost impossible to maintain with curly hair. For a while, he let his hair grow as long as he could, ending up with a soft afro. Just before college, he decided to try dreadlocks. Since his hair was still too short for that look, he looked more like a porcupine.

Academically, he had no difficulty maintaining A-levels. He was extremely driven. At the end of his junior year in high school, while attending a summer internship aimed at introducing young people to medical careers, he was also playing football. The schedules conflicted, but he refused to give up either one. We had to take a trip at the same time as his internship, so he stayed home alone. Every morning, he woke up at 4 a.m., walked to the local high school, played football for a couple of hours, and then took a bus to the hospital, where he stayed until 5 p.m. When he returned home, he did a large amount of homework. We still don't know how he managed, but he wouldn't have it any other way.

His efforts were admirable but also perplexing. His drive seemed almost excessive, and, unlike his older brothers, he never wanted to ask for help. When we returned from our trip, we were appalled by the conditions of the house. With a large family, we were used to a mess, but what we found was extreme. He had left food to rot in various parts of the kitchen.

Teaching him to drive was also different from anything

I had experienced with my other sons. He didn't seem to concentrate on the road ahead and often stopped just inches away from objects or people. I usually returned home shocked and frazzled. "You take him from now on!" I would tell my husband. We were surprised when he passed the driving test.

During his senior year, Jonathan attended a program designed to help minorities to get into college and won a modest scholarship. He had several options. For example, he was admitted at West Point Military Academy, where pursuing a medical career would have been financially easier. He had some interviews with other prestigious colleges, as well. In the end, he chose to attend UC Merced, a fairly new college in a quiet and scenic place.

We continued to see changes in his behavior. He became quieter. A few times, he went out with friends at night without telling us. It was unusual, but due to his past behavior we continued to trust him. We were puzzled, however, to see him cry when my husband talked to him about his new habits, as he did during my husband's later talk about his slackness in contacting colleges.

As he prepared to leave, he gave his faithful, huge, raggedy teddy bear to his girlfriend Anna to keep while he was gone. Anna had been his girlfriend for almost two years. She was a very sweet and polite young girl from a good Christian family. Jonathan was extremely fond of her. We often joked that, out of all our children, he might end up marrying at the youngest age.

The church also gave him a formal farewell. As is customary when someone leaves the church, either to transfer to another church or to move away temporarily, we all prayed for him at the end of the Sunday service and finished with the song "In Christ Alone."

No power of hell, no scheme of man,
Can ever pluck me from His hand;
Till He returns or calls me home,
Here in the power of Christ I'll stand.[1]

As usual, our pastor, Rev. Michael Brown, handed him a book. What was unusual was the book itself. Normally, young people going to college received a book on apologetics. Jonathan received *Too Good to Be True*—a book by Michael Horton, who is also the assistant pastor of our church, on understanding suffering and following by faith the difficult paths God may lay before us.

Jonathan came back from Merced a few times. Each time he was disheveled, holding his laptop under his arm without a bag. We thought it was all part of his absentmindedness. The final visit was at Christmas. He told us he had failed two classes and been expelled from college.

We were shocked but tried to encourage him to move on. Tom suggested he appeal to the college.

"If you don't, you'll end up living at home and going to the local community college," Tom said. "Your mother thinks you should stay home."

Of course I did. I am Italian. I think all my kids should stay home forever.

"I want to stay home," he said. I was comforted, but it was definitely strange to hear from our free-spirited eighteen-year-old.

After the holidays, everyone resumed school. Jonathan

1. "In Christ Alone," words and music by Keith Getty & Stuart Townend copyright © 2002 thankyou music. Used with permission.

signed up for a couple of classes at Grossmont College and waited for the new semester to start. In the meantime, he spent most of his time in his room quietly.

That's when I received a shocking phone call from Pastor Brown. He had discovered that Jonathan had been smoking marijuana. Jonathan? Really? We had never suspected it. Not from him. And how had our pastor found out?

Church Discipline

Apparently, Jonathan had been smoking for some time and had convinced Anna to smoke with him. His "theological" grounds (which I discovered later) were that the Bible didn't expressly forbid marijuana, so it could be included in the same class as wine—a substance "to gladden the heart of man" (Ps. 104:15). Anna agreed to try it, but her mother caught her and, after hearing the explanation, decided to contact Pastor Brown to see whether this "doctrine" was taught in our church.

Initially we hoped this was just a passing fad—something he had tried at college and would easily put aside, especially since it had obviously affected his grades. For sure, he would listen to our pastor and stop.

Things were not so easy. Pastor Brown took him out for breakfast to talk to him, then discussed the matter with the elders. Since Jonathan seemed intent on continuing his habit, two elders talked to him separately. Finally, the church consistory (the administrative body of the elders and pastor) decided to ban him from the Lord's Table in order to impress on him the seriousness of his offense.

Church discipline has become a foreign concept in most contemporary churches. To outsiders, it has an ominous sound, reminiscent of the Inquisition or—at the very least—of narrow-minded intolerance. In reality, it is simply a system of pastoral correction for those who stray in doctrine or in life. It is exercised only on those who have previously agreed to submit to it, and it's done with the goal of guiding the individuals and leading them back to the obedience they have professed to desire.

In other words, if our church government determined that, in Jonathan's case, smoking marijuana was a sin, he could accept it, contest it (by appealing to the synod—a meeting of church leaders), or simply move to a church that allows such behavior.

Jonathan was visibly disturbed by the church's decision. Still, he didn't say much and was not ready to admit that smoking marijuana was a sin.

To me, as a Christian mother, the whole situation was devastating. What did it mean? Did he still have faith in Christ? Was it just a difference of opinion? Is marijuana usage really a sin?

Pastor Brown explained that, first of all, marijuana was still illegal, so Jonathan was breaking state laws—which, according to Romans 13, Christians are supposed to keep. The main issue, however, was Jonathan's desire to get high. "Using a drug to get high is the same thing as deliberately using alcohol to get drunk," Pastor Brown said. "It's the sin of drunkenness and does not produce the fruit of the Spirit. It does just the opposite." This was something that Jonathan was not willing to admit.

Just a few weeks later, Anna came to return Jonathan's teddy bear and break off their relationship, maybe as a result of her parents' suggestion. After she left, Jonathan stayed in his room. He told me what happened only a few days later, when I asked him why she had stopped coming over.

Within a month, Jonathan has now been expelled from school, been disciplined by the church, and lost his girlfriend. Emotionally, the last blow has probably been the hardest. He was deeply in love.

Depression and More

It's around this time that Jonathan tells me about his problems with his "life extension." By now he has sunk into a very recognizable depression. He spends most of the day, every day, in his room, playing chess online. Sometimes he sits in the living room with the TV on with no sound, not really watching. Other times he turns the volume up as high as he can and stands there without apparent emotion. Frequently my husband has to get up in the middle of the night in order to turn off the blaring TV downstairs.

He eats little and bathes even less. He stays up all night and sleeps during the day. He seems nervous, often bouncing his legs or tapping his hands on something.

I talk to Anna. She tells me she had noticed some changes in his behavior when he returned from college but thought it was just because he had been away for a while. She is sorry he is having problems and decides to take him out to lunch. Her parents had taken her to a Christian counselor, and she really likes him. Maybe she can suggest him to Jonathan.

I am thrilled. A few days later, Anna tells me that Jonathan is not the same person she knew. "He was pretty quiet," she says. "He definitely seems different. I don't know how to put my finger on it, but he seems a bit disconnected. I got the impression he was depressed, because all he had to say was that he doesn't do much of anything these days and doesn't get out much." He didn't respond to her suggestion to see a therapist.

We watch him carefully. He seems to be off drugs but still on another planet. It breaks my heart to see him this way. If I hug him, he hugs me back tight. If I talk to him, he thanks me. His sweet disposition makes me suffer even more. If he were rebellious, I could steel my heart. I am not sure whether he realizes he needs help, and that hurts me even more.

I feel lost. Sometimes I sit by him and say nothing. I am normally a very busy person, juggling a few tasks at the same time, but now I stop everything and sit in our back-yard with him, staring with him at the distance. If this were the sixties, I tell him, we could wear some colorful bands on our heads and look perfectly "groovy."

College starts, so we encourage him to attend his classes. He drives by himself, but we aren't sure whether he makes it to the college. Finally he stops going altogether. We ask him to cancel the classes, to salvage what is left of his academic record, but he doesn't. We try to find him some part-time jobs to make use of his time.

My friend Kris says that her husband Bill might be able to use him. Bill is a landscaper, and Jonathan has worked for him in the past. The physical work and fresh air may help. Jonathan works for a few days without putting in much effort. Then he never contacts Bill again—not even to pick up his pay.

Brian, an elder at our church and a manager at In-N-Out, tries to find Jonathan a job in one of their branches. It seems like a great opportunity—easy position, good pay. Brian tries to coach him on how to present himself and how to dress. Jonathan used to know this well. In the past, he went to many important college interviews. This time, he nods but never shows much interest. Finally, Brian sets up an interview.

"I am risking my reputation," Brian tells me. "I am recommending Jonathan, but he needs to be everything I know he can be."

Jonathan still has his struggling dreadlocks. In-N-Out cares a lot about appearance, so they have to go. I explain it to him, and he agrees to cut them off. Since they are not well done (they don't start close to the scalp), I conclude that a regular barber can do the job. I ask if he wants to make an appointment.

"No; I'll just go before the interview."

I give him some space. He spends the day on the living room couch, with the TV on and the sound off. A couple of hours before the set time, I start to nudge him.

"Shouldn't you go now?"

He nods.

"Let's go, then."

I am sure few things are as bothersome as a nagging mother, but his responses frustrate me.

"Do you still want to go?"

"Yes."

"Okay, then; you should go."

Finally, I drive with him to the barber shop—in a separate car so he can go to the interview right after the haircut. He parks and sits in his car.

"Are you going in?"

"Yes."

He finally stands in front of the barber shop, still hesitating. I push him inside, then sit in my car, feeling terribly guilty. When he comes out, looking like a ruffled brown chick, he unsuccessfully tries to start his car. He apparently left the keys in the ignition, partially turned, and the old battery didn't make it.

By that time my husband is home from work, so I call for help and leave Jonathan with him while I go to teach Italian. It's too late for Jonathan's interview. He has to call and cancel. My feelings of guilt mount throughout the evening. What if he had a strong emotional attachment to those dreadlocks?

At home, I find Jonathan sitting on his bed, in semidarkness, staring at the wall. His fingers whirl one of the tiny dreadlock stumps that are left on his head.

"I am sorry I pushed you," I say.

"It's okay."

"Did you make another appointment?"

"Yes."

"When?"

"Tomorrow."

No change of motion, no eye contact, no display of feeling—just the same absent stare at the wall in front of him and the same whirling of the same truncated strand.

Seeking Help

Jonathan eventually makes it to the job interview but, needless to say, doesn't pass. He is well dressed and groomed. I have bought him new clothes and shoes for the occasion. He has, however, another problem.

"He didn't say anything," says Brian. "He just stood there and stared."

At home, he keeps displaying strange behaviors. His handwriting, once small and neat, becomes huge and messy.

He draws large scribbles on paper or writes apparently senseless sentences. Even his speech stops making sense. Once, we find him sleeping on our roof—a typical, slanted, tiled roof. Another morning, my husband finds him in a hammock outside. The weather is cold and humid. Tom brings him a blanket, and Jonathan thanks him.

We are confused and distressed. He is supposed to meet again with the elders at church in a few days, but I can't see how he will manage. I email a dear friend at my church who has had some struggles with depression.

"If Jonathan is having a difficult time thinking straight, then until that is addressed I don't believe he can represent his views on his circumstances properly," she says. "I have the name and number of a psychiatrist in Encinitas, if you would like it. I have had a session with her myself and have been helped."

I also talk to one of my students, a therapist. He recommends a family counselor closer to our home. Taking my son to any professional will be difficult because he doesn't think that he has a problem, but a counselor may be an easier choice than a psychiatrist. Somehow, I convince Jonathan to try.

"Is this a career counselor?" he asks me in the car.

"No—it's a life counselor, just to see what we can do to help you."

Upset, he insists that we go back. I beg him to try. He squirms in the seat. In the meantime, I get lost and have to ask for directions. My level of frustration mounts as Jonathan continues to demand that we turn around. Finally, I park by the counselor's office. Jonathan refuses to go in.

"Okay; I'll go by myself, because we have to pay no matter what," I say.

I get out of the car and start walking. Jonathan follows me.

Peter Lautz is a welcoming man with a wide smile and a warm personality. He asks Jonathan if he can have me sit in on the session. To my surprise, Jonathan agrees, and he candidly answers all his questions. Pressed to display his lucidity, he plays the part well. He tells Peter that he has friends he sees regularly. I smile when he compliments my cooking.

"Are you going to school?"

"No; I stopped."

"Why?"

"I thought there was more to life."

"So what do you do now?"

"Play video games, watch TV . . ."

What a life, I think. Actually, he doesn't even do that. He watches TV without sound or stares at walls.

"Have you used any drugs?"

"Yes—marijuana."

"How much?"

"A lot."

"Any other drugs?"

"I had mushrooms twice."

My eyes widen, but I remain silent. Jonathan is still emotionless, but his body starts twitching. He incessantly bounces one knee and rubs his hands on his arms nervously.

"Have you stopped?"

"Yes."

"For how long?"

"Six months."

"Do you find that your mind is clearer?"

"Yes."

Then Peter asks an unexpected question.

"Do you ever hear voices?"

"Yes."

This statement shocks me to the core, but I don't show it. Peter wants to know more.

"They come from inside me, but they bounce back in the fish tank's bubbles," Jonathan explains. "Also, when someone talks to me, I hear something else. Sometimes I hear two or three voices at the same time."

Stunned, I try to understand what he is saying. I imagine other voices covering mine as I speak to him. What does he really hear?

Peter recommends a doctor's visit and some tests, just to rule out any physical cause. He tells Jonathan to exercise, preferably outside, and to try some creative activity—maybe painting.

As soon as we leave the building, Jonathan turns to me. "What a waste of time!"

"At least he gave you some ideas about exercising and painting."

"I could have come up with the same things."

For a few days, he looks upset. "I can't believe you took me to a therapist," he says. Again, I feel guilty and lost. Am I doing the right thing? How do I know what's right? Tom and I have been discussing Jonathan's care, but most of the time Tom lets me follow my instincts. I have never liked to make decisions.

Tom and I decide to follow Peter's orders. First we put Jonathan on Tom's HMO insurance. The premiums are expensive, but we foresee long-term care. Then we make an appointment with a general practitioner. I ask Tom to take Jonathan this time. I have antagonized my son enough.

Jonathan puts up a little struggle but finally gets to the doctor's office. The doctor orders tests and schedules him to see a psychiatrist. Taking our son to the mental clinic is harder, but my husband acts calmly and pragmatically, and Jonathan complies. A few days after the initial evaluation, I return with Jonathan to hear the results. Physically, he is in perfect shape. Mentally, it's another story.

His case manager proceeds to explain that Jonathan has schizophrenia. Surprised by her bluntness, I ask her to clarify. I've always thought of schizophrenia as a dual personality. She briefly describes the illness, gives me a list of resources I can use to find support, and hands Jonathan a fact sheet and a prescription for Risperidone. Very prudently, she asks him to sign a consent paper allowing his parents to be aware of his appointments, diagnosis, and medications. He signs without much concern.

2

Following the Signs

God works even in darkness and in secret.[1]
(S. G. De Graaf)

Coming to Grips

Initially the diagnosis gives me hope. At least Jonathan has some pills to take. I expect that they will work and everything will be fine. The casual attitude of the case manager corroborates this thought. I still don't understand all the implications of this illness, but I trust that the doctors know what they are doing. After all, schizophrenia has been around for a long time.

Others encourage this hope. "I talked to a psychiatrist who told me that, with medication, schizophrenia is very manageable," an elder at my church tells me.

The case manager told us it will take a few weeks for the medication to take effect, so I watch my son, hoping to catch a hint of improvement. He still sleeps most of the

1. S. G. De Graaf, *Promise and Deliverance*, vol. 1, *From Creation to the Conquest of Canaan*, trans. H. Evan Runner and Elisabeth Wichers Runner (St. Catharines, Canada: Paideia Press, 1977), 31.

morning. I try to meet him when he first gets up so we can read some Psalms together, which are cries from the soul.

At the same time, I am also uneasy and impatient. I want to wake him up, to talk to him, hoping for a word of reply or a sign that he is still there, that he is looking up to the God he knew so well.

I think that most Christian parents want to "be the Holy Spirit" for their children. We want to enter their minds and direct their thoughts, especially when we see them stray. This desire is magnified in my situation, when my son's thoughts are absolutely unintelligible and unfathomable—just like the voices he is hearing.

A verse rings in my mind: "The voice of the Lord breaks the cedars . . . of Lebanon" (Ps. 29:5). I read the whole psalm and find it encouraging. God's power—so terrifying in itself—is a great comfort if we are in Christ. For sure, God's voice is stronger than any voice my son hears.

I also find a helpful quote in *Promise and Deliverance* by S. G. De Graaf:

> At first the earth and all that was under heaven was an undifferentiated mass lacking order and form. It lay in darkness. Yet God was at work there; His Spirit was moving over the waters. Under the cover of darkness God was preparing what he was about to bring to light. Yes, God works even in darkness and in secret; the fruit of His work becomes visible later. In the same way God is working at this very moment in the hidden depths of many a human heart. Perhaps He is at work in your heart, teaching you to have faith.[2]

2. De Graaf, 31.

I think of Jonathan and realize that God is at work in my son's sleep. God is preparing what he will bring to light. I should just trust and wait. But it's easier said than done.

As I wait, I research the subject. The pamphlets that the hospital gave us are short. I look through the list of support groups. The closest one is the National Alliance on Mental Illness (NAMI). I call them. Their meetings are once a month. I just missed it.

Genetic factors are high on the list of causes of schizophrenia. I call my sister in Milan, Italy, and find out for the first time that one of my cousins had schizophrenia. Apparently the social stigma was so strong that my aunt placed him in an institution and told very few people about it. My sister found out much later, after my aunt had already died.

My sister also tells me that one of her best friend's sisters was diagnosed with schizophrenia when she was already married with kids. This made it more difficult for her in many regards, but she also had a very strong motivation to get better—and she eventually did. I'm keeping these things in mind.

Some days pass. In spite of these discoveries, the seriousness of the illness has not hit me full force, and my friends' somber reactions surprise me. Those who know the illness look as if I have told them my son has cancer.

"I am sorry," Pastor Brown says gravely. He has had some experience with this. Two of his uncles have lived with schizophrenia, and he has seen other cases in our congregation. He recommends that I talk to Alex, a pastor who used to attend our church. His son Britton, a bright and personable young man, has been living with schizophrenia for twenty years and has gone through several nightmarish experiences.

"The most important thing you can do is find a good doctor," Alex says. "It took a while for us to find the right one, but it made all the difference."

How do I know who is a good doctor? With an HMO insurance plan, we have limited choices. I ask my friend Gigi, who is a retired psychiatrist and used to work for the same medical group. She doesn't know the psychiatrist my son is seeing, and she suggests another, who is practicing in a location that's far from our house. We decide to stay with what we have for the moment and give it a try.

Gigi thinks the medication dosage is too low, but our psychiatrist says that she is planning to increase it after a while. Good sense seems to tell us to wait and see.

We tell our other children. Three of them—Kevin (age 17), Raphy (15), and Reny (13)—are still home with us. Having lived with Jonathan for the past few months, they are aware of the problem but don't seem to fully grasp the meaning and implications of the diagnosis. Like us, they hope that the medication will work.

One of our older sons, Dustin, is deployed in Afghanistan, and we can't reach him. Christian, Simon, and David, who live on their own, refuse to believe it. They think Jonathan is just going through a phase. He was always a bit odd. He is probably reacting strangely because he is so sensitive. Two of them offer to keep him at their house.

The gravity of my son's condition stares me in the face one month later, when we visit Christian and his family in a small scenic village near Fort Bragg, North Carolina. The area is much greener than most of San Diego, and I enjoy the change. Jonathan spends most of his time with his brothers, playing or watching them, but his expression is always vacant.

We take a walk through some woods near the house, headed for the lake. Christian's wife Nicki leads the way, walking briskly and holding her two-year-old daughter. Like Christian, she is a West Point graduate. We all tag along behind her. As the vegetation gets thicker, Jonathan seems disturbed. He looks all around him with fear, then pulls his hood over his head and comes close to me. I think of some words I saw in his medical papers: "paranoid schizophrenia." They seem fitting.

Jonathan eventually calms down but remains absent and quiet, even a few days later when we all go to Orlando to spend a few days at Disney World. His empty stare is in stark contrast with the excitement of the place.

Once, we have to leave him at the hotel because he says he doesn't want to go out. We see him standing disappointed and confused at the entrance as the bus drives off.

I look at Tom. "He's okay," he says.

Is he? It's hard for me to believe it. I wish Disney World were really a magical place where I could fly back to Jonathan and make everything turn out well. I try to share in my granddaughter's delight as we move from ride to ride, but my mind is fixed on Jonathan's disheartening look.

Eventually we go back and take him out for dinner. While we are eating, Christian tries to encourage him to do something exciting or take a trip somewhere. He doesn't invite him to stay with him because he is about to deploy, but he says he's willing to have him at a later date if Jonathan chooses to go to college near his house.

We return to San Diego a few days later. As soon as we get home, Jonathan runs frantically through the house, checking every room and looking out the windows. Again, he seems frightened. The San Diego summer heat welcomes us full force, and we cool off in the pool—everyone but Jonathan. He has never entered the pool since his return from college.

Thankfully, he continues to take his medication. I watch him discreetly as he swallows it every night. To stave off the side effects, the doctor has given him Benadryl, which is supposed to calm him—but since it's optional he rarely takes it.

A Self-Protecting Medical System

Soon after we return home, he visits his new counselor, Tammy, as part of his treatment. Tammy is a welcoming, passionate woman who obviously loves her job and cares for her patients. She gives Jonathan her recipe for success: regular usage of the correct medications, a supportive family environment, and abstinence from illicit drugs and alcohol. She explains that some people can use marijuana without any problems while others suffer permanent brain damage. Jonathan says he has stopped using it, which is a relief.

Science is still uncertain about marijuana or other hallucinogens as causes of schizophrenia. They may not cause it, but they could be a trigger in predisposed individuals. Other possible triggers are stressful events such as the loss of a job, the end of a relationship, or the death of a loved one. In Jonathan's case, the usage of drugs combined with the loss of his girlfriend and the end of his studies at Merced could have triggered or worsened the illness.

Jonathan seems to like Tammy. As with Peter, he is candid about his experiences and feelings. Yet he refuses any suggestion of attending a support group. She doesn't insist.

After the first two sessions, we are surprised by a phone call, as the clinic calls to inform us that Tammy has left the group and Jonathan is scheduled to see another counselor. Shocked by the unexpected news, I search Tammy's name on the internet, find her private practice, and call her to leave a message of appreciation. Surprisingly, she calls back to thank me.

"Good luck with Jonathan," she says. "He is a very special young man."

"You can talk to him if you want to."

I hand him the phone, describing the situation.

"What happened?" he asks immediately.

"It's a matter of politics," she explains diplomatically.

He listens quietly, responds affirmatively to some of her questions, and then gives me back the phone, without any expression on his face.

The new counselor assigned to Jonathan is a rather impersonal woman with a reserved smile. Unlike Tammy, she asks me to stay out of their session. She returns a few minutes later to announce that Jonathan has decided to discontinue therapy. My mother-bear instincts are ready to pounce. She lets me into the room to hear the explanation.

"So Jonathan has decided to stop seeing me," she says without changing expression or tone. Turning to him, she asks, "How will you know if you need therapy again?"

"If I fail school," he replies.

Wait a minute, I think. *We are dealing with a very ill young man. His mind is not functioning, and you leave the decision to him?* I can't say this in front of my son, but I know the answer: "He is nineteen."

I'm told this all the time. Yes, he is in an altered state of mind. Yes, he could potentially harm himself and others. Yes, we know about the potential dangers of untreated schizophrenia: suicide, homelessness, incarceration. . . . But he is nineteen, an adult in our society, and no one can infringe on his freedom.

In the car, Jonathan tells me that he wants to stop taking medications, too. He is planning to tell the psychiatrist at his next appointment. I ask him why, and he says he doesn't like what they do to his brain. Somehow I convince him to continue until he sees her and pray that she will be more sensible.

She is not. We are back at square one.

Self-Medication

It takes some time for the medication to wear off completely, but it finally does; and Jonathan spends his days totally self-absorbed, trapped in a circle of desires and frustration. He scribbles on paper, writes a few messages, sends some tweets—mostly short poems.

Somewhere in this mess of lies
Someone can tell time.
From there just follow the signs.
Head to the reason and where we got this rhyme.

These are not existential questions. When I talk to him, he still believes God's sovereignty in our lives and his overarching story of redemption. What he can't understand is the tangle of voices, perceptions, and paranoid fears that are battering his mind.

"What do you do when you hear voices?" he asks me.

44

"I don't hear voices," I have to reply, begrudgingly. I wish I could say that I hear them and have a solution. That's what parents do. We cross rivers before our children and then try to guide their steps. I feel that this answer has just deepened the gap between us. We are on two different levels, or in two different states of mind. But what else can I say?

Just before Halloween, he wants to return to see his friends at Merced. We tell him that it's not a good idea, but he doesn't listen. He manages to get a little money by working for Bill and packs his bags. I ask how he is planning to travel. He says he wants to rent a car. I tell him that no one will rent him a car without a credit card, but he doesn't believe me.

On the last day, just as he is ready to leave, I suggest that he call the rental company he plans to use. Only then he learns the ugly truth. No credit, no car. He begs me to rent it for him. Then he begs me to let him use our extra car. He can't; his brother uses it most of the time. Besides—though I don't tell him this, we would never feel safe letting him drive that far.

Finally he ends up frustrated and depressed on the living room couch, with the TV on and the sound off. He takes some Benadryl—the same drug he refused to take when he actually needed it. He looks pitiful.

I wish I could spare him all these disappointments, but he wants to have his way. Over the course of several months, I drive him to countless job interviews that he sets up by phone and see him return to the car disheartened. Finally a student from my Italian class offers him a job cleaning up her yard. As usual, he shows no emotion. I drop him there and drive back home.

My student calls me a couple of hours later.

"I am sorry, but he has been standing in the yard talking to a tree," she says. "You have to come and get him."

I pick him up, fearing his reaction, but he is still emotionless. We drive quietly home.

A few days later, he asks if he can work for me. He used to help me with translations and did a stellar job. Now he gets confused and changes language halfway. I ask him to scrub my floor tiles instead. He cleans half of the floor and never returns to do the rest.

Bill still gives him a chance to work with him once in a while. Finally he calls me to explain that he cannot take the responsibility. "He walks out in front of moving cars."

After a couple of weeks, my son sends Bill a message, begging him to take him back. He blames his absentmindedness on lack of exercise and promises that he will do better. Then, at the end of the message, he forgets what he is writing and starts rapping.

Red Corvette
Fires to it
We don't need participation
We need firemen

Once in a while he still goes to school. The semester at community college is not over, and he has not officially dropped his classes. I suspect that he is acting fine in front of his teachers—at least part of the time.

One day I receive an email message from his teacher that is addressed to him. He has used my email account to send her an essay, and she has replied. "This is a fascinating and well-written essay," she writes, "but unfortunately, it does not remotely address the tasks required in the prompt."

I am not sure what the subject of the essay was, but he wrote about technology and social networks. The beginning is well written and makes a lot of sense. Then suddenly the tone changes.

> You get the eerie feeling of déjà vu. You look up, and see you laughing at you. Personally, I feel myself becoming deliberately diagnostic analytical at a mouse click speed. I also find myself feeling like Chris Griffin hiding from the evil monkey in the closet avoiding that thing and its earthly problems. . . . The thoughts going through my head in this essay feel like the ones I've used a thousand times for this same point. The monotony is endless through-out the day. I find myself saying, 'I'm here' in my thought process with uninterrupted efficiency. . . . With so much progress comes so much conformation and secrets swept under the rug.

I know that all this makes perfect sense to him. I wish I could understand.

During the day, the voices seem friendly. I see him walking around our backyard, talking to unseen characters and smiling. During these long conversations, he moves his arms to make his points more clearly. If I join him, however, he gives me a scary look—angry and vigilant, ready to pounce.

He is very suspicious of me, ever since I took him to doctors and therapists—and especially after I told our pastor he has schizophrenia. That's something he has not been able to forgive me. Our relationship is definitely strained, but most of the time he is too absent to show any emotions.

Yet sometimes the poems that he scribbles on paper are strangely encouraging.

Lucky to have so many people still pushing on me
helping me through 'cause I know I can't see
I thank God for the question and the places I want to be
I thank you for saying I and not we.

In another poem he said, "When I'm in my home I know God's cooking breakfast."

During the Christmas holidays, Tom finds him a job ringing bells for the Salvation Army. It's something that Jonathan has done before, so we don't foresee any problem. After the second day, he is fired. Apparently he spent the money that we gave him for food to buy marijuana. Then he came home to eat. At 2 p.m., I find him asleep in a car full of smoke. I wake him up, and he drives back to work, only to find that someone has reported his absence. He had left his donations and bell in front of the store the whole time.

So he is still smoking marijuana—when he can find money. We have already limited his driving, but now we forbid it altogether until he can produce a clear drug test. He is furious.

When he is calmer, I talk to him about marijuana. He tells me it helps him to calm down. I have noticed that he often tries to self-medicate with whatever he can find at home. He has finished the Benadryl that the doctor prescribed and has taken a bottle of Tylenol PM from our bathroom. We start locking our door so he can't come freely into either our bedroom or our bathroom.

Finding Information

Since Jonathan refuses to see a doctor, I try to find as much information as I can by myself. Studying the problem and living it at the same time is not easy. I don't have time to digest and organize the information I get, and I don't have anyone to consult for medical advice.

I decide to go slow, reading only as much as I can absorb and praying that God will continue to work behind the scenes. After all, Jonathan is his son, and I know that he loves him more than I ever could.

Almost every paper that I read tells me there is a much higher chance of beating this illness if it's caught early and cured with medication. Every month Jonathan spends without medication apparently worsens his condition.

If he could only admit that he has a mental disorder, there would be many more opportunities available to him, especially with the Department of Rehabilitation—a government agency that provides employment and independent living resources for people with disabilities. Also, the colleges he has attended would wipe out his negative record and give him a fresh start, and even provide him with special services. But Jonathan categorically refuses.

His refusal to acknowledge his condition is another part of the illness. It is called *anosognosia*, and it explains in large part why many people with mental illness don't want to take medications. They don't consider them necessary, and of course any unnecessary medication can be potentially harmful.

I contact various centers and organizations that specialize in helping people with mental illness and their families. Finally I am able to join one of NAMI's monthly group meetings at a nearby library.

The meeting is well attended. In fact, there are almost too many people for the small room, and everyone seems eager to talk. They are all desperate people with very challenging stories. They ask me how old my son is.

"He's nineteen."

"Oh, he is a baby!"

Most of them have loved ones in their thirties or older, who live on their own. I hear horror stories—a son living with excrement splattered over his walls, a daughter sleeping somewhere in the streets and showing up at home once in a while, another daughter obtaining bank information and draining her mother's accounts dry. Some people cry. A daughter asks what to do with a mother who refuses to admit that she needs help. There is hardly any time to speak, because everyone seems desperate to share their stories and to obtain some information. I prefer to listen anyhow. As does every support group, this helps me to see that there are other people with similar problems—in fact, problems that are even much worse than mine.

The facilitator explains the process of coping with a mentally ill loved one. NAMI lists "hope against hope" as one of the first reactions that parents experience—part of a preliminary phase of denial that parents are supposed to outgrow. We take turns saying where we are in this process. I tell them I am just at the beginning, but I feel I am going through both the first and second phases at once: I'm in shock and denial, and I'm learning to cope. I am definitely not in the third phase: advocacy. I am not ready to be an advocate for anything. I am just learning.

A parent says, "I am in phase three, but sometimes I still hope against hope."

I will always hope against hope! I think. I don't want to

ever leave this "phase." I understand that NAMI sees it as a sign of denial, but we have a God who can act beyond all our hopes and dreams. It might be a painful "phase" to prolong, but I don't care. Pain is an intrinsic part of the Christian life in this earthly pilgrimage.

I continue to attend the meetings for a couple of months, but they are much less organized. Fewer people attend, and no facilitator is present. I meet new people. For some reason, at least in this branch of NAMI, few people attend the meetings regularly. At the last meeting, instead of talking about sons and daughters who live outside the home, we focus on how to cope with those who live with their parents or how to send them to an institution. One mother says she can't take it anymore. A couple talks about their son who has almost set the house on fire.

They talk about the Psychiatric Emergency Response Team (PERT) that follows 911 calls. Someone mentions a program called IHOT (In-Home Outreach Team), run by Telecare Corporation, which specializes in home visits and support for people with mental illness who refuse to seek medical care as well as for their families. I take their number and call them the following day. They put me on a waiting list.

I also call NAMI to sign up for their instructional classes, but they are not very convenient. They mostly occur at the same time as my Italian classes. I put my name on their waiting list as well, hoping for a better schedule. The operator suggests that I read a book, *I Am Not Sick, I Don't Need Help!*, by Xavier Amador. I order it through my local library.

I contact some Christian organizations. One of them puts me in touch with the mother of another young man with schizophrenia. She immediately calls me. I am hesitant to open up, but she encourages me with her warmth and compassion. We talk for a while about common frustrations and hopes. Her son is not taking medications and is not attending church. She suggests that I keep a list of useful numbers ready to call in case of an emergency, and I do it immediately after the call. The way things are going, an emergency might be just around the corner.

Mounting Frustration

As time passes, frustration increases on both sides. Jonathan is frustrated because he can't do what he wants, and I am frustrated because I can't help him or even understand him anymore. Sometimes he has last-minute demands. He needs a book for school or needs to use my computer immediately. If I say no, he stays in my room or sits at my desk in the well-lit walk-in closet I have turned into an office and refuses to leave. If I insist, he bangs his hands on the desk and shouts apparently senseless sentences.

I beg him to wait, trying to explain that I don't do well under pressure. I need time to think before I react. I look at him in the eyes as I talk. He stares back as if trying to penetrate my thoughts. Or maybe he is hearing something else.

I sit in front of him, because we can't trust him anymore. I am not happy about letting him use my computer because I don't know whether he will download something harmful onto it. I just don't know what to expect anymore. Besides, he had two laptops and ruined both. With the first, he pulled every key off its keyboard and lost most of them. The second computer was ruined by water. He may have accidentally spilled some, because there was an empty glass next to the computer, but he blamed his brother and sister, saying that they went to his room on purpose to pour water on it. We couldn't dissuade him. In fact, his anger became so frightening that my children locked themselves in their rooms.

I have become a prisoner in my own house. Besides locking our door at night and when we leave the house, I have to lock it every time I am in my room.

One day, quite unexpectedly, Anna contacts me again. She is very concerned about Jonathan. He has started to send her countless messages—all of them very strange. Once, he sat outside her house for hours in the rain.

"I don't think our friendship is going to continue, unfortunately," she says. "He has said a lot of rude things to me recently. I don't know what changed all of a sudden. He seems to really be struggling, so I don't hold it against him. I wish him all the best, though, and I hope he can find himself some help in some way.

"He had a lot of questions about our relationship," she continues, "but it struck me so strange that he would ask the same question maybe five times and not remember ever asking it before. He has a lot of anger about it, so one minute he talks like he hates me, and then the next minute he just wants to be friends."

He does the same with us, becoming angry and abusive, and a while later acting very sweet. It's heartbreaking, because it seems he can't help it. I thank Anna for letting me know and tell her that all we can do for Jonathan is pray.

Britton, Alex's son, explains to me that it's normal for people with schizophrenia to feel unbearable anger. "We just want a way out," he says. After several years of treatment and a few hospitalizations, Britton has finally learned to contain it.

When our twenty-two-year-old, David, visits from his Air Force post in Washington, we try to convince him to encourage Jonathan to seek help. At first David refuses. He is not convinced that medications or even therapists would help. I call him to my room while Jonathan has a psychotic attack. Once again, Jonathan sits at my desk refusing to go.

"What do you want?" David asks him.

"Stamps; stamps; I want stamps—lots and lots of stamps!"

There are some stamps on my desk, so Jonathan probably said the first thing that came to his mind. David thinks he is just being sarcastic, and it could very well be. Of course he can have the stamps, but that's not what he wants.

Having seen Jonathan's episode, David starts to believe that there is reason for concern. He is still reluctant to intervene, since it's a delicate situation. Finally he agrees to talk to his brother. I sit next to him. First he promises to take Jonathan out. Jonathan smiles. While he rarely goes out alone, even to the closest store, because his paranoia has reached an all-time high, Jonathan is always happy to be with his older brothers when they come to visit.

David adds that there is a requirement. We want him to see a therapist again. Jonathan refuses. The more we talk to him, the more agitated he gets. I know I should stop, but I don't. David is going to leave the next day. I really want this to work.

Jonathan gets up and storms out of the house. He doesn't come back at bedtime. I check his room periodically through the night. In the morning, he is still gone. I am frantic. I imagine him somewhere in the streets, with his blank stare. He must be cold. He never notices changes of temperature. A few times he has slept all night outside on our hammock without a blanket.

I feel terribly guilty for pressuring him. I should have left at the first sign of discomfort. From the looks on David's face when he leaves, I know that he feels guilty too, and maybe a little resentful because we pushed him into that difficult situation.

I finally text Jonathan. "Come home, it's OK. You don't have to go where you don't want to."

I am giving in. Is it right? I realize I am in a very difficult predicament. Many people, even at NAMI, have been telling me to give him an ultimatum: "You either take your medicines or you're out." I just can't do it. I can't live knowing that he is homeless somewhere. At the same time, I don't feel capable of caring for him at home.

He doesn't respond to my text message. Frantic, I try to contact Jered, his closest friend from high school. I know he still sees him occasionally.

"I am Jonathan's mom. He got angry yesterday and didn't come home last night. I know you are his best friend. Please let me know if you see him. Also, if you have any idea of what he wants and how I can help him, let me know."

Jered replies to my message. "Hello. I am sorry to hear that and I will let you know if I find him. As for what he wants I am not sure because he doesn't talk anymore I don't know if it's the same at home but it seems like he just doesn't want to speak at all about anything."

Yes, it's the same at home. Thankfully, Jonathan returns around noon. He goes to his room and curls up under his blanket.

3

Taken Away

Remember that thing screaming in your ear?
Turns out it's still there.
(Jonathan Carr)

Nearing a Crisis

For a while Jonathan continues to come to church, even if his mind seems to be on a distant planet. After prayer, counsel, and research, Pastor Brown and the other church elders agree that it's very important for Jonathan to be on medications. One Sunday, after the evening service, two of the elders take him aside to talk. After expressing their concern for his health and wellbeing, they ask if he is following the doctor's prescriptions.

He tells them the psychiatrist has agreed that he doesn't need medications. They ask me if it's true, and I find myself once again in the uncomfortable position of having to contest what my son is saying. The psychologist agreed to let him discontinue therapy, but discontinuing the medications was his own decision—presumably against medical advice. I know that Jonathan will not react well. He grows restless.

57

"Even if you think you don't need medications," one elder says, "you can at least go for a second opinion."

As the elder continues to talk about the benefits of medical care, Jonathan starts to shake uncontrollably. The elders try to encourage him but soon realize that they have to stop the conversation altogether. When we finally get to the car, he seems relieved. He talks for a while, which is unusual for him.

After this, he often refuses to go to church. On most Saturday evenings, he tells us that he will come with us the next day, but when morning comes he changes his mind. Once he complies but leaves church after ten minutes and walks home.

This is very hard for me. I miss him at church. Most of all, I know that he needs to hear the gospel—the good news of Christ's finished work of redemption—now more than ever. When I return home, I peek into his room and tell him about the sermon. I tell him that the elders send their greetings and miss him. I ask him if he will come next week, and he always says yes.

As time progresses, so does his anger. He starts to use foul language—something he has never done before. Once he directs a torrent of insults directly at Tom, who instinctively slaps him. We have never allowed this behavior. For a moment, I fear for their lives, but nothing happens.

Something has to change. As I find half-burned paper in the hallway and in his room, I almost wish that he would start a fire—nothing threatening, just enough to bring the crisis to a head so it can be resolved. I know it's a terrible thought, but I feel there is nothing I can do. God has to intervene somehow.

My twenty-nine-year-old son, Simon, agrees to take

Jonathan with him for a day. Simon lives here in San Diego with some friends and works as sous-chef at a popular downtown restaurant. He takes Jonathan to lunch and tries to force him to order on his own.

"Why are you mean to me?" Jonathan asks, a puzzled look on his face.

Back at Simon's apartment, Jonathan spends most of the time lost in his world, as he does here. Once he breaks the silence by asking if he can live there. When Simon says no, he returns to his thoughts. After a few hours, another one of my sons goes to pick him up and take him back home.

Simon sends an email to some of his brothers and sends a copy to us.

"We need to do something," he said. "He spent the day staring at my walls."

No one responds. It's hard to believe it unless you see it. Jonathan had always been our brightest son.

My husband keeps a picture by his side of the bed of a younger Jonathan holding a bunny.

"I wish I could have him back," he says.

Can Jonathan see how much he has changed? The photo shows a happy boy with neatly curly hair and lively brown eyes, holding the bunny close to his chest. We had baby bunnies in our backyard. Through many ups and downs, we ended up keeping two.

When one of them became injured, Jonathan begged me to go to the vet. It had a simple cut, but a large one, and he didn't want it to be infected. Then he followed up daily with the treatment, injecting antibiotics under its skin.

These days Jonathan's eyes are dull, staring into nothing. Once in a while, if he is scared or angry, his gaze becomes terrifying. His hair, as well as is general appearance, is messy.

Jonathan, age 14, with one of our pet bunnies

Most of the time, he doesn't seem to care about anything. Then, suddenly, he gets a compelling urge and wants something right now.

I am different from my husband in many ways. Maybe I am more pessimistic, but I don't even think about having our old Jonathan back. I am willing to live with the Jonathan we have now. I would be willing to spend my life getting to know him and helping him . . . if he only wanted help.

I am reading the chapter on schizophrenia in the book *Far from the Tree* by Andrew Solomon. The opening paragraph includes one of the best descriptions of the illness I have found, comparing schizophrenia to Alzheimer's as "an illness . . . of replacement and deletion." This may come as a surprise to many. "Initially, parents almost universally believe that schizophrenia is invasive, an added layer masking their beloved child, who must somehow be liberated from its temporary conquest."[1] As painful as it is, they will ultimately have to accept that some of their child's mental faculties, memories, and even personality traits may be sorely erased in this life, even if many things stay the same.

So it is for Jonathan. He is still very kind and has a special proficiency at playing chess and solving math problems, but many of his social skills, interests, and emotions are gone. He still has an amazing sense of humor, but only in the rare moments when he is not busy battling voices in his head—which, as Solomon points out, "are usually cruel and often encourage bizarre and inappropriate behavior." And this is what makes schizophrenia particularly painful to a caretaker who has to watch its developments. "The person who hears them is commonly terrified and almost always paranoid."[2]

This constant mental struggle gives account for the strange messages Jonathan writes everywhere and the look of fear he has in his eyes while he peeps behind curtains to make sure all is clear outside.

The book also helps me to understand Jonathan's desire for isolation, as "the fading of the nondelusional world puts [people with schizophrenia] in loneliness beyond all reckoning, a fixed residence on a noxious private planet they can never leave, and where they can receive no visitors."[3]

It's frightening, but there is not much I can do, because this illness impairs Jonathan's ability to distinguish illusion from reality—so much so that, as Solomon points out, "having an idea and having an experience are not particularly

---

1. Andrew Solomon, *Far from the Tree: Parents, Children, and the Search for Identity* (New York: Scribner, 2012), 295.
2. Solomon, 296.
3. Solomon, 296.

different." That's why depression is most frequent in the earliest stages of the illness, when the person is suddenly confused and frightened by voices and delusional thoughts. "In later stages, emotional capacity altogether is reduced, and people may seem vacant and emotionless."[4]

Jonathan fits this description to a T. Something needs to be done. We ponder the idea of having an intervention. But, judging by his reactions when David and the elders talked to him, we are afraid it might make things worse.

I call the nurse at the mental health clinic to share my concerns. As in the past, she tells me there is nothing she can do because he is of age. He is now twenty years old. If he poses a danger to himself or to others, I should call 911. I hear this over and over. Still, it's hard for me to understand why we have to wait until then. There is no answer except that "he is of age."

Finally, I convince the nurse to talk to him and invite him back for a visit, since it has been a while. She agrees, and I hand him the phone. I can hear his responses. He says he is doing well. He is going to school and working for a landscaping company. Somehow, when he is forced to react normally, he is able to do it.

I call the nurse back, who says there is nothing else she can do. She can make an appointment for him, but he will have to agree to go. I ask if they could make a house call. I am willing to pay. She is surprised and says no. I tell her they should think about doing it. It could be part of crime prevention.

Once again, we feel powerless. We can only watch our son's deterioration and desperately pray for God to intervene.

---

4. Solomon, 296.

A Difficult Decision

By this time, I have read Xavier Amador's book a few times. Like many other professionals, he agrees there is no way to treat schizophrenia without medications. His book takes parents step by step through a call to 911, hospitalization, and the patient's return to his home or transfer to a halfway house. This is all very foreign to me, but I understand the wisdom behind it.

Pastor Brown agrees. "If it were my son, I would take him to the hospital by force, even if I had to take two or three men with me to do it."

It's easier said than done, because Jonathan is twenty and cannot be forced to stay in a hospital. At the same time, the principle is very valid.

Things continue to get worse. Once, Jonathan spends all day in bed, awake but with his eyes closed. I take water to him, but he doesn't touch it. I call a crisis hotline, but there is not much they can do. In the evening, still without any food or water, he walks to the local college.

On another occasion, he fills the room with lighted, scented candles that he finds around the house and seals the door with masking tape. In the morning, I find by his bed a cracked bowl that he had placed on top of one of the candles. He is an accident ready to happen.

His anger continues to explode whenever he feels we are denying him something. A few times he threatens to kill me. My other children stay away from him.

"When he threatens you, you have a reason to call the police," my husband says.

I still can't bring myself to do it. Deep inside, I don't think that my son means what he says. He always apologizes. Still, at times his eyes are scary. They open very wide but maintain a blank stare as he fixes them relentlessly on me. I stare back, feeling a courage that I never knew was there. Or is it just reckless behavior?

I hate to do something so drastic against his will. He is still often sweet and compliant. But what's best for him? Should I just let him vegetate ... or worse?

Once, my husband makes a strange and unexpected prediction.

"I don't think he will live one more year."

I am quiet. I have never heard him talking this way. Could he be right? I refuse to believe it. I continue my life and take care of the usual events—taking the other kids to school, cleaning the house, cooking, making phone calls, teaching Italian, translating, and writing books or articles.

As I sit at the computer, trying to concentrate on my work, Jonathan comes and asks to use it. This time I have a ready answer. My husband and I have decided to give him another laptop—the third in a row—hoping that he will be more responsible with it and maintain some independence. It's a fairly old laptop. It belonged to my father-in-law, and I have been using it when needed. I can do without it.

I tell my son of our decision but ask him to wait because I have to connect it to the home Wi-Fi. My husband has given me the password, so I set it before me and start working on it.

But Jonathan has no intention of waiting. Tired of my slow efforts to type a long code, he grabs both laptop and password from my hands and leaves. A few minutes later, he storms into my room again and goes through my husband's toolbox. Before I can say anything, he grabs a power drill and leaves again.

He then heads, with the power drill, for the door at the bottom of the stairs from our room. With rapid movements, he unscrews the handle from this door and takes it to his own bedroom. At least he is not drilling the laptop.

I try to push his door open. His lock has not been working lately, and we thought this was a good thing, as we wanted to make sure he was okay. Still, he is pushing from the inside and is much stronger. I hear the constant sound of the drill. Then suddenly there is quiet. I try pushing the door, but somehow it is locked. I call him, but he doesn't answer.

It takes me some time to figure out he has drilled the handle between the door and the wall, locking it shut. I also realize he has taken into his room the TV and PlayStation we have set in the garage for our children to use during the weekend when they have done their homework and chores. For Jonathan, we had already lifted any restriction and he had been free to use both devices at any time.

I wait for my husband, because I certainly can't do anything. But even when Tom returns, Jonathan doesn't open the door. I knock and ask if he is hungry. There is no reply. Everything is quiet. There is no indication that he is watching TV or playing. We go to bed around ten. He is still not out.

I sit back at my computer and notice he has left his Facebook page open. I read some messages:

Remember that thing screaming in your ear? Turns out it's still there.

I hate my life and all who enter it
stupid people who wouldn't want to answer this

they ask me what my problem is. I tell them that
to taste the wrong end of a baseball bat.

In this life there's no room for anyone else.
It's why I sit alone at night and break into my self
until it hurts.

The next day, his door is still locked and there is no sign
that he has been out of his room. In the kitchen, everything
is as we had left it the night before. I start to panic. Is he
even alive? Around ten, I knock at his window and tell him
I am going to the bookstore. He likes books.

"Do you want anything?"

He opens the window. With no expression on his face,
he tells me the name of a book he would like. I am elated.
I will have one more chance to see him when I bring the
book back. On the way home, I stop at Jack in the Box and
get him one of his favorite combos. He opens the window,
takes everything, and thanks me. That's it for today. At least
he is alive.

Over the next few days, he rarely opens the window.
Even my attempts to lure him with Jack in the Box meals
fail. I ask my daughter to try. He opens to her and takes the
food. One more day of life.

My husband and I wonder how he goes to the bathroom. Thankfully we discover he goes out at night, because
now we start to find a mess in the kitchen every morning.
I have never welcomed a mess as gladly as I do now.

By Saturday, my anxieties have reached their limit. I go
and teach two classes at the Italian Cultural Center and
return around noon. His door is still locked and there is no
reply. I knock and warn him that if he persists I will have to

call the police. Still no answer. I call my husband, who is at work finishing some important business.

"If he doesn't reply, I will call 911."

"Go ahead," Tom says.

I never thought it would come to this, but I am just too concerned for my son. Am I exaggerating? My older sons might think so. I have a tendency to worry too much. Still, this time I see no other way.

9-1-1 . . .

An officer arrives within the hour. He doesn't look too concerned. He has probably seen many worried mothers like me. He hears my explanation and knocks on my son's window.

"Jonathan, I am a police officer. Open up." His voice is strong and authoritative.

Jonathan opens. He acts and speaks coherently, replying to every question. When the officer is done, he closes his window.

"He sounds very lucid," the officer tells me. "There is nothing I can do—but if you want, I can refer him to the PERT team. But they will probably just talk to him."

I remember PERT, the Psychiatric Emergency Response Team, from the National Alliance on Mental Illness meetings. They are special officers who are trained to deal with mental illness. And anyone who wants to talk to him is welcome!

"That would be great," I say.

An Unlikely Scene

The PERT team doesn't show up until Tuesday evening. Apparently, in spite of the "emergency" portion of their name, they only work Tuesday to Friday. They also don't seem too concerned. In the meantime, Jonathan has unlatched his door and has been out of his room. Still, he spends most of his time in bed, often curled up under his blankets.

I explain to the officers that since he has been out I have checked his room, and that he at least never used it as a bathroom, which is a relief. I have heard horror stories from mothers of other people with schizophrenia. I have however found lots of uneaten food—in fact, most of the Jack in the Box meals were untouched.

The main officer seems particularly concerned by the fact that Jonathan took food only from his sister. "Some schizophrenics are afraid that others want to poison them," she said.

I also tell them I found a kitchen knife stuck in the wall by his door. He might have used it as screwdriver.

They knock on Jonathan's door, get him out of the room, have him sit on a chair, and check his room. They inspect the area where the knife was placed, but there is hardly any mark. Then they start to talk to him. As usual, he is very honest about his medical condition and his refusal to take medications. He tries to maintain an air of credibility.

I am sitting in the next room because I am not allowed to be with him. They ask him if he is afraid we might want to hurt him. He hesitates, then says, "Not really."

His answer triggers a new response, "We want to take you for a medical examination. It might just take a few hours, or the doctors might decide to keep you for a couple of days."

"I don't want to go."

"You need to come anyhow."

I hear some banging and bumps. A chair falls. I run outside the house, feeling extremely nauseous. I pray desperately for God's help. Before long, I see Jonathan emerge. His eyes are closed, and he is handcuffed. Two officers escort him to the car while one comes to talk to me.

"When you go back into the house, you might cough, because we had to use pepper spray. He was resisting."

I can't believe what I am hearing. They explain that he will be taken to a hospital, wherever they can find a bed. Normally they can't keep anyone longer than three days, but sometimes the doctors request a two-week extension. That seems to be the maximum stay.

Another officer asks me for some water to pour on my son's eyes. I see him in the car, struggling to pull his legs through his handcuffed arms, probably to reach his teary eyes. The officer tells him that he has to stay still or things will get worse.

I get some water, still utterly shocked. This is the same baby I delivered in a natural way, making sure that the lights were dim to avoid any distress as we welcomed him into the world. It's the same boy I nourished with whole grains and fiercely protected from emotional and physical injuries. I keep looking at the police car, thinking, "What have I done?"

As my husband returns, we get the last instructions from the officer.

"I am not supposed to tell you this," she said, "but we are taking him to Aurora Hospital. You can try to contact him there tomorrow."

That night, I cry uncontrollably until I exhaust my strength and fall asleep. A few hours later, I am wide-eyed again. "Lord, help him. Be with him. He is in your hands," I keep repeating.

Through the Valley

I call the hospital early in the morning.

"I'd like to talk to my son. He is a patient there."

"How old is he?"

"Twenty."

"Do you have his number?"

"What number?"

"His patient number."

"The police just took him there last night. I don't have any number."

"You can't talk to him without a number."

"How do I get the number?"

"He has to give it to you."

"Okay, then—can I talk to him so I can ask him for the number?"

"No, I am sorry; you can't talk to him without a number."

I am not giving up. Finally, I convince the operator to connect me to his department so I can try begging someone else. The answer is the same, but at least I can implore the person on the phone to ask my son to give me this magic number.

"I can't tell you if your son is here."

"Okay—but without telling me anything, if he is there, can you please ask him to give me the number?"

They agree. I have a moment of doubt. What if he is not there? I call again and ask for the financial office, and I tell them I want to know how to pay his bills. Immediately they give me all the billing information. And yes, he is there. Then, suddenly, they have their moment of doubt.

"Do you have his number?"

"Not yet."

"Oh; I was not supposed to tell you anything then."

I thank her and reassure her that I will not abuse this bit of information. At least I know he is there. That's all—until he gives me his number.

The same evening, I go to the weekly prayer meeting at my church. I have been attending it for a while, asking for prayer for my son without giving any detail, because he had reacted so furiously when I let our pastor know his diagnosis. This time, however, I tell everyone what happened. The prayers of my brothers and sisters in the Lord are a great comfort.

"I am glad you told everyone," Pastor Brown tells me later. "It's important to have everyone praying for this."

Suddenly I am hearing from other people who have similar problems. A young man tells me about his mother who has schizophrenia but refuses to take medications. A woman tells me about her daughter who lives with bipolar disorder. By God's grace, during a recent visit, she was able to detect some hidden messages in her daughter's words and convinced her husband to take her to the hospital. They saved her just in time, because she was going to commit suicide.

Where have these people been? Only now they open up their hearts. How many more are suffering like this? Of course, these are not things we share in the few minutes we meet for coffee break—but how wonderful to be able to pray for each other!

On Friday morning I receive a call.

"I am Jonathan's social worker. He has given me permission to talk to you this one time. He is going to see the judge in a couple of minutes and wants to know if he can come home."

Once again, I am pressed to do what I hate most: make a decision—and a very important one.

"I don't know; I haven't talked to him yet. Can he come home?"

"We don't recommend it."

I try to get as much information as I can. Is he being treated? What do they recommend? Surprisingly, this person answers my questions, and we talk for a while. I learn that if we don't take him out, he will stay there for two more weeks. They recommend a longer stay because they found him incapable of caring for himself. In fact, the medical tests showed he was undernourished. Also, until his stay there, he was not medicated; but if he stays they will be able to force him to take medications.

This makes the answer easier. I finally say we cannot take him home against the doctor's orders but would love to have him back as soon as he is stable. I also ask the social worker to please tell him that we love him very much. I know my expressions of love are not going to amount to much in this situation, but I still want him to know.

The social worker tells me she can't give me any more information, but she gives me her phone number in case I want to contact her. I can give her all the information I want, and they can definitely use it.

My heart sinks as I hang up the phone. Still, I know I made the only possible choice.

I call Tom to tell him what happened.

In the afternoon, I try to call my son, but I find he has left a message with the operator saying he does not want to talk to his parents. There is nothing I can do, but I write a long letter to the social worker to let her know everything that has happened until now.

I also write a personal message for Jonathan (I still call him Branch) and send it by Facebook. I know he can't read it, but writing it makes me feel better.

Branch, I know you can't read this now but one day you will. You gave permission to your social worker to talk to me only once and I had to answer her question very quickly. She said you are not ready to come home and if you do so it will be against medical advice. I really wanted to talk to you and see if you were willing to come home and see a doctor but she didn't give me that option. She said you were about to go into the court hearing. Branch, I am very sorry that all this has to happen. I just want the best for you. I hope you will forgive us one day and that you will be able to live here again as happily as you did in the past.

Mom

Surprisingly, Jonathan calls me a few days later. There is no emotion in his voice. He wants me to bring him his phone and laptop. I tell him I need his number. I hear him asking someone, and then he gives it to me. I feel empowered.

Tom asks me to go by myself the first time. When I ask why, he just says, "I will come next time."

Even the drive to the hospital is an adventure. I have a terrible sense of direction and lose my way very easily. Somehow I get there. When the emotions mount up, I pray, "Lord, help me." I feel like Bilbo Baggins—shaken out of my comfortable hobbit hole.

The hospital has a pretty name and a fancy website. In reality, it's a dull, faded rectangular building in a grey industrial area. At the initial check-in, I am informed that no phones or laptops are allowed in the building. I have to take them back with me. Thankfully, I have another bag with some clothes. He left our house barefoot, and his clothes got wet when they poured water in his eyes.

I walk through a barren corridor to the section where Jonathan is kept. They examine my bag and return most of the clothes. I am not allowed to bring them in because the pants cannot have strings and the shoes cannot have laces. Then they let me through the door.

The lights are dim. A few people stand by their doors, staring at me. A tall, handsome young man falls at my feet and lowers his head, as if he waits to be knighted. I don't know how to react, so I don't do anything. A nurse calls my son. He appears after a while, wearing a hospital gown. He looks clean, for a change. He asks about the phone and laptop.

"They didn't let me take them in," I say.

He takes the bag, turns around, and leaves without a word.

I return the next day with my husband. This time I bring shoes without laces and pants without strings. We go through the door. Jonathan comes halfway toward us and asks if we came to bring him home. We say that we can't. He cusses and turns around.

After this, he doesn't come out to see us anymore. Still, we visit almost every day. At home, we clean out his room. We also set up a TV and give him a DVD player, laptop, and PlayStation. It touches my heart to see my husband fix the shelves in Jonathan's room, hang the TV on the wall, and move in a new chest of drawers. We are building his nest in hope. When Jonathan returns, he will have everything in his room and won't need to take anything from others. We also put a lock on his door so he will not feel the need to barricade himself. Of course, we have a key.

We don't know what to expect. He could come back at the end of the two weeks, or he might decide to move somewhere else. Just in case, Tom calls our oldest sons to see if anyone wants to take him. Most of them disapprove of our actions. They don't think it was necessary to call the police. Still, they hesitate when we ask them to take him.

Our oldest son has a young daughter, so he doesn't want to expose her to this situation, but he agrees to take Jonathan for a couple of weeks. Another son can take him after that. At least we have alternatives. We also look into halfway houses, but it seems too easy for their residents to just leave and move to the streets. We don't want Jonathan to be homeless!

In the meantime, I try to focus on the rest of my life—the other kids who have gone neglected while I've been focusing all my efforts on Jonathan, my work, and so on. I sleep little. To find comfort, I keep repeating to myself that Jonathan is not my own, that he is on loan, and that God knows what he is doing.

As much as I try to tell myself that everything will be well, my body is reacting badly. I always have this problem. My mind reassures me while my body falls apart—especially my intestines. Maybe if I cry enough tears the diarrhea will stop. I am casting my anchor in God, who is greater than both my mind and body.

4

Through the Unknown

Poor though I am, despised, forgot,
Yet God, my God, forgets me not
(William Cowper)[1]

The Heavy Weight of Guilt

My husband and kids go away for a few days, and I have some time alone to read, think, and pray. I think of some books I have read about mental illness even before Jonathan became ill—for example, an interesting book about Lisa Miller, wife of Hugh Miller of Scotland, a geologist who was affected by mental illness (probably schizophrenia) and took his life in the 1800s. I guess God has been preparing me.

The truth is that I don't want to be prepared or taught. I just want my baby back. I know I have allowed his illness to deteriorate right inside my house because I couldn't let go. Now I've finally realized I can't do that to him. But this hospitalization hurts both of us. I am almost positive he will

---

1. William Cowper, "God of My Life, to Thee I Call," 1779.

not respond well to us if he comes home, at least for a while, but I can't think about that.

I look for advice anywhere I can. I go back to the National Alliance on Mental Illness (NAMI), where the other parents congratulate me for managing to hospitalize my son. They tell me it's highly unusual for the police to take someone away on the first call and for the hospital to keep someone longer than a month.

"How did you do it?" they ask.

I tell them, feeling far from successful.

I also go back to see Peter, the family counselor. I realize I should have seen him—or some other professional—sooner. I am not trained to deal with these sorts of problems, and in order to get sufficient knowledge from books I would have to stop everything else I am doing and devote all my time to studying mental illness. I bring a notebook with a list of questions.

Peter answers with great wisdom and patience. He cautions me to be careful about taking Jonathan back. He reminds me to think of my other children. I know they are relieved to have him gone.

I tell him that my husband and I have decided to take him back only if he can abide by some simple requests: he needs to be under medical care and follow the doctors' advice, and he needs to stop burning anything in the house. Peter recommends putting this in writing. He also suggests that we welcome him into a peaceful atmosphere. "Schizophrenics don't do well with intense emotions," he says, "even good ones, like joy."

"*Now* you tell me," I reply. "You know I am Italian, don't you?"

He laughs and says that his father and grandparents

were Croatian, so he understands passionate expression of feelings. He encourages me to take care of myself: to eat, sleep, and exercise.

Exercise comes easy. I like to stay in motion—it takes my mind off my fears. Sleep is more difficult. Computer work is even harder. I try to concentrate on my translations, but my mind gravitates toward the gloomy hospital, the uncertain future, the unexplainable past. In Italy we say, "La lingua batte dove il dente duole" (The tongue is drawn to the aching tooth).

Guilt is a steady companion, finding constant occasions to sneak back into my mind and open endless windows into my past. It is a common response for parents of the mentally ill, because it provides some of the rare explanations that seem to make sense—even if they are untrue.

I begin questioning every decision I have made as a parent. Have I loved Jonathan enough? Have I been too strict? Too absent, when he went to college? Why didn't I notice the early signs? And, especially, did I handle his illness well? Could I have been more understanding? Why didn't I study this subject more, from the very start? Was the call to the Psychiatric Emergency Response Team a mistake? Could I have done anything to prevent this downward spiral of events?

Sometimes even words of encouragement depress me. When Pastor Brown tells me God is doing this for our sanctification, I feel terrible thinking that God had to inflict this pain on my son to get through to me. If I could just be less stubborn and learn some easier way . . .

My older sons don't help the situation. They still think that hospitalization was not the answer.

I know that mulling over the past is a waste of time. Most

of all, I know that God is sovereign and works in spite of our mistakes. Still, I have a strong need to hear it from others. I write Alex, who can relate to emergency calls because of his experience with his son. He identifies with my feelings. "I felt the exact same way as you," he said, "because of my self-centered (and very sinful!) lifestyle when Britton was a teenager. I lived a 'me me me' life after experiencing a broken family. Thus, I battled deeply with guilt. But God used this for me just like he used the devil to 'sift Peter' so he would understand his identity (*nothing* good dwells in me!) and thus understand God's immeasurable grace."

"The thing that freed me from this and many other kinds of guilt is the gospel," he explained. "I now realize that there's nothing good in me and that God uses everything, including my sins, to work everything together for good."

I know that it's true. The well-known promise that "all things work together for good" is for all "those who love God" and "are called according to his purpose" (Rom. 8:28). This includes Jonathan. God is using this experience not just for my sanctification, but for Jonathan's too—for my good and his good.

It's not just a simple assertion that "everything will work out in the end." In fact, everything may not work out at all in this earthly life. It's not even a general promise of God's sovereign providence, because that holds no comfort for those who are not in Christ. It's a promise that a very specific God, the God who sent his Son to die on the cross for us, will work all things together for our salvation—which is what ultimately matters, even if we don't understand how.

Alex quotes Romans 8:38–39: "For I am sure that neither death nor life, nor angels nor rulers, nor things present nor things to come, nor powers, nor height nor depth, nor anything else in all creation, will be able to separate us from the love of God in Christ Jesus our Lord." I add mental illness to the list. The promise still stands.

A Mother's Calling

As incompetent as I feel, I have to come to grips with the fact that God has not dismissed me from my duty as mother. My younger kids are afraid to face Jonathan when he comes back. They think he will be much worse and will try to hurt us or them. As much as I want him back, as much as I would like a second chance to take better care of Jonathan right here in our house, I have to seriously take my children's feelings into consideration and protect them.

It's one of the hardest things to do. Normally I try to make everyone happy, and I hate making decisions. And yet calling 911 and the Psychiatric Emergency Response Team (PERT) was my decision, and so was leaving Jonathan in the hospital. These were decisions I had to make on the spot, without a chance to discuss them with my husband. God has definitely been asking something new of me.

My son's mental illness has invaded my world with the force of all the troubles of Job combined (or so it feels). One of the things that makes it so difficult is that I can't even find a category for what has happened to him. Jonathan is not dead. He has not openly renounced Christ. He is just gone. His eyes often betray his disease—one that doesn't fit into any biblical category except maybe demon possession or Nebuchadnezzar's temporary insanity in Daniel 4 (that's why in the past so many Christians have equated mental illness with demon possession).

There is very little literature on this issue that is written from a Christian standpoint. Even medicine is uncertain. A few decades ago, schizophrenia was the parents' fault—especially the mother's. Now it's a chemical imbalance. Does anyone really know? Since some medications are working (mostly dopamine blockers), there may be some truth to the imbalance theory—but it's all still experimental, and it varies from person to person.

With so much uncertainty, I am praying that God will give Jonathan competent doctors and will heal him through the scientific means he has provided, which is how I believe he usually works today.

I also pray that God will give Jonathan peace and will help us to parent him correctly. I have often seen confusion and even terror in his eyes. The medications might help, but what if he stops taking them again? How do you nurture a mindless soul?

I discuss this question over e-mail with two Westminster Seminary students, Brenden and Tim, who have been lavishing me with compassion and encouragement since the beginning of this new turn in my life. They help me to understand that sometimes modern Christians put too much emphasis on the mind.

"Doctrinally, we know that faith presupposes knowledge and assent before being able to qualify as trust," Brenden explains. "But that's only 'ordinarily.' The Reformed loved that word because they realized their systematic categories needed qualifications to allow for the 'extra-ordinary' work of God—his sovereign moving, especially within the covenant community. This is how the Reformed believed that the children of believers are 'holy' even though they don't necessarily have knowledge and assent."

"Whether or not one's mind is functioning," Brenden continues, "doesn't ultimately matter for the Holy Spirit, who has already united believers to Christ and carries them through the death of their bodies and minds, into paradise. You can bank everything on the sheer mercy of God, who identifies himself as 'The LORD, the LORD, a God merciful and gracious, slow to anger, and abounding in steadfast love and faithfulness, keeping steadfast love for thousands, forgiving iniquity and transgression and sin' (Ex. 34:6–7)."

Tim adds some very helpful advice: "Your loving actions toward him, especially if he cannot understand the gospel, speak the love of Christ to him, even if he cannot understand why. He may not be able to understand why you are letting him stay where he is in the hospital, but that doesn't mean you should relent in loving him by helping him get what may help. Your and your family's relentless love to him speaks of Christ's relentless love for us when we were in no condition to love him back."

Brenden and Tim's emphasis on love resonates with my motherly instincts. My love has to rely, of course, on the power of God's Spirit. I have learned already that I can't place my trust in my love. In spite of the charm of the Beatles' song, love is not all we need. My love will not in itself "work wonders." Still, it occupies a large place in Scriptures. "Above all, keep loving one another earnestly, since love covers a multitude of sins" (1 Peter 4:8).

In the quiet of my home, I have time to reflect and pray. I ask God to expand my mind, which is so narrow, so tense—a mind still holding on to its fears and trying too hard to fit this strange new experience into a mold, to reduce it to easy terms: illness, medications.

Deuteronomy 29:29 comes to mind: "The secret things belong to the LORD our God, but the things that are revealed belong to us and to our children forever, that we may do all the words of this law." I need to leave the secret things—the things I can't understand—in the Lord's hands, while I love my son as he is now, even if I will never again see the Jonathan I once knew.

What is schizophrenia, really? Maybe I will never know—not in this life. Maybe scientists will find out one day. What I know now is redemption, the gospel, and the solid hope that is in Christ for me and for Jonathan and all my kids. I think of the cry of Jonah from the belly of the fish, "Salvation belongs to the LORD" (Jonah 2:9), and of the cries of Job from his bed of ashes, "I know that my Redeemer lives, and at the last he will stand upon the earth" and "in my flesh I shall see God" (Job 19:25, 26).

The future is still frightening. I don't even know whether Jonathan will ever come home again. Either way, there are fears—fears of losing him and fears of facing another unbearable struggle at home.

Somehow I find an inspiring song online. It's a rendition of William Cowper's poem "Friend of the Friendless," beautifully sung by Gerhard Wagner.

God of my life, to Thee I call;
Afflicted, at Thy feet I fall;
When the great water-floods prevail,
Leave not my trembling heart to fail.
Friend of the friendless and the faint,
Where should I lodge my deep complaint?
Where but with Thee, whose open door
Invites the helpless and the poor?

I especially find comfort in the next portion, which reminds me that Christ "always lives to make intercession for" me (Heb. 7:25):

Fair is the lot that's cast for me;
I have an Advocate with Thee.
They whom the world caresses most
Have no such privilege to boast.[2]

Cowper suffered through periods of severe depression and spent much time in what was then known as an "asylum." Many of his poems and songs reflect the experiences of his life and his strong reliance on God as his only hope and comfort.

Slow Progress

Jonathan responds erratically to phone calls. Sometimes he answers, sometimes he refuses; other times he says hello, listens for a few minutes, and hangs up. Once he replies to my question about medications and tells me he is taking Valium and Haldol.

For days, he has been convinced he will be out on Sunday. We try to see where he could safely go.

In the meantime, some patient at the hospital must have given him some strange information. Suddenly he calls to ask us to take him off our insurance. For some reason, he believes that if he is on private insurance he will be in the

---

2. William Cowper, "Friend of the Friendless," 1779; music and vocals by Gerhard Wagner, video, 4:15, July 25, 2011, https://www.youtube.com/watch?v=GPLsK3I-VIE.

hospital forever. I try to convince him this is not true, but he doesn't listen. He calls repeatedly, sounding extremely anxious. He calls my husband's cell phone and repeats the same request. When Tom stops answering, Jonathan leaves a message saying that if Tom doesn't take him off the insurance he will kill him.

Tom asks me to stop answering his calls. Jonathan keeps calling throughout the afternoon—probably ten times. Finally I call the hospital and ask the nurse to please calm him down. He never calls back. Tom and I decide to let the social worker know about this threat. Even if Jonathan didn't give her permission to talk to us, we can leave her messages. In fact, she encouraged it and is always thankful to know more about his history and his behavior at home. In this case, she lets us know that Jonathan will remain at the facility for a full month.

"We can't discharge patients who make threats to hurt themselves or others," she says.

This is a definite setback in our relationship, but we believe it's in his best interest. We keep visiting him, and he keeps rejecting our visits. In spite of this, he surprises me by calling me on my birthday. He forgets Mother's Day a few days later.

One day, he allows me to visit. I find him sitting in the common room, playing chess with another patient. I sit between them.

The other patient is a very sociable young man.

"Jon is so smart," he says. "He beats me at chess every time. He also writes great songs."

I listen with interest. My son keeps playing, without lifting his eyes. Other patients circle around us, smiling at me. A few minutes later, the nurse comes and gives Jonathan the bag I have brought for him. They have checked it and kept the pants, because they have a string, and a hardcover book, which is also not allowed.

Jonathan looks through the bag.

"I will bring you another pair of pants and another book, with a soft cover," I tell him.

He doesn't answer but opens a note I have placed in the bag. It's an explanation of what happened and why I called PERT—I was worried for him and thought they were just going to talk to him and persuade him to see a doctor. The note also explains that we will be glad to have him back when the doctors think he is ready. He reads every word, still silently. He puts down the bag, moves a chess piece, and wins the game. Then he gets up and goes back to his room, carrying the bag with him.

He calls me a few days later, asking when he can come home.

"You want to come home?" I ask, surprised.

"Is it not obvious?"

"Not really. You said you want to kill us."

"I didn't mean it."

I explain that if he wants to come home he has to talk to us. He finally agrees to meet us.

My husband and I both agree that taking him back is the right decision.

Tom has not said much throughout this experience, but the little comments he has made have been very wise and often moving. I have always heard that men are more reticent to share their feelings.

Once, however, Tom tells me why he has hesitated to allow Jonathan to come back. It's not just to protect the other children. It's to protect his own feelings. "I don't think he will live more than a year," he says. "If he died, I don't know how I would cope."

In some ways, distance dulls the pain. Or so it seems.

I am different. I could never bear the thought of having my son live on the streets. I would move out with him just to keep him safe.

Back Home

On the meeting day, we park in the crowded hospital lot and walk hesitantly, once again, into the dim facility. This time we are both allowed into the common room, where Jonathan meets us. Another patient looks at me intently, then kneels by my side and lowers his head. Since my son is completely ignoring him, I decide to do the same. I wish I knew what to do in these puzzling situations.

My husband explains to Jonathan what we expect of him when he returns. Jonathan nods as he plays solitaire with cards. He keeps playing the whole time. We talk a little longer, until he leaves abruptly and returns to his room.

We come back a few days later for Jonathan's discharge. Since he never gave the hospital permission to divulge any details of his condition, the social worker can't give us too much information. She warns me his recovery will take a long time. He has a very advanced case of schizophrenia—he is considered "gravely disabled"—and the hospital can only do so much. He will need to continue to take his medications. She adds that most people with schizophrenia return to hospitals over and over again. It's called "revolving door syndrome."

She suggests that we consider requesting conservatorship for him—appointing us as his legal guardians. I have actually looked into the procedure already. Following the advice I found on the NAMI website, I have recorded a detailed history of his illness and behavior for the courts to see, if need be. The social worker gives me the number of the person who has been his official conservator for the time he has been hospitalized. This person suggests that we don't apply for conservatorship right now.

"If you think your relationship is strained, think how much worse it will become if you are his conservator," she explains. She understands my concerns. At home, with full freedom of choice, he will most likely make many wrong decisions.

"Keep a record," she encourages me. "Most likely he will be back in a hospital, and then it will be easier for you to obtain conservatorship."

These are bleak perspectives for parents. Still, my trust is in the Lord. Only God can move Jonathan to comply with treatment and make the right decisions—or he can heal him in other ways, as he pleases.

We attend a pre-discharge meeting with Jonathan and the social worker. A tall, strong male nurse stands by the door, ready for any emergency. Jonathan looks annoyed. He obviously doesn't like the social worker and replies curtly and crossly to her questions. Still, he agrees to our requests, and we set a date for his release.

I have almost memorized the suggestions in Amador's book. He encourages us parents to show love and to sympathize with the pain of being institutionalized, without ever suggesting that we won't commit our children again. It's a promise we just can't make. He says we can ask for forgiveness, while understanding that we may never receive it.

On the set day, we sit nervously in the facility's waiting room, wondering what will be his reaction to us and to his renewed freedom. The wait is longer than we expected. The delay is compounded by our apprehension.

Finally, the double doors open and Jonathan walks out, hugging a clumsily packed bag of his items. He doesn't turn to look at us. A nurse follows him, hands him his discharge papers, and pats him on the shoulder.

"Take care of yourself," the nurse says, betraying a sincere care and the pain of seeing many young men walk out still unprepared to face the world.

We walk in front of Jonathan, leading him to the car. The silence is uncomfortable. Before we open the car's doors, he surprises me with an odd request.

"Mom, can you speak to me only in Italian?"

My heart leaps. My schizophrenic son just asked me to speak to him—never mind in which language! I am sure that psychologists could offer some interesting interpretation, but at this point it doesn't matter.

"Certo! Come stai?"

"Bene."

"Sei felice di tornare a casa?" (Are you glad to be coming back home?)

He hesitates. His Italian is not proficient.

"Sì."

In the car, he hands us his papers and tells us he needs to buy his medications. We stop at the pharmacy on the way back home. The list is quite long—Zyprexa (an antipsychotic), Ativan, Trazodone (to aid sleep), and a muscle relaxant (to offset the side effects of the antipsychotics). On top of this, every two weeks he will receive an injection of Prolixin, another antipsychotic. I am surprised at the amount of medication, but the doctors must know what they are doing.

Jonathan sits, quiet and compliant. I glance at his other papers while my husband goes to bring the prescription to the pharmacist. They point out some of the problems still to be resolved. Mostly, he is still not coping well and doesn't have social skills. I feel confident that these issues will be overcome with time.

When we finally arrive home, we show him his room. It's clean. The bed has new sheets and blankets. His clothes are organized in his closet and drawers. We have hung a TV on the wall, and his laptop and phone are on his bed. He is still inexpressive. As I leave the room, I turn around and ask him for a hug. Surprisingly, he holds out one arm. I cling to him tightly. "Oh, Jonathan!" is all I can say.

After dinner, Jonathan sits at the table in our backyard, smoking a cigarette. That's a habit he has picked up in the institution, where cigarettes were given freely to patients. I have read and heard from more than one source that nicotine acts as a medication, temporarily blocking some of the hallucinations. Of course, no doctor has actually prescribed it, but apparently cigarettes were handed out at every break. It's quite ironic. And yet at this point this new addiction ranks low on my list of concerns.

I sit next to him and ask a few questions in Italian. He answers briefly, still showing no emotion. He is relaxed and seems content. I don't know how long it will last, but I praise God for it.

I continue to sit quietly. I don't want to force him to speak. There will be plenty of time for that. I breathe the cool evening air. Strangely, I am no longer interested in trying to fit Jonathan into the "normal" world. Of course, there is a need for that. When the mind is so far off, it's really detrimental in every way. But now that the medications are controlling the illness to a certain extent, I want to explore his world, as much as he will allow me. Hopefully, by God's grace, I am slowly winning his trust. Maybe, if God sees fit, I can help him find, even in his world, the "light that shines upon our paths and leads us to the Lamb," to use William Cowper's words.[3] Or he might help *me* to see it.

3. William Cowper, "O for a Closer Walk with God," 1779.

5

Entering Your World

So shall my word be that goes out from my mouth;
it shall not return to me empty,
but it shall accomplish that which I purpose,
and shall succeed in the thing for which I sent it.
(Isaiah 55:11)

In God's Hands

This would make a great ending for our story: Jonathan is back, all is well, and we can live happily ever after. But those are fairy-tale endings. This life is messy. The ever-after happiness has to wait.

I move circumspectly as I try to adjust to this beloved stranger. He is not the Jonathan we knew, and yet my love for him has increased. He is meek and compliant—probably an effect of the medications—but looks fragile, and I am afraid I might break him.

For a few days, I take him to the psychiatrist and the therapist at the former HMO facility. I ask for a new therapist, and surprisingly they acquiesce to my request—even if, at twenty years old, Jonathan should be making the decision.

The new therapist, Lisa, suggests some group therapy but doesn't insist. There are no people with schizophrenia in the groups, and all the participants are older than Jonathan. She assumes he will not like them. I ask if there are other alternatives, but she doesn't know of any. The papers from the hospital strongly recommend intensive group therapy, so I suggest that Jonathan should at least try, but she doesn't extend the offer to him.

Once in a while, he twitches uncontrollably. I call the hospital, and the nurse tells me that it's normal—I just need to increase his muscle relaxant. I am not comfortable with the amount of medications he has to take. I try to discuss them with the nurse, but she tells me that it's up to him and the doctor—I am out of the picture. The only reason that she talks to me is because he signed a release, but that's just to inform me about his therapy and appointments. I have no say in any of this.

This doesn't stop me from calling the nurse repeatedly, until she tells me they are all very busy. Since my son has no intention of using his doctor-patient email system, and since I have set up his user name and password, I use that venue to keep the doctor informed of what's happening. They probably hate me by now.

I have read that in Europe the whole family is offered therapy together with patients, and it really should be done this way in the United States, too. Mental illness affects the whole family, and we need to face it together. It would be great if help were offered to all, but most insurance companies don't cover it and (apparently) parents don't demand it.

Lisa normally allows me in the consultation room after she's talked with Jonathan for a while. At that point I have time to express my concerns and ask questions. I try to be discreet. Once, however, I go overboard in my attempts to be a good parent and ask what I can do better. She passes the question to my son. From his facial expression, I realize I have opened a can of worms.

"Sometimes you are pushy," he says.

"Well, thank you for telling me—now I know. I will try to do better."

He is right, but the first thing that pushy people like me need to learn is to leave well enough alone. My husband would have wisely stopped there. Not me. I have to dig deeper.

As I start the car, I bring up the subject again, "Let me know if I am ever pushy, because I don't want to be."

"You are pushy," he says.

"I know; but tell me when I actually do it."

"You are doing it now."

At this point, any person with an ounce of common sense would stop talking. Not me. I continue until I totally irritate him. I lean back to take my bag, and he jerks. He probably thinks I am trying to get close to him, so he takes a piece of paper and starts to hit me with it. "You are pushy! You are pushy! You are pushy!"

I have to leave the car in order to catch my breath and find a little sanity. I walk into the hospital and write a short note to Lisa, just to let her know. When I return to the car, Jonathan is gone.

I frantically look around the hospital grounds. When I am sure he is not there, I drive away, following the road I imagine he would take to walk home. There is no sign of him. I try other streets, then turn around and follow the same route again, scanning each side of the street. Maybe he is not coming home. But where would he go? Actually, he could go anywhere. I can't rely on logic anymore. Nothing is predictable.

Finally I return home, and he is sitting on his bed with his door wide open. I am not sure how he could have walked so quickly. The hospital is about four miles away.

"I am glad you are back," I say. I wait in vain for an answer. "I am sorry I got you upset."

I leave quickly. Tomorrow he needs to see the psychiatrist and get his injection, and I pray that I didn't mess everything up.

Maybe he is especially tense because the shot is due tomorrow and the medication is low in his blood? I am not sure. I am taking it as a lesson to keep depending on the Lord hour by hour. I have to learn to be less "pushy"—or whatever my son considers pushy. I also pray that God will override my sins and mistakes. On the positive side, I now know what bothers Jonathan and can try to do better. Joel 2:25 continually comes to mind: "I will restore to you the years that the swarming locust has eaten." While the context of the verse is not the same, it gives me confidence that God can undo any damage.

It's also humbling. It's easy for us to think that our motherly care is the main influence in our children's lives, when in reality they are in God's hands and he uses our parenting efforts for his glory. I can pray for wisdom and do what I can to fulfill my job as mother, but ultimately God is the one who directs Jonathan's life. This is both a source of comfort (do I really want to have the ultimate responsibility in the life of my son?) and a reminder to recognize my role in God's overarching plan.

I often remember that "the king's heart is a stream of water in the hand of the LORD; he turns it wherever he will"

(Prov. 21:1). That goes for my son's heart too. Every heart, knowingly or unknowingly, is subject to God's will—both my son's heart and the hearts of doctors and nurses. I believe the Heidelberg Catechism when it says that "all creatures are so in [God's] hand that without His will they cannot so much as move."[1]

I remember these promises in prayer before I call the HMO's member services department to talk about their performance. I tell them that while I am not a medical professional, it seems to me that they need to work with more urgency in this case—my son did just come out of the hospital. I explain how last year, when someone told him that he didn't have to take his meds, he ended up in the hospital. Now his therapist is telling him that he doesn't have to attend the intensive program if he doesn't want to, and it brings back painful memories.

The operator asks me what I want specifically—I guess she just wants a few words to fit in the form they gave her. I tell her that I just want the medical staff to consider things a little more carefully, and if they truly believe that he doesn't have to attend the program that was recommended by the hospital, I want to know why.

I hang up, replaying the conversation in my mind. I have an uncomfortable habit of questioning my decisions. Was I too confrontational? I normally try to avoid conflicts, but then when it comes to my kids I end up acting impulsively, trusting my motherly instincts. I finally decide to stop questioning the call and my tone of voice. Even if I didn't explain things right, or even if the whole call was a mistake, things will work for good because of God's promise.

1. Heidelberg Catechism, answer 28.

Progress

Jonathan's case manager calls and offers him a place in their group therapy program three times a week. She is doubtful that he will agree, but she is willing to talk to him about it, since his seemingly compliant manner puts us at an advantage.

I ask Jonathan if he would like to try the group, and he says no. I suggest that I could pay him a few dollars for every session he attends. Amador's book mentioned this—and if it works, why not?

He agrees. Lisa is surprised but is willing to have him. Jonathan continues to attend the group three times a week and even participates in the discussions—once, I see him outside the facility, talking with some women who attend the program. He does all his homework, and once again things look promising.

His writings are still mostly confused—they mention Satan, goblins, "scary gargoyles," haunted trees, and "monsters under my bed like Calvin Hobbes, the ones that rip your face in chunks and gobs and leave it puddled in a bloody gob." Sometimes I find him hiding behind our tool shed, inside the shed, or outside a side door we rarely use. Once in a while, he still writes messages about his long-gone girlfriend. The wound has not closed. "Everything reminds me of you, from the TV to the air conditioner. I can't believe how much I'm missing you. I can't believe how much I'm missing."

Yet the papers he writes for his group therapy are very clear. The handwriting is neat, and he expresses his feelings articulately. I find a note about the "ascension" he experiences "with the only person who'd listen and pay attention when I'd mention this aggression." He might be referring to his arrest—he has always seen it as an unjustified aggression. I understand how important it is for him to be heard and understood.

Almost every day, I take him to the hospital for either a visit or a group meeting. The shot of Prolixin is every two weeks. He doesn't talk much—he mostly stares into space. Sometimes he smiles, and he seems content. If I want to elicit some response, I talk to him in Italian, which snaps him out of his silence.

Seeing him taking his meds gives me peace, but he doesn't like it when I watch him. I know I can't put my trust in medications, but right now they are the means that God is using for his healing. I'm still not sure whether they are the right combination, but they seem to work. He still has moments when he is totally gone, but most of the time he's his sweet old self—plus a confused mind.

He has become very much like a young child, and my heart yearns over him. I am back to basic parenting: cleaning his room, making sure he has clean clothes. I haven't practiced this type of nurturing for a while—once my children grew up, I stopped being a hands-on caretaker and became more of an encourager, applauding their independence. But things are different with Jonathan. I try to learn the subtle dance of being present while giving him space, watching without hovering. It feels odd at my age—the age of empty nests and grandbabies. God had something else in mind for me.

I send him a personal message on Facebook. He may or may not see it.

Hi Branch, I hope you read this. I just want to thank you for taking your meds. They will help you so much in the future to lead a happier life. Let me know if you need any-thing. Mom

I am proceeding slowly, but I am encouraged. Things may get shaky again, but this realization keeps me close to God. I try to be there for Jonathan when he needs me, with-out being pushy or "invasive" (a new word he has started to use). He was probably told to use it in the support group. At least it helps him to express his feelings.

He likes to write, so I encourage him to do that in order to keep him occupied in a creative way. Sometimes he takes the trolley and goes to the beach alone. I think about giving him a ride one day and seeing if there is something he can do there. He sometimes goes out without telling me and doesn't answer his phone, but he always comes back. He remembers most of his appointments.

He leaves the house without warning on Father's Day, and I wonder if he will be back in time to go to the restau-rant for dinner. Just as we are about to leave, I find him on his bed, dressed up and ready to go. He is quiet, but his eyes shine, alert and alive, like polished obsidian.

We have to take two cars, and he climbs into mine. I feel honored and touched that he'd want to ride with me, in spite of my "invasive" nature. He is quiet, but I have learned to let him be this way. I try to limit my nagging to his meds and doctor's appointments.

I pat him on the leg to show that I'm happy he is com-ing with us. The mellowing effect of the medications causes his muscles to relax, and he doesn't react. He once told me he doesn't like to be hugged or touched, so I try not to do it, but once in a while I sneak a light pat on his leg or shoulder, or a soft kiss over his head on the tip of his dreadlocks. It feels so good, and I want it so much, but I have to remember that I don't need it—not if he doesn't want it. The only way to accept it is to keep my eyes on the Lord and to get my satisfaction from him. I thought I was done learning most of my lessons about motherhood, but no . . .

On Sunday, Pastor Brown preaches a good sermon on Luke 14:12–24.[2] At the end he mentions how those in Christ are free to love the unlovely without expecting anything in return. I need to remember this and not expect anything from my son. He is in God's hands, and my job is just to love him and pray for him, no matter what he does.

It's something I have been learning very slowly and imperfectly—taking two steps forward and one (or sometimes two) backward. It's easy for me to act impatiently with my kids and talk to them like "meek" Moses addressed the Israelites when he finally lost his temper: "Hear now, you rebels: shall we bring water for you out of this rock?" (Numbers 20:10). Once again, it's a reminder for me to simply do what God requires of me as a mother and to trust him for the results.

In the meantime, I read books and ask experts for their advice. One of my friends, an acupuncturist with a PhD in psychology, has a very simple suggestion: "Feed him." That's Italian wisdom. I prepare the dishes that Jonathan likes and make sure he eats regularly. I offer food when I see him tense or afraid, and it works. This is probably not the best idea for a person who struggles with obesity, but my son has always been thin, and the food I offer is healthy.

2. See Michael Brown, "The Banquet Is Ready" (sermon, Christ United Reformed Church, Santee, CA, June 16, 2013), available online at http://www .christurc.org/sermons/the-banquet-is-ready.

The nurse at his clinic suggests, "He needs a regular schedule. That's why people with schizophrenia thrive best in hospitals or prisons." I understand the comfort of regularity, but I don't want to turn into a jailer. And actually, experts have repeatedly debunked the notion of people with mental illness thriving in jail. Far from being helpful, punitive confinement is actively counterproductive for them. Dr. Richard Warner, medical director of the Mental Health Center of Boulder City, Colorado, believes that "people with schizophrenia can get worse if treated punitively or confined unnecessarily. Extended hospital stays are rarely necessary if good community treatment is available. Jail and prison are not appropriate places of care. Yet, around the world, large numbers of people with schizophrenia are housed in prison cells, usually charged with minor crimes, largely because of the lack of adequate community treatment."[3]

Sadly, it's easy to place people with mental illness in confinement and then close the doors so we can feel safe in our ignorance and indifference, and this is often what happens. The fact that nurses are trained to think of prisons as positive environments for people with mental illness is alarming.

The Reappearance of Pot

Jonathan has been coming to church occasionally—he says that he likes the sermons. The very first Sunday after his release from the hospital, he greeted one of the elders enthusiastically with a bright smile—the same elder who

---

3. Richard Warner, *The Environment of Schizophrenia: Innovations in Practice, Policy and Communications* (London: Brunner-Routledge, 2000), 14.

made him feel uncomfortable in a past session. I had felt encouraged and relieved.

Now, just a few weeks later, I smell marijuana in the house.

"Are you smoking again?"

"It helps with the anxiety—better than medications."

"How did you pay for it?"

"With the money you gave me."

This puts me in a difficult position. If I stop giving him money, he will stop going to therapy. I send a message to Lisa to see what she thinks, and I talk to Jonathan about the dangers of addiction.

"I know I am addicted."

He has always been very truthful, but the illness has made him more so.

"You know?"

"Yes; we had a program at the hospital."

"Did it help?"

"Not much."

We talk for a while about the anxiety. He says he has to constantly monitor what is around him and determine whether it's real or not, and this makes him anxious and tense. The medications he is taking also make him restless. I have noticed that. It's one of the side effects, and one of the reasons why they gave him a muscle relaxant. He says it doesn't help.

I suspect that he also likes to escape reality—but I might be wrong. I tell him he should lean on the Lord instead of drugs. He smiles. Is he high right now?

"You know it's illegal," I add, trying a different angle.

"I have a medical card."

This is surprising. "You do? How did you get it?"

He tells me that one day, instead of going to the beach, he took the trolley to a doctor's office—one of the many doctors who give marijuana prescriptions. It's easy to find them online. Apparently this one has told Jonathan that marijuana is "very good for schizophrenia." Anything I say now is useless—in his case, it's not illegal, and he believes that it's actually good for him! He's probably thinking, *Who says that the doctors she's chosen are better than the one I found?*

With a marijuana card, he can call a dispensary (the numbers of which, again, are listed online), and they deliver to the house. I think back and remember a very nice, clean-cut, well-dressed young man coming to our door a few weeks ago. Initially I had thought it was a missionary asking for donations. When he asked for my son, I figured he was someone from school. I didn't think much of it when they talked very briefly outside our door. He was probably the delivery boy.

I'm seriously concerned about how the marijuana will interact with all his medications. I ask him if he has discussed his current prescriptions with the "new doctor," and he says no. I call the nurse at his HMO clinic, but she never calls back. I try the clinic's pharmacy, but they can't legally give me any information. Eventually the clinic's case manager calls back and impatiently tells me that they don't have time to answer all my calls. She tells me to call the National Alliance on Mental Illness.

I insist, explaining the problem. "I just want to know if there are dangerous interactions. I would think that this is the type of information a nurse or pharmacist could give."

"If he collapses, you can call 911," she replies.

I thank them, hang up the phone, and cry. I understand that even professionals don't always know what to say, and we are all fallen people, but I am terribly concerned for my son. Maybe they are right—maybe I should just relax and wait until he collapses, but it will take a lot to get me to that point.

What frustrates me is that I have no support in telling him to stop smoking. The nurse said, "What can you do?" and the counselor told him, "I don't want to be your mom and tell you not to do it." Then this new doctor told him that marijuana is actually good for schizophrenia. I need to pray that the Lord will show him that pot is not the answer.

I'm also frustrated because this HMO clinic seems to take things lightly, limiting Jonathan's doctor's appointments to once a month and leaving things up to him, while the Psychiatric Emergency Response Team and hospital had realized there was reason for serious concern and had put him into intensive care programs. I'm scared and angry, but I need to remember that God is present—even in the midst of fearful pharmacists and lax medical service—and that things aren't always what they seem.

I look online to find information on drug interactions, but the results are confusing and contradictory. Then I remember my friend Jay, who runs a compounding pharmacy—I know he is busy, but maybe he can help.

He replies promptly to my e-mail. "The mixture is not dangerous. The marijuana will fight the anti-psychotics, diminishing their potency. It will also magnify the soothing effect of drugs like Ativan or Trazodone, making him sleepier."

I am happy to know it's not deadly, but it's definitely something he needs to avoid. Thankfully, Jonathan has very little money and pot is expensive. I continue to point him to the Lord as our only source of peace and comfort, but my words seem inadequate. Or maybe I am just impatient. I keep waiting for some heaven-rending effect of God's Word, but I need to remember that it never returns empty and will always accomplish what he has purposed (see Isa. 55:11).

The Puritans often talked about the danger of looking for "creature comfort," or comfort in other people. As people have let me down and my son has continued to become a new entity (even many entities) before my eyes, I have realized I cannot put my trust in others, nor in my own attempts. Over and over, God has been grabbing my chin and turning my eyes toward him. I close my eyes and think about the triune God—not only as a helper and a comforter of sorrows, but in all his greatness and the perfection of his attributes. When I do this, things are re-dimensioned.

Further Help

I receive a phone call from IHOT—the In-Home Outreach Team. I have been on their waiting list for a couple of months. The caller, Jenny, tells me that my case has been approved.

"Thank you," I tell her, "but my son has been hospitalized and is now taking medications, so it might be too late."

She is surprised. "Do you want to cancel?"

"I don't know. He is taking his meds."

"It's not easy to be approved, and your son is in our program. Why not take advantage?"

I agree. Normally the program is limited to people who are refusing medications, but since my son has already been accepted, it's a providential opportunity.

IHOT starts their programs with a visit to the parents

or caretakers in order to formulate a plan with them, so I make an appointment.

My husband and I meet three caseworkers at the local library. Two of them, Jenny and Asheka, will work with us, while the third one, Sasha, will visit Jonathan. We are grateful for the help but concerned about Jonathan's reaction to a new and unexpected program in his life. Sasha reassures us that she will simply explain how their group follows up with people who have been hospitalized—how they offer support and resources without coercion and in full respect of his rights to confidentiality.

Asheka asks what we're hoping this program will accomplish. It's an unexpected question.

"I just want him to be happy . . . to be able to cope with his illness," I say hesitantly.

My husband has a larger dream. "I wish we could have our son back—the son we have always known," he says. "But I know it's not realistic."

They smile. "What do you want Sasha to accomplish?" Asheka continues.

Again, I am not sure. I haven't thought about goals. I have been happy just to see him take his medications and live day to day.

"It would be good for him to have some social interaction," I say. I know that this social awkwardness is one of the symptoms of schizophrenia that medications cannot cure.

"Do you have a youth group at your church?" Asheka asks.

"Not really. There are many young people, and they meet informally, but Jonathan leaves immediately after church and sits in my car," I reply.

They formulate a plan. Sasha will visit Jonathan, the two

can get acquainted, and then she can suggest a youth group. Asheka tells us we can call them any time.

Things are looking up. It's comforting to know we have someone on our side. I have a short moment of regret— if I had only waited a little longer, maybe we could have resolved the situation without resorting to a forcible hos-pitalization. As usual, I have to chase these thoughts from my mind and look to the God who is sovereign over all. His plans are never fouled by our mistakes.

Overdose

Tom takes the two youngest kids to Los Angeles to spend the Fourth of July with his brother. I stay home with Jonathan and Kevin. On the evening of the third, I go out to teach Italian—a three-hour class at a community college.

I come back at 9:30. As usual, I look into Jonathan's room. He has been leaving his door open, and I have gotten into the habit of checking on him, pulling up his blankets, closing the window if it's raining, and picking up things off the floor so he will not trip when he gets up in the night.

Tonight I find his legs lying half on the bed and his head and torso dangling toward the floor. His head is stuck between the bed and a chair. It looks like half of his room is on the ground: a laptop, his blankets, the TV. . . . He proba-bly fell and dragged everything down.

Whatever happened is not important now. I act quickly, trying to wake him up, but I don't get a response. I try to pick him up. He is very heavy, but I manage to get his head on the bed. Now what? Can I leave him like this?

He is alive. I see him breathing. I check his medica-tions. The bottle of Ativan is open. I count the pills. He is supposed to take one every night. I do some quick mental math—he has taken more than one, for sure. How many? Ten? Fifteen? My mind is not working fast enough.

I have to get him to the hospital, so I ask Kevin to help me and we take him to the car. He leans on us and walks but isn't awake. We place him in the passenger's seat. I still feel uneasy.

I call the HMO's emergency number and explain the situation.

"You shouldn't drive him. What if something happens on the way? You should call 911," they suggest. Just hearing the number evokes terrible memories.

Reluctantly, I do what they say. The paramedics arrive quickly, write down the information, take the bottle of Ativan, move Jonathan to the ambulance, and drive away. I follow closely. Kevin comes with me. I can see Jonathan sitting up on the stretcher, finally awake. He looks out of the window—I feel he is looking at me.

"Do you think he hates me for calling 911?" I ask Kevin.

"Hates you? You're the only one who talks to him."

I follow Jonathan into the emergency room, but he's fallen back asleep. I wait one hour for the doctor, and then I decide to leave. He's safe, and I will come back in the morning.

After a few hours of sleep, I return at 6 a.m. He is still sleeping, and the nurses tell me he is fine. The doctor has seen him during the night and will come back later. I sit next to him, enjoying the feeling of knowing he is peaceful and safe.

He wakes up at 7 and looks around. "Where am I?"

"At the hospital. You took too much Ativan, remember?"

No answer.

"How many did you take?"

"Ten."

"Why?"

"I wanted to see what it felt like."

The doctor arrives. He repeats that Jonathan is fine. Last night he was able to answer a couple of questions. He said he had taken fourteen Ativan pills—fourteen grams in all.

The doctor explains that an overdose of Ativan is not usually deadly. The danger comes from the fact that breathing can slow down considerably, leading the patient to asphyxiate in his sleep. I am glad I called 911.

"I assume he should stop taking it for a while," I say.

"He needs to see his psychiatrist. In any case, he should not stop abruptly. Definitely he doesn't need any today." The doctor adds that we have to wait for a social worker to come and talk to us. It's common procedure.

We wait for an hour, but no one comes. I'm hungry and ask Jonathan if he wants anything to eat. He says he does, so I go to a supermarket that is just around the corner. I leave my cell phone number at the nurse's station in case the social worker shows up. I am in line to pay when the phone rings. "I am coming right away," I say.

When I arrive, they tell me that the social worker has come and gone. "She couldn't wait, but she will come back." We wait for hours. Jonathan grows restless, so I let him play with my phone. I have very few games, which I never use. I think of the many hours I spent in waiting rooms when my kids were young. I reach for the doctor's blue gloves, blow them up, and tie a knot. I show him my five-finger balloon.

"What is it? A turkey?" I ask him.

"It's an elephant." An elephant? I turn the balloon around. I guess it could be an elephant. I draw a pair of eyes.

We talk about nothing for hours. Once in a while, I check with the nurse. Apparently the social worker is still making her rounds. I keep trying to find subjects to discuss with Jonathan before he gets totally frustrated.

"Can we go now?" he asks from time to time.

Finally the social worker arrives. Her main concern is to make sure Jonathan's overdose was not a suicide attempt.

"I am not suicidal," he replies.

She asks me if I want him back home.

"Of course."

She suggests I should manage his medications and asks for his approval. Surprisingly, he agrees.

We are free to go. The nurse prints out the discharge papers and lets me know that the doctor has detected a urinary infection and prescribed an antibiotic.

Jonathan asks if he can sit in the car while I wait at the pharmacy, and I let him. The wait seems endless after a long day at the ER. I am also uneasy about my decision. He has the car keys—what if he drives away? Finally they call his name and give me a bottle of red pills to take twice a day. I pay and leave in a hurry. I give him one in the evening.

The next day Jonathan looks disoriented. He stumbles through the house, losing his balance, and can't hold anything in his hands without dropping it. Tom is home, and together we decide to take him back to the ER. Jonathan doesn't question it.

As we wait for the doctors, he starts talking about football. He's in an unusually good mood. He continues talking to Tom for a long time.

The doctors arrive but don't know what to say. They ask him some questions—where is he, what's the date, who's the president—but only some of his answers are correct.

111

His heart is racing and his pupils dilated, but the doctors don't know why and don't seem to know what to do. They give him another Ativan. Finally they diagnose him with an "altered state of consciousness."

They don't know whether the Ativan overdose caused this or whether the altered level of consciousness caused him to overdose. The ER doctor tends to think that it's the latter. He consulted a toxicologist who said that one of Jonathan's antipsychotic medications (Zyprexa) can cause disorientation. He says we need to take all medications away from him and keep him within sight until he is stable.

Now we just have to wait for the nurse to discharge us—with no answers and no solutions. Tom leaves, and I wait with Jonathan, who is increasingly impatient. I ask when the nurse will come, and they tell me she is very busy.

In spite of my protests, Jonathan gets dressed and walks out of the room, pulling aside the curtains that divide each room in the emergency ward.

"Can you do something?" I ask the nurse at the desk. "I can't hold him any longer!"

Within minutes, the nurse comes with the discharge papers—apparently Jonathan knew what to do.

As we leave the hospital, he continues to talk as he hasn't done for years.

"Is Kevin going to Cal-Poly?" he asks.

"Yes."

"It's a good school. Are you still writing children's books? Are you going to write one about Michael Horton?"

At home, he gets in the pool for the first time since he has been ill and plays with his brother and sister. I ask my husband to film them. It's like having our son back. I don't know what's happening, but I enjoy these brief moments.

Before dinner, I prepare his medications—the usual ones, plus the antibiotic. Now that everything is peaceful, I check the bottle: Fluphenazine. Is that an antibiotic? I look it up and discover that it's the generic name for Prolixin. What happened?

It takes me a while to understand. Because of a shortage of Prolixin injections, the psychiatrist has prescribed pills to take their place, and the pharmacist handed me those pills even though I had given him the prescription for Cipro. I call the pharmacy and they calmly tell me they will prepare the other prescription. I point out their mistake, but they tell me I should have checked the bottle. My sense of urgency is constantly clashing with their nonchalance. They are probably used to mistakes.

Is that why Jonathan is behaving so differently? Since the injectable Prolixin is still in his system, he had an extra dosage. Is that why he is looking "normal" in some ways? Part of him is still not here—in fact, it's more distant than ever—and the "altered state of consciousness" is definitely not a good sign. It's a sobering revelation of what psychotropic medications can do.

I feel terribly guilty for the mix-up. Since it's a weekend and the clinic is closed, I call poison control to see what they have to say. They are very kind. Apparently, what I gave him was not too much, even if it has side effects. I hope that his regular doctors understand when I tell them what happened, because they normally seem to resent my interferences, and this mistake may disqualify me in their eyes as a capable caretaker. Their priority seems to be to give Jonathan autonomy, but he can't have full autonomy right now.

But the ER doctors have suggested that I keep the medicines away from Jonathan and dispense them to him.

In spite of my mistake, I know they are safer in my hands than in his. This is a positive outcome of this distressing accident.

The next morning, Jonathan is back to what he was a few days ago—silent and completely uninterested in anything around him. He doesn't remember anything at all. The blue plastic glove "elephant" means nothing to him.

At first he protests against my holding of his medicines. He doesn't remember agreeing with the social worker about it and doesn't remember the doctor's orders. I show him the hospital's discharge papers and the diagnosis of "altered state of consciousness." I explain that the doctor advised I dispense the medicines for now. He gives me a long, questioning look, then leaves the room quietly. My heart runs after him. I want so much to fill his searching void. I wish I could.

6

Successes and Failures

Trapped in my mind and I'm a mean jailer.
(Jonathan Carr)

Family Environment

I have been reading many books on schizophrenia and other mental illnesses. Warner's *Environment of Schizophrenia* is particularly encouraging. In his words, "The popular and professional view that schizophrenia has a progressive, downhill course with universally poor outcome is a myth. Over the course of months or years, about 20 to 25 per cent of people with schizophrenia recover completely from the illness—all their psychotic symptoms disappear and they return to their previous level of functioning. Another 20 per cent continue to have some symptoms, but they are able to lead satisfying and productive lives."[1]

Warner lists some elements that are helpful in this recovery. "Medications are an important part of treatment

---

1. Richard Warner, *The Environment of Schizophrenia: Innovations in Practice, Policy and Communications* (London: Brunner-Routledge, 2000), 5.

but they are only part of the answer," he says. "They can reduce or eliminate positive symptoms but they have a negligible effect on negative symptoms."[2] In other words, they can reduce or eliminate hallucinations and "voices," but they can't help the patient to regain what seems to be lost or missing—lack of social skills, responsiveness, motivation, and healthy emotional reactions.

Likewise, hospitalization "is mainly reserved for those in an acute relapse." What works for a sustained treatment is family involvement and social rehabilitation (including "training in basic living skills; assistance with a host of day-to-day tasks; and job training, job placement, and work support").[3]

I like to think we are providing a good family environment, but, according to Warner, a series of studies has shown that "the relapse rate is higher for people with schizophrenia who live with critical or over-involved relatives."[4]

I am definitely over-involved. I have become his shadow, so I try to step back. As a Christian, I have the advantage of knowing (and believing) that everything is part of God's plan.

Going from this knowledge and assent to a full trust that allows me to sleep at night is not as simple as it sounds. But I have lived long enough to know that I will never reach that trust and peace of mind by really, really trying to get it. Faith, like everything else, is a gift from God. We can strive to get it, but ultimately God's Spirit works it in us through external means, such as the preached Word. We have to learn to accept it and claim it, then rest.

It's easier said than done. Most of us have an inborn

2. Warner, 13.
3. Warner, 13.
4. Warner, 30.

desire to act, to fix things, to take matters into our hands, as if our hands were the best and the strongest—as if our love and passion could automatically translate into expertise, ability, and success.

The Therapeutic Value of Work

According to Warner, "Work helps people recover from schizophrenia. Productive activity is basic to a person's sense of identity and worth. The availability of work in a subsistence economy may be one the main reasons that outcome from schizophrenia is so much better in villages in the developing world. Given training and support, most people with schizophrenia can work."[5]

Tom and I contact the San Diego Department of Rehabilitation to see if they can find Jonathan a job. He has an initial interview. When asked, "What do you want to do?" he replies, "I want to work at a cash register."

My husband tries to encourage him to do more. He has always had such a bright mind. The department could help him to get back to college and find a career, but Jonathan is sure of his choice. Is he discouraged or just realistic?

While we wait for the slow wheels of government agencies to turn, I try to keep Jonathan busy in other ways. In high school, he loved pole vaulting. I Google "pole vaulting teams in San Diego." I can only find some for children, so I email one of these contacts to ask if they know of any team for young men. They give me a phone number. When I call, I discover that the man in charge of the team is Jonathan's high school coach. Quite a surprise!

5. Warner, 13–14.

The coach remembers Jonathan. I explain the situation, and he is eager to help. They have free practice in the summer, but if Jonathan wants to continue in the fall he will have to enroll in the community college where the team normally plays. I give Jonathan the good news. As usual, he doesn't react.

I take him to his first practice. He seems a little confused—he is not jumping as high as he used to. I tell him he has to exercise, to build up his strength, but I'm not sure whether that's all. Has he lost some of his coordination or his ability to gauge distances? He is quiet but continues to go to all his practices.

I tell him I am proud of him, and he is surprised. "I really couldn't do what you do," I add. I mean it. I don't think I could fight on as quietly and resignedly as he does. I know that God gives grace as we need it.

During the day, Jonathan checks job ads and sends off applications. I encourage him to wait a little longer. The Department of Rehab should answer soon. He doesn't want to wait. Occasionally he asks me to drive him to interviews. Each time, he comes out knowing he has been rejected. Each time, I wish I could go inside and explain the situation to the managers, but I can't. I have to let him do this on his own.

He gets a call from Home Depot—one more job interview. This time he seems convinced he will make it. We go to buy some new clothes. Before the interview, he asks me to drive him to the support group. He doesn't have time to attend a full session, but he seems eager to show off his new look, and the group is encouraging and praises him.

We drive to Home Depot. Once again, I sit in the car during the interview, praying that God will spare him another disappointment or allow him to bear it. Jonathan comes out with some papers in his hands—he passed. I am surprised. As usual, he shows no emotion. Next hurdle: a urine test to detect the presence of drugs.

I know he still smokes marijuana, and I am pretty sure he will fail. As much as I hate to see him hurting, the rejection might help him to understand that drugs can limit his opportunities.

I take him to our HMO clinic for the test. Only after the test does he tell me that he has to go to a specific place and that Home Depot will pay. We arrange to go in the morning, but at the last minute he tells me he has lost his ID, which he needs to complete the test.

We spend a couple days madly searching through the house. After the Home Depot manager calls a few times and issues an ultimatum, we find the ID in the pocket of one of Jonathan's pairs of pants and drive to the appointed lab. I wait in the car, correcting some papers—working is therapeutic for me, too. I have to think of something else or I'll lose my mind.

Jonathan doesn't show up, so I walk around the block a few times to exercise. I clean the car. Still no trace of my son. Finally, I enter the lab and find him staring at some notices on the wall.

"Are you done?"

"No."

"Why not?"

"I can't pee."

I give him some water, but nothing happens. He's probably nervous. The water is cold and he starts shivering violently. Finally, I take him home and hope for a better day.

At home I find the results of the first urine test. It

119

detected traces of marijuana. Trying again at the lab will only serve to teach him a lesson.

The next day he manages to take the test, and we get an answer from Home Depot a few hours later. He passed the urine test and has to report to work. How did he pass? He couldn't possibly have cheated, because they screen everybody very carefully. My husband thinks they have a limit of tolerance, and Jonathan was probably below those numbers.

Emotionless as ever, Jonathan tells us where he will work: about twenty-five miles north of our house—half an hour by car. He has to go to sign some papers, and his shift will start at 4 a.m. every day.

"How will you get there?"

"By bus."

"There is no bus that early in the morning."

"Then I'll walk."

My husband and I look at each other. We know that he means it. He will walk.

"You can't possibly walk that far in the middle of the night. It will take you hours. It's dangerous. The police might even stop you."

No answer. We sit in silence for a while.

"I'll take you," I finally say. "I wake up in the middle of the night anyhow."

Thankfully, after the initial trip to sign papers, his manager decides to move him to their Santee branch, a short walk from our house. God is good!

I continue to wake up around 3 a.m. anyhow. I stay awake until 3:30 and make sure that Jonathan gets up in time. I prepare his clothes and a snack every night. I might be babying him, but he needs help. Warner's book does say that assistance for people with schizophrenia "can include training in basic living skills" and "assistance with a host of day-to-day tasks." I just wish I had understood this sooner.

Andrew Solomon gives a clear explanation of this new dependence on others, as "schizophrenia can take away the ability to connect to or love or trust another person, the full use of rational intelligence, the capacity to function in any professional context, the basic faculty of physical self-care, and large areas of self-awareness and analytic clarity."[6]

I still leave Jonathan the responsibility of setting his alarm clock and waking up on time, getting dressed, and taking his apron, name tag, and snack. I just check and see that he does it and help him if he forgets. Occasionally I wake up late and find him still in bed. Then I drive him to work. I enjoy every minute with him, even when he is silent—but deep inside, I don't know how long any of this will last.

Back to Full Communion

Jonathan's social skills are still lost. Once, he asks me to take him to a high-school friend, but less than an hour later he calls me and asks me to pick him up. He used to stay for hours. Now he can't last too long.

I wish someone at church could take him out and be his friend, but I can't force anyone. So far only some elders from the church have reached out to him, but I think he interpreted it mostly as "checking on him." Even his brothers are distant, at a loss for the right thing to do or say.

I am grateful for all the brave souls who engage in a small conversation with him. I know it can be intimidating—he

---

6. Andrew Solomon, *Far from the Tree: Parents, Children, and the Search for Identity* (New York: Scribner, 2012), 295–96.

usually looks down and absorbed in serious thoughts, his face covered by a rebellious forest of dreadlocks. He looks impregnable and hostile—but, unlike other situations, when someone talks to him at church he lifts his head and his face brightens into a wide, sincere smile. He happily answers every question with concise replies. In some cultures, people with mental illnesses are considered wise—and maybe they are, in some ways.

I talk to Pastor Brown, who agrees that we can't force anyone to visit Jonathan. Once again, God has to turn hearts. He does, however, make an announcement before the Sunday service. "If anyone is looking for a ministry, you don't have to look too far. We have lots of opportunities right here. You can visit the elderly or those who live with physical or mental illnesses." Within days, Mike—a young man with gentle eyes and a warm, infectious smile—tells Pastor Brown he would like to help, and our pastor suggests that he visit Jonathan.

Jonathan greets Mike kindly and agrees to go out with him. They go bowling, together with Taylor, another young man who is preparing for the pastoral ministry. Apparently they have a good time. "He referred to us as 'my friends,'" Taylor tells me.

Mike continues to visit other times. Once, when my husband and I have to attend a family function in LA, Mike takes Jonathan to church. They seem to get along, even if Jonathan is still mostly quiet.

Pastor Brown starts visiting, too. He arrives on his motorcycle, takes off his helmet, and sits at our table in our backyard where he plays chess with Jonathan. They play together for a while, saying little about anything else. Jonathan beats him almost every time—his ability to play is astounding.

Jonathan and Pastor Brown playing chess in our backyard

After his second visit, Pastor Brown tells me that Jonathan wants to go before the church elders and ask to be readmitted to the Lord's Supper. The appointment is on a Tuesday evening. I can't take him because I am teaching an Italian class, so we decide that my husband will take him and that I will pick him up.

I am not completely surprised by the announcement. Recently Jonathan has been more eager to come to church and more relaxed while he is there. He sings and reads along with the others and doesn't seem as lost in his thoughts as he has been in the past. Just a few days ago, after church, he told me that he wants to stop smoking and thanked me for what I am doing. I am afraid to get my hopes raised, but I am extremely thankful to God.

On Tuesday evening I feel distracted while I teach.

I shoot up constant prayers to God—will Jonathan be honest in his talk to the elders? He has talked to them twice before but could never get past his compelling desire to use marijuana. Even my ride back to church is a never-ending prayer.

I arrive minutes before he is done. He soon comes to the car, still emotionless.

"How did it go?"

"I can take the Lord's Supper this Sunday."

I quietly thank God for this miracle. I am not using this word lightly. Even today, in an age far removed from the apostles who were directly appointed by Christ, when God dispenses his protection, provision, and healing through ordinary means rather than prodigious signs, turning the hearts of men to him is still a miracle of his grace.

"We need to celebrate," I tell Jonathan. "Do you want to eat out?"

"Okay."

"Where do you want to go?"

"Olive Garden."

The suggestion of Olive Garden rubs roughly against my purist Italian tastes, but anything is great at this time. At the local restaurant, I watch him gulp down forkfuls of fettuccine alfredo while I patiently refrain from commenting on the amount of tomato sauce they used in my minestrone.

"What did they say?" I venture to ask.

"The same questions as before."

"So what changed this time?"

Without changing his expression, he explains with surprising clarity. "Before, I was really rebellious. I wanted to have my way."

That says it all.

Relapses

Jonathan's progress is never a linear line. There are many ups and downs. After a period of peace, I smell marijuana coming from his room. Now that he gets paychecks, he can buy it with no problem.

This has been a stressful week. The day before yesterday I said something that upset him—something related to medications—and he went to his room, turned off the light, and put some music on full volume. Then yesterday he seemed to be in another world again—even before getting the marijuana.

I think there is so much happening with the job and track that he feels overwhelmed. He keeps forgetting things everywhere. I'm sure that it frustrates him, and he finds some peace when he smokes. I ask him how it helps him, and he says, "In every way." The soothing effects of the drug are familiar and comforting.

Relying on God's grace is difficult for everyone, and I imagine it's worse for those who have a mental disability. While the struggle against sin is often fierce for all of us, it's starkly visible in the life of my son, and it hurts to see. I know that the Lord is faithful with me, bringing Scriptures back to my mind when I need them, and I am praying He will do the same with Jonathan.

I am, of course, very concerned—not only because of the damages that marijuana can have on his mental health, but also because he has just talked to the elders and, to my knowledge, has promised to stop smoking. I let Pastor Brown know.

Jonathan gets angry when I tell him I contacted our pastor. He also looks extremely scared, which is normal with paranoid schizophrenia. I try to reassure him, telling him that all he has to do is repent and try again—because our righteousness is in Christ (not in our perfect performance), God's mercy toward us knows no end.

Sadly, I find him smoking again a few days later—this time sitting by the side of our house and using an apple as a pipe.

"I thought you were going to stop," I say, disheartened.

"I talked to the pastor. It's okay," he says.

I am surprised, but Pastor Brown tells me that they are having patience because of Jonathan's condition.

One of the elders, Aaron, gives me a longer explanation. As our pastor already told me from the start, the problem is in the addiction and the drunkenness, which is a lack of self-control.

"Jonathan's case is unique," Aaron explains, "because of his overall circumstance. There is definitely a spiritual war raging around him, and we want to pray for his protection and that he hears God's voice/Word and places his confidence in it." In other words, the elders decided to be gentle with him, encouraging him to remember who he is in Christ and to walk according to the Spirit and not the flesh. "We all struggle with this tension in some way or another," Aaron adds.

He reassures me that the recent meeting with Jonathan went very well. "There has no doubt been a major improvement in Jonathan, and his spiritual life seems to be stronger now than it has been over the last two years. The quality of his desire to be in full communion—or, to put it another way, his affection for the Lord—was evident at the meeting, and we saw that, spiritually speaking, Jonathan's eyes were looking toward heaven and the promises of God."

He advises me to "load him up with gospel"—"He knows what he did wrong. He needs to hear that God loves him, despite his sin, because of Christ. This setback can be seen as discouraging, but I would remind him of what Christ has said is true of him through the gospel."

Since Jonathan has just changed some medications and the doctors are waiting for him to adjust, I appreciate the elders' compassion. I pray that the doctors can find the right balance of medications so that Jonathan will not feel so restless and try to self-medicate with other substances.

Struggle at Work

Each week that Jonathan continues to work at Home Depot I am surprised. At home, he can barely finish one task without getting distracted, and if he gets more than one instruction at a time he ends up forgetting them all.

I would much prefer that he work through the Department of Rehabilitation, but Jonathan has told them he has a job, so they've had to take him off their list.

I think Jonathan feels the pressure at work but is determined to continue. As usual, he expresses his thoughts in a short poem.

Jon Carr pulling trailers
overflowing with my successes and failures
Trapped in my mind and I'm a mean jailer.

Then one day he skips work altogether, without notice. In reality, it is due to circumstances that are quite out of his control.

The day beforehand, a friend came to pick him up to go

to a Chargers' game. He is a high school friend who Jonathan has not seen in months, if not years. I am glad that Jonathan is finally getting out, but I worry when he doesn't come home at night.

I try to call him, but his phone is turned off. I vacillate between a general malaise and outright panic—even when I try to repress my worries, my stomach growls and I feel nauseous. Worry always affects me physically, tying knots in my intestines and bringing shivers through my body.

"He's probably staying with his friend for the night," says Tom, who could probably sleep through a hostile invasion. He makes a lot of sense, and his calming tone of voice, along with my exhaustion, finally silence my fears. With a last, desperate prayer, I slip into a deep sleep.

Jonathan returns early in the morning.

"What happened?"

"I was arrested."

Finding out the details is like pulling weeds from hard ground. Finally, I get a general picture of what happened. Apparently Jonathan got separated from his friend and walked through the stadium looking for him. Somehow the guards thought he was drunk, so they arrested him and placed him in the stadium's "jail" until morning.

I am full of angry questions. Why didn't his friend look for him? Couldn't the guards use a breathalyzer before coming to such a conclusion? I know my son can look disoriented.

I wish I could have told his friend about Jonathan's condition, but my son would have hated me for that. He still feels the weight of stigma. Our society, of course, doesn't help. Kids often use words such as *schizo* or *psycho* in a derogatory way. Stereotypes about people with mental illness are all

around us, and the media, TV, and movies repeat them—
and even distort and magnify them—unashamedly.

So I don't blame my son. Who wants to be known as
schizophrenic in a world that equates the illness with split
personality, unpredictable behavior, and violence?

There is a red mark around his neck. Did someone grab
him by the neck? I ask him and he says no.

While we are talking, his boss calls him from work.
I notice the number.

"Tell him something happened. Don't be specific,"
I advise Jonathan as he answers the phone.

"I was arrested," he says without hesitation.

I smile. His illness has brought out an unusual honesty.
I suppose when a mind is cluttered with voices and different
perceptions of reality, honesty has a refreshing simplicity,
and prudence takes second place.

"You told him you were arrested?" I asked after the call.

"He's a good guy," he replies.

A few days later, Jonathan receives a letter announcing
that he is banned from attending Chargers games again
unless he first attends a special course. My husband calls
to explain, and also to find out what really happened. He is
told that our son looked like he was under the influence of
some substance, and the guard was only following the customary procedures.

Did my son and his friend smoke something before the
game? I don't really know his friend and don't feel that I
can knock at his door to find answers. The matter is not big
enough to upset my son, but I am left with the utopian desire
to live in a world where all illnesses and imperfections are
fully understood and treated with compassion. As a Christian, I know that in reality there is something better ahead

of us—a world where all illnesses and imperfections will be gone forever, when God will make all things new—but the travail throughout this sin-broken life is unavoidable.

The Ghost of Harder Drugs

I keep my eyes on Jonathan every time he manages to buy marijuana. Most of the time he is moderate, but today I find him sprawled on the couch, almost comatose. I find a dispensary's receipt in his room that lists a couple of marijuana-infused candies, free of charge.

At this time, in California, there is no way of knowing how much tetrahydrocannabinol (THC) is in each marijuana candy or whether other substances have been added. This is one of the incongruences of medicinal marijuana regulations: doctors are allowed to prescribe this substance without limiting or monitoring its dosage. A medical marijuana card is not a prescription—it's a license to use as much marijuana as one wants.

At this time, states in which marijuana is legal have a few more regulations—for example, each container has to state the ingredients and the amount of THC and other active compounds in the product, the way other states mandate the number of calories, proteins, and fats in packaged foods.

Some marijuana candies are so potent that they can produce scary reactions even in seasoned smokers. Most websites advise users to consume them with prudence, starting with a small amount until their effect is clear—but what happens if you give two powerful candies to a person with a mental impairment, who is likely to forget if he has taken the first one? What happens when a normally absent-minded person leaves them in open view of children?

I pray that my son makes it through the night, and he does. In the morning, I explain the danger of these "treats." If this "doctor" truly believes that marijuana is good for schizophrenia, then Jonathan needs to treat it as a medication and consume it only in limited amounts. I still believe that abstinence would be ideal, but I'll take what I can get.

I give him a weekly medicine dispenser for the rest of his marijuana and encourage him to split it into days. Even if he doesn't care for his health, this would ensure that it last until his next paycheck. For once, I am thankful that the prices of marijuana are still quite high.

Jonathan agrees and seems to follow my advice. A few days later, however, he asks me to get him a book from the library: *Tweak*, by Nic Sheff. He says that a friend recommended it to him. I don't get books from the library for him anymore—the last book I checked out for him was left out in the rain all night. I buy a used copy online—the full title is *Tweak: Growing Up on Methamphetamines*.

I tell Jonathan I have ordered the book and ask the question that's weighing on my mind. "You are not thinking of using meth, are you?"

"No," he says.

I try to believe him and pray that God will protect him.

When the book arrives, I read it quickly and anxiously. It is a painful first-person account of the life of a young man caught in the relentless grip of drug addiction. I turn each page uncomfortably, frightened by the realization of how easily anyone could slip into that deadly downward spiral. One syringe, one snort of cocaine (even less than a snort) might be enough to trigger the habit.

After a while, reading becomes too disturbing and I skip to the last pages. Thankfully, the story has a happy ending—the young man goes through rehab and is reconciled with his parents.

The last scene is particularly moving, with Nic and his father both asking for forgiveness, hugging, crying, and saying "I love you." Maybe it's okay for my son to read it after all.

I give him the book, but I still monitor his reading—I watch him turning the pages or marking his place when he leaves the book on his bed. I want him to get to the end. I want it to be our ending, too—love, peace, and happiness. We all want that, don't we?

In the meantime, I continue to help him through his daily routine. I give him meds, make sure he gets to work, make sure he has food to eat, and drive him to pole-vault practice. Almost every day, a young player greets him with a big smile.

"Hi, Jonathan!" she says.

He replies softly, his eyes lowered, but I know he feels appreciated.

I usually leave him at the field and let him take a bus back. He doesn't like it, but I teach Italian in the evenings, and I have to get dinner on the table before I go to work.

Sometimes I am able to stay, and he likes that. I sit in the car, parked next to the field, and watch him jump. He is still not as good as he was in high school, but he is persistent, as he has always been. Before each jump, he looks toward me to see if I am watching.

His phone rings while I am there. It's a text—I glance over and see the first lines of the message: "60 bucks." He will hate me for this, but I just have to look—anything involving money is suspicious. The only money he receives is from work, and they would not text him. I open the message and read, "For 60 bucks you can get three pills. Take them all at the same time for a maximum high." I look at the thread—it's obviously his supplier. There is a message from Jonathan asking if they sell acid. Acid?

I feel the panic rising in my chest but stay in the car and continue to smile when he looks at me. What do I do? I want to call the suppliers and yell my frustrations—are they even allowed to sell acid? They sell "medicinal marijuana," but I'm sure that acid is not medicinal at all! I am tempted to call the police, but I know that would not solve my immediate dilemma. I pray desperately, trying to keep calm while my heart pounds. Finally, I decide to call Asheka at the In-Home Outreach Team. Thankfully, she answers the phone.

I explain the situation, and she comes up with a plan. Her promptness makes me wonder if this has happened before. "Take him out to dinner," she says. "Then talk to him casually." It seems like a strange plan, but I decide to follow it. I call my husband—he was going to be out at my daughter's water polo game, so he can take the others out as well.

Jonathan helps the team to clean up the field. It's wonderful to see him working well with others. When he comes back to the car, I ask him if he wants to eat out. He says yes.

"Where do you want to go?"

"In-N-Out."

"No, I mean an actual restaurant. We can sit there."

"Olive Garden." I should have known.

We sit in the restaurant quietly. I have come to appreciate the power of silence—it's definitely better than speaking just to say something. I watch Jonathan eat heartily, his face lowered over the plate. I am not sure if he has seen the text message yet. Once in a while, I ask him about pole vault and practice. His answers are short.

I mention drugs only as we are driving back home. It's better that way. My Italian heritage has taught me that food—even food from Olive Garden—has to be enjoyed without awkward conversations.

"Branch, I know you're still smoking pot, and I hope you are doing it in moderation, but I just wanted to make sure you don't use harder drugs."

"I am not," he says.

"They can be very dangerous, even acid," I insist.

"I know."

At home, I wait anxiously to see how the evening will enfold. No one comes to the door. The next day, the usual supplier arrives with a small package. As Jonathan walks back to his room, I grab the receipt he has left behind. It's only marijuana. For today, at least, this crisis was averted.

7

Hard Providence

I know it's your will so I won't question.
(Jonathan Carr)

For a while, things seem to go well—at least on the surface. Jonathan has a job, practices pole vault, takes his medications, and seems to be more moderate in his marijuana intake. To be on the pole vault team, he had to enroll in college, but he was allowed to take only one class in the fall: physical education, which is practically weight training. He will have to take more classes next semester, but since he finally admitted his disability in his college application, the school is not making the same demands that they make to able students.

He is receiving disability checks—$600 dollars a month—that help with his expenses. Thankfully, the state has made me the executor of his money, so he can't spend it on drugs. Since the disability checks were retroactive, he has enough money to buy an inexpensive car. My husband finds one through a friend, and our mechanic is amazed at its mint condition. Jonathan enjoys the independence that driving gives him.

He is also more relaxed and seems to trust me. He allows me to clean his room, even if he is not there. He even allows me to fix his dreads. I have to look up dreadlocks online to see how to twist them, but I soon get the hang of it. I am just amazed that he lets me touch him.

All seems well. In reality, I am not completely satisfied. The amount of medications Jonathan is taking still makes me uneasy. In spite of many promises, the doctors have kept the same dosage. I see books on the danger of psychiatric medications, especially antidepressants and antipsychotics, but I don't have the heart to read them because I can't do anything about it.

I wish I could take Jonathan to a new psychiatrist for a second opinion, but he refuses to do it. Online, psychiatrists claim to be able to treat schizophrenia without drugs. Dr. Warner, the author of *The Environment of Schizophrenia*, has a center in Colorado called Colorado Recovery that also seems promising, but Jonathan will not agree to try it. Besides, we can't go there for a visit or two. He would have to be admitted into their program.

I consider taking him to Italy, where psychiatric care is supposed to be more advanced. He has always wanted to go back to Italy, and as Italian citizens we wouldn't have medical expenses. But, once again, we couldn't possibly go for a visit. We would have to stay for some time, and—providing we receive a good treatment there—we would have to find a psychiatrist in the United States who would agree to continue the same program.

I look for other options. Acupuncture doesn't have a record of efficacy in the treatment of schizophrenia, but it's good for anxiety; and if Jonathan could be less anxious, he would have less of a need for medications like Ativan or for drugs like marijuana. My acupuncturist friend is located nearby. I ask Jonathan if he wants to try. Surprisingly, he says yes.

He is relaxed as we prepare for his first visit to my friend's office. After we arrive, he sits quietly in the waiting room, staring at the walls. I see another woman who looks disturbed, possibly by a mental illness. She stares at him.

When the acupuncturist's assistant calls her name, the woman gets up and follows her. Before leaving the room, she moves closer to Jonathan and asks, "Are you in a band?"

"Yes," he says.

"Are you?" I ask him, perplexed. He nods.

"What's the name of the band?" she continues.

He replies without hesitation: "Kid Nobody." That's the name he has handwritten on the side of his tennis shoes. I guess that's his band. A one-man band. I know he likes to write rap music.

My friend comes out in person to escort Jonathan to a room. Then, when Jonathan is settled and enjoying the treatment, he comes to talk to me.

"I didn't know he was so beautiful," he says. "He doesn't like to talk, but I got him to open up a little. I asked him where he would like to be if he could choose one place on earth, and he said Merced."

Getting to know my son is a never-ending adventure.

As we drive back home, I ask Jonathan how the session went.

"It put me in a better place," he said.

I wish the effects could last longer, and that he wouldn't need to resort again to marijuana, but it's just a wish. Still, at least he knows he has an alternative, and we can come back whenever he wants.

Back to Merced

The word *Merced* comes back again as we sit at a table on the side porch of our house, where Jonathan likes to spend much of his time.

"I want to go back to Merced for Halloween," he says.

He hasn't given up on his dream of returning to see his friends, and now that he has a car, who can stop him?

It gets worse.

"I want to move back there."

"Do you mean go back to school there?"

"No—just move there with my friends."

"How would you support yourself?"

"I can use the money from Social Security."

"Branch, first of all you need to talk to the Social Security office, because they made me in charge of that money. Besides, that's not going to be enough. And what about your job? Pole vault?"

"I can do it there."

"Will you see a doctor there?"

"I don't know."

Anxiety mounts up inside me again. That's the danger of feeling better. He has made so much progress lately that he feels he can cope on his own. I really wish he could, but he is not ready. I want him to have independence—but one step at a time. Besides, Merced is about 800 miles from home, and I am not comfortable with letting him drive on his own.

"Are your friends from Merced?"

"No; they're from LA."

"Then why don't you wait until they come down here to visit their parents?"

"No."

I talk to Tom, who feels the same way. We want to tell Jonathan not to go, but we don't know how. We don't want to say, "It's because of your illness." At the same time, we remember what happened at the Chargers game. Besides, these are the friends who introduced him to mushrooms. Who knows what he will do there? And I can't expect him to take his meds. I guess I need to let go. I can't possibly oversee him indefinitely. But I still worry.

I email Asheka, from the In-Home Outreach Team, and talk to Lisa, Jonathan's current therapist. Asheka thinks letting him go is a terrible idea and encourages me to keep trying to persuade him to stay. Lisa thinks the trip is a great opportunity for him to be more independent. I tend to agree with Asheka, because the thought of my son traveling alone is still terrifying. In fact, worry keeps me awake at night. Tom always tells me that worries are useless, but sometimes they produce ideas. I think and think.

I also talk to my friend Grace—one of the dear people who have been by my side through this ordeal.

"I am so sorry," she says. "Probably reasoning with him just doesn't work the same as 'before.' I will pray for you and for him. Road trips seem like a lot of fun. All the kids are doing it these days . . . at least a lot of our friends' kids. Usually, though, they are with another person or two. I wonder if there is someone he trusts enough to go with him. Who could be gone for a while?"

I lighten up. What a great idea! What if we rent a car and ask our son Dustin, who is now back from military service, to drive Jonathan to Merced? At least Jonathan will be safe during the trip. Then Dustin can take the time to visit Kevin at Cal-Poly—something he wants to do anyhow.

I talk to Tom, who thinks it's a good plan. Dustin agrees to do it.

Jonathan refuses.

I continue to beg him, to no avail.

On the day he has set for the trip, he fills the car using the last of his money and asks me for some pocket change. It makes sense for him not to leave penniless, but I can't do it.

"I am sorry. I told you I'm not supporting this trip, and I can't give you money. If you go with Dustin, I will."

"I am not going with Dustin."

For the first time in many months, I see him angry. He hits his laptop's keyboard with both hands. "It's stupid! It's stupid!"

The next morning, he prepares to leave. I cannot dissuade him. I go to the shop and buy some healthy foods so he will not be forced to survive on junk food. I give him his meds in a pill container and make sure he has his driver's license and enough clean clothes. He thanks me.

I follow him until he is ready to get into the car. At the last minute, I give him sixty dollars. I can't let him go without money—not in his weak state of mind. I would feel too guilty if anything happened.

I make him promise to call every day and remind him that we expect him back for his dad's birthday in five days' time. I steal a hug from him. It might be our last.

He drives away. "He is in God's hands now," I say to myself. Immediately I realize how stupid that sounds—as if he had been safer up to now just because he was with me. I change my refrain. "He is in God's hands! Nothing to worry about."

A few hours after he leaves, I find a letter for him in

the mailbox. It's obviously a paycheck. It's strange, because Home Depot sends direct deposits to his bank. I text Jonathan. "When you stop for lunch, call me. There is a paycheck here for you."

Of course, he calls me back immediately. Money is important to him.

"Are you driving?"

"No."

"There's a paycheck for you. Do you want me to open it?"

"Yes."

There is a letter with it—this is the last paycheck. He has been fired. I give him the news.

"I know," he says.

"When did they tell you?"

"Yesterday."

"Did they say why?"

"They said I didn't work fast enough."

I comfort him, telling him that finding work is hard for anyone right now. I tell him not to worry. When he comes home, we will reapply to the Department of Rehab, and they will find him a better job.

He asks me to deposit the money. I regret calling him, but, after all, the sixty dollars I gave him are not much. If he spends it on food, he will not have gas for the way back. I agree to do it, reminding him to call me in the evening to let me know he has arrived.

He doesn't.

Tearing Away

Nights are always difficult for me. I wake up around 3 a.m. every time, probably because of my age. To avoid thinking about my worries, I use an MP3 player with soft, gospel-filled songs that remind me of Christ. If I am particularly awake, I listen to a sermon. I need to keep my mind on the big picture. In the large scheme of things, this is just a "light momentary affliction" that is "preparing for us an eternal weight of glory beyond all comparison, as we look not to the things that are seen but to the things that are unseen. For the things that are seen are transient, but the things that are unseen are eternal" (2 Cor. 4:17–18).

A portion of a song by William Cowper strikes me.

The dearest idol I have known,
whate'er that idol be,
help me to tear it from thy throne
and worship only thee.[1]

Have I turned my son into an idol? For a Christian, an idol is anything that takes priority over God. This case is a little difficult because, as any caregiver does, I have to revolve my life around my son.

I think of him when I wake up at night. Sometimes I check to make sure he is in bed and pull up his covers. I think of him when I wake again in the morning and review his schedule to make sure he is making all his appointments. I like to do it, and I believe that he needs it, at least for now.

The problem comes when he doesn't follow my plans—when he takes too much marijuana, when he decides to stay home from church, or, as in this case, when he stubbornly follows a dangerous course. Janie, my pastor's wife, has a great definition for mothers: she says we are "fruit

---

1. William Cowper, "O for a Closer Walk with God," 1779.

inspectors." We tend to inspect our kids' "fruits" as a proof or measure of their faith. We get our noses too close to their problems and faults.

Now that Jonathan is gone, it's actually easier for me to let go. I lie on my bed and relax. I think of messages I hear all the time from friends: "Let it go. Think positive thoughts." Right now it could work, but it still seems useless. I can let go of the thought, but it will come back. I can't just get my son out of my mind, because he is, after all, my son and my responsibility. The answer is not to eliminate thoughts or to resort to a stoic unattachment. It's to put things into perspective. It's to keep my mind on Christ, "the author and finisher of our faith," and on his bigger plan.

The balance, it seems, lies in accepting what God has placed in my path while doing at the same time what I know I should do to make things easier for my son and my family. It's not easy, because emotions are strong.

I eventually fall asleep. The next day, Jonathan calls. He has had a small accident. He rear-ended a car and needs the insurance information. We have asked him to buy his own insurance, so he should have the papers with him, but he doesn't. I look in his room until I find the papers. I ask if he is okay. He says yes but doesn't add any details. Apparently there is a friend with him.

After this call, silence. He never calls or texts again. It's unnerving. Once in a while I send him a message.

"Remember you have your shot on Wednesday."

"I am sure your coach misses you by now . . ."

I even wrote in Italian, reminding him of his father's birthday the next day.

"Branch, *domani è il compleanno di tuo padre. Festeggeremo verso le 6 o 7.* Will you be here?"

No reply. I try to call, but it goes straight to voicemail. Maybe his phone is not charged or he turned it off. I am starting to worry again. What if something happened? How would I know? What if he decides to stay there, since he has been fired? His doctors and medications are here. I'm sure I wouldn't be as worried if he didn't have schizophrenia, because I'm not worried about any of the others, but we don't know what could happen if he doesn't take his meds . . .

As I clean his room, I find some troubling words scribbled on paper.

> So I haven't started yet but lately I'm on edge.
> Sometimes it makes me wanna rip out a dread.
> But you can't stop me.
> Monster says, wanna bet?

My anxiety mounts. I remember the name of one of his friends at Merced and look him up on Facebook. I can read his latest posts, but there is no mention of my son. I am tempted to write, but I decide to wait. I will feel better when he returns, but this uncertainty keeps me looking up to our only Hope.

An Eerie Look

Jonathan returns, suddenly and surprisingly, on my husband's birthday. It's the day that he promised to come, but I'm still surprised because of the long silence. He calls from the freeway exit because he has run out of gas. My husband goes with a gallon of gasoline. When they come home, I go downstairs to greet them.

Jonathan stares at me. He might be expecting a rebuke for his silence, but I am just too relieved.

"Welcome home!" I say.

He has come just in time to celebrate Tom's birthday. We're going to a Thai restaurant. As usual, Jonathan chooses to ride in my car and sits next to me. He looks very odd, almost disoriented.

We have Thai food quite often, since we spent a few years in Thailand. This is a new restaurant that just opened nearby. It's not too crowded and seems nice. We're all together, except for my oldest son who lives on the East Coast and another son who is in the Air Force.

The waitress takes our orders but skips Jonathan. I call her back, "Excuse me, you have skipped one person."

She looks at me. "What would he like?"

I want to tell her to ask him, but she is as frail as he is at this moment. He lowers his head, lost in his world, and she looks away, afraid to face that world. I lean toward him and take his order. It's easier this way.

Jonathan at a restaurant we often visited as a family

Jonathan's disoriented look continues after we get back home. The next day, I clean his car. I find all the food I gave him—some is rotten. His clothes are all there, still folded. He has worn the same outfit the whole time. I also find his medicine case, still full. He has never taken his meds. It's disappointing but not totally surprising. Could this be the reason for his look?

I ask him about his trip. He says it went well. I am not shocked to hear he has been smoking marijuana.

"Did you take anything else? Mushrooms? Acid?"

"No."

I believe him.

We take the car to the mechanic to be checked. One woman stands ahead of us with her small dog on a leash. Immediately the dog starts growling at my son, then barking incessantly. Jonathan ignores it. The woman looks at me and I look at her, but none of the three of us moves. The situation feels surreal. Is she expecting me to take my son away? Finally, she quiets the dog, and the mechanic comes.

Something has heightened Jonathan's malady to the point that even dogs can sense it. Could it be the fact that he hasn't been taking his medications?

I find out that he managed to keep all the money in his paycheck but has just ordered more marijuana. Once again I lecture him about the danger of drugs. I am especially concerned about the addiction.

"We all have addictions of some kind," I tell him, "but we have to fight them." I pause to think. "I'm not sure what my addiction is."

"Work," he replies at once.

I laugh. "No, not really. I work a lot because I have to,

but I don't crave work. I could easily do without it. Maybe I'm addicted to worry."

His face lights up in a rare smile. "Yes—yes, that's it! Worry."

"Okay; you fight your addiction to marijuana, and I will fight my addiction to worry. Deal?"

He nods, a charming, soft smile still lingering on his lips.

Car Accident

Jonathan agrees to call the Department of Rehab and reapply for their program. In the meantime, he rests in the mornings and goes to pole vault practice in the afternoons. On Wednesday he drives himself to the clinic to get his Prolixin shot. I check with the clinic, and they confirm that he was there.

The next day, I find him asleep in the afternoon and wake him up to send him to practice. Startled, he jumps out of bed and gets his car keys. I tell him I will go later with Dustin and watch him play.

He looks particularly odd. Maybe he is still half asleep. Or is he high? I have a strong premonition, and I run outside to ask him how he feels. Maybe he shouldn't drive in this condition. I can take him. But he has already left.

I feel terribly guilty for not acting sooner. It takes me a while to respond to intuitions, and I saunter when others would leap. I pray desperately for Jonathan's safety.

When Dustin arrives, we drive together to the college, but Jonathan is not there. The coach says he never came. I am very worried, but Dustin is not concerned.

"He probably changed his mind and went to see a friend," he says.

I know he would never do that—not on a day we had said we would watch him. Unsurprisingly, Jonathan doesn't answer his phone.

I wait restlessly at home, but he never comes back. My husband tells me to stop worrying. He agrees with Dustin's theory that Jonathan has changed his mind and gone to see a friend. Finally, I go out to teach Italian. I have a conversation class every Thursday with a group of women who are about my age. I have been teaching them for years, and we have become friends. We meet at someone's house, and one of them, Jackie, gives me a ride there and back.

During the class, I chase worries out of my mind as a farmer fends off flies in his stable. On the way back home, I tell Jackie about my concern. "Is there a way to find out if he had an accident?"

"Calling hospitals is difficult," she says. "There are so many regulations to protect the patients' privacy. There is a way to find out if he was detained, even if that's probably not an option. There's a government website called 'Who's in Jail.'"

Jail? It's a terrifying thought—but anything is possible. I remember all the frightful stories I heard about convicts who are mentally ill. For a split second, I have a terrible thought: "He would be better dead."

I guess I am tired of all this pain—for me and especially for my son. I remember a popular saying: "A parent is only as happy as his or her most unhappy child." It's true, as far as our tendencies go. We would like so much to take on their sorrows, even if that won't do them any good. The only answer is to ask the Lord to give us all strength. He can sustain us while he works in our children's troubled minds.

Jonathan is still not home. Tom and Dustin still don't

seem concerned. I have a tendency to worry, so they are used to minimizing my fears. Undeterred, I try the website that my student suggested, and Jonathan's name appears.

"He's in jail," I tell Tom.

"How do you know?"

I show him the website, then call the jail to see if they can share some information. The clerk is very kind and helpful. She says that my son has been arrested for DUI and has been involved in an accident. He is well, but the car has been impounded. She gives me the address of the place where we need to retrieve the car and suggests that we contact a bail bondsman.

I tell her he needs to take medications, but she says we can't bring him anything. They have a doctor on staff, she adds.

This is a whole new experience for us. Thinking that we may need to see a bail bondsman in person, we call one near our house. It's 9:30 p.m., but these people are ready to work at all times. He explains the process, and we pay the deposit by credit card.

We discuss the logistics of picking up our son from jail and getting back his car. Finally, we fall asleep, exhausted, with a prayer still on our lips.

Jonathan calls at 4:30 a.m. I am not sure why it took him so long. He says he is in jail and that he had a car accident. He is well, but the car was destroyed. He says that he hit another car but that everyone was fine. We tell him that we posted bail, and we arrange to go and pick him up in the morning. He doesn't know when he will be out—and, of course, his phone is dead.

The bondsman told us Jonathan would be out at 8, so Dustin goes to wait in front of the jail at that time. No one comes out. Dustin continues to wait. He is a little unnerved, because there is no parking in front of the jail, and he has to keep driving around the block.

At 11 a.m., Jonathan arrives home. When he came out of jail, he didn't see anyone, so he took a trolley home. I am not sure whether he had any money. We call Dustin back.

We bombard Jonathan with questions. He says that he started a four-car pileup. Oddly, he says no one asked him for his insurance information. He didn't have his wallet with him, so he had no license and no insurance.

I am concerned about his experience in jail. "Did they treat you well?"

"Yes." That's all I will ever know about it.

Later I call a lawyer to see if he can make any sense out of this. The problem is, we really can't pay him for his services. We already had to pay to post bail and to get the car out of the pound. The car is partially destroyed. It looks like something went under the frame, and we can see tire marks on top. We try to understand how that could be possible. Jonathan is not helpful.

He says, however, that he was not high. They took a blood test, and because he had been smoking earlier on, it shows that he was under the influence. Marijuana stays in the blood stream for days. In any case, we don't know the full story.

We tell him he has to stop smoking marijuana at least until the trial, which is in two weeks. Of course, we want him to stop entirely, and we hope that the court will mandate a program for substance addiction. Something good may come out of this.

But Jonathan looks shocked and confused. The car was his taste of freedom, and the job too. In just two weeks he lost both. I try to comfort him, but my words sound hollow against his pain.

I tell him he could have lost more—his life, or a limb. I tell him he is back at square one, but that just means that he needs to continue to square two, three, and so on. Still, I know it's very hard for him. This is the time when he would look for comfort in marijuana. He needs to look for it in Christ. The most effective thing I can do is pray.

As I clean his room, I find a comforting sentence he has scribbled on a piece of paper: "I know it's your will so I won't question." I assume he is talking to God. I just wish I could always have the same attitude.

On Sunday, I find out that the owner of the largest bail bonds company in California attends our church. I normally call him by his first name, and even when I saw his last name I didn't make a connection. He offers to help us.

His first advice is not to hire a lawyer. Not yet. The state will give Jonathan an attorney, and we can start from there. He tells me to go to the police and get the transcripts of the accident and give him a copy. Then he will contact people who he knows at the courthouse and find out as much as possible what goes on behind the scenes. It's a huge relief!

I go to the police station with Jonathan, who looks totally uninterested. He lets me read the report while he stares peacefully into space. I learn that the accident involved five cars, as Jonathan's collision had a domino effect. There were no physical injuries.

Apparently, when the police officer arrived on the scene, my son was still in his car, unresponsive. The officer ordered him to come out and performed a sobriety test, which was negative. Unconvinced, the officer took him to jail, where he took a blood test and found traces of marijuana. In the report, he noted that my son had taken a dosage of Zoloft that morning.

Zoloft is one of the medications that were prescribed to him by the hospital and that I have been begging the doctors to decrease. I am sure they want to be careful, since depression is quite common in people with schizophrenia, but at this point my son doesn't show signs of this illness.

I call the nurse at the clinic, explain what has happened, and ask once again if they can decrease the dosage and eventually take him off. I just feel he is taking too many medications. She says he can start taking it at night. Since I am not the patient, I can't fight too hard.

I tell my son we'll be moving Zoloft to the evening. Once again, I try to convince him to change doctors, or at least to get a second opinion, but he refuses. I am quite sure that it's not a matter of love for his doctor. I think he is afraid of changes.

By now, he has been sober (from marijuana) for a couple of days, and his mind is much clearer. Still, he thinks that marijuana is not a problem in his life. I pray that God will show him. Anyhow, I read that people with schizophrenia have twice as many car accidents as people without, so maybe we can't just blame a substance. I remember again our early driving lessons and his difficulty with stopping on time. I am just thankful he didn't have any accidents before, that he is still alive, and that no one else was hurt.

8

Moving Forward

Quickly trying to get to Zion.
(Jonathan Carr)

Jonathan is back to his quiet daily life, as if the accident never happened. We talk about it occasionally. I remind him of his court appearance, and he nods. He seems free from worries. I don't know if it's the effect of the medications.

He doesn't want us to get involved. On the appointed day, we take him to court and he talks to the public attorney alone. We sit and watch from a distance. Finally, he has his turn in court, and the judge reschedules the trial. These things take time.

In the meantime, my husband takes Jonathan's car to Mexico—the only place where we can get it fixed at a reasonable price. The mechanic takes his time too. Everything moves at a slow pace.

I don't mind giving Jonathan rides. In fact, I prefer it, since I know he is safe. Besides the rides to practice, I often take him to the gym where he can get extra training.

I watch him sitting next to me in silence. He often breaks into a smile, as if he has just seen or heard someone.

At least it's pleasant. The terrified look in his eyes is a thing of the past. Is he happy this way? His goal seems to be to forget and ignore anything negative.

"What do you really want?" I ask him. "Do you want to get a job and function in society, or do you just want to feel better?"

"To feel better," he says promptly.

I understand, but I have heard that people with schizophrenia recover much faster when they have a strong motivation to do so—for example, a wife and children to care for. As a Christian, he should think of others instead of being wrapped up in himself and his world—but how much can I expect? How can I steer him in that direction?

Most of the time he seems serene. Once in a while his face darkens with melancholy. "I don't know why I do certain things," he says, "things I don't want to do."

It reminds me of the words of Paul in the Bible: "I do not do the good I want, but the evil I do not want is what I keep on doing" (Rom. 7:19). I tell Jonathan this is a battle for every Christian, because of the sinful nature that's been ingrained in us since the fall of Adam. He nods. He knows. All the theology he has learned over the years from biblical instruction, catechism, and listening to sermons is still there, and it's a relief for me to recognize it.

I leave him at practice and go back home to my regular activities. I feel heartbroken because of what he is going through. I can walk away from him and go about my business, but he lives in that situation all the time. As I drive back, I listen to music to calm my apprehensions.

Be thou my vision, O Lord of my heart;
naught be all else to me, save that thou art—

thou my best thought by day or by night,
waking or sleeping, thy presence my light.

Ultimately, Christ is my only true comfort and my only anchor in this sea of uncertainty. I sing along, turning the lyrics into a prayer. The last stanza seems particularly fitting:

High King of heaven, my victory won,
may I reach heaven's joys, O bright heav'n's Sun!
Heart of my own heart, whatever befall,
still be my vision, O Ruler of all.[1]

Fire!

Sundays are particularly peaceful. Jonathan comes to church with us, and I love to have him next to me and to walk behind him as we go to the front of the sanctuary to partake of the Lord's Supper. Christ is an anchor for Jonathan too, and his eagerness to be readmitted to the sacrament has reassured me that he appreciates this tangible manifestation of the gospel.

At home, Sunday is a welcome day of rest—the only day of the week when I manage to take a nap. This week is no exception. Our bedroom window, on the second floor of the house, opens up to the backyard. As I lie in bed, I can see the trees in the park behind our fence and our overgrown palms waving slowly in the breeze.

Today there is an unusual sight—a thin stream of smoke

---

1. "Be Thou My Vision," translated by Mary E. Byrne (1905), versified by Eleanor H. Hull (1912).

rising against the late autumn sky. Sometimes afternoon naps leave me even sleepier, so it takes me a while to realize that this is not a fruit of my imagination. As I get closer to the window, I see a partially burned tree. My husband and some firemen are standing next to it, talking.

I rush outside. Apparently, Jonathan was smoking a cigarette while lying on the hammock and fell asleep, dropping the cigarette on the dry leaves underneath. The ensuing fire was quite serious, burning the right side of a tall tree and a large portion of our fence. In fact, the flames were so high that three of our neighbors saw them from a distance and ran to the rescue.

The neighbor on our left rushed into our backyard with a bucket of water while the neighbor on our right used his hose from behind his fence to put out the fire. In the meantime, the man living across the street from us called the fire engine and rang our bell to see if we were okay. All this while I was sleeping.

Even my husband had been totally unaware. He was in the kitchen fixing something to eat, and the curtains on the windows facing the backyard were closed.

"Where's Branch now?" I ask Tom.

"In the house."

"Is he okay?"

"He said yes. I found him here, with his shirt in hands. It was burnt to shreds. Then he just walked inside. He didn't seem to be hurt, just very confused."

Tom keeps talking to the firemen about the potential disaster we just missed. The area behind our house is rugged, with only a small section groomed into a park. The rest is wild trees, bushes, and piles of dead branches and leaves, which follow a long, dry riverbed. If it hadn't been for our neighbors, the fire could have easily spread, causing damage to a large portion of our city.

I rush to Jonathan's room. He is on his bed, curled up in the fetal position and wearing a different shirt.

"Did you get burned?" I ask.

"Yes."

"Can I see?"

"No."

"Go and take a cold shower."

Thankfully, he does.

I run to the backyard to talk to the firefighters, but they are already gone. I rush to our front door. They are about to leave. I stop them.

"Can you come inside and look at my son? He got burned."

They seem surprised. I am not even sure they believe me. Maybe, after talking to my unruffled husband, they see me as a hysterical mother.

"Talk to the paramedics. That's their job," one of them tells me calmly.

I stop the paramedics, who are also about to leave, and they get their equipment. I tell them that he has schizophrenia, to prepare them for any unusual reaction.

To my relief, Jonathan agrees to talk to them and lets them examine his burns, which are spread all over his left side from his armpit to his hip. Basically, he had been roasting over the fire.

"He has second-degree burns over a large area of his arm and torso," one of the paramedics tells me. "He should go to the hospital. We can take him, or you can drive him."

I turn to him. "What do you want to do? Do you want to go with them?"

"Yes," he says.

He does? Both the paramedics and my husband are surprised. It's much better this way. He will be taken care of all the way to the hospital and will be seen sooner, skipping the waiting room. Thankfully he now has Medi-Cal because of his disability.

Once again, I follow the ambulance in my car. When I arrive at the hospital, I thank the paramedics for their care and sign up at the desk, waiting for them to allow me in. When they do, I find Jonathan lying in one of the rooms, already bandaged up.

I ask the nurse how he is doing, but she just hands him the instructions for home care. "It's all written here."

I read the paper quickly. Jonathan should not take off the bandages but should see a nurse in any related clinic. The burn will take a few weeks to heal, and the clinic will tell us when he can stop going back for treatments.

"Does it hurt?" I ask him.

"No."

As usual, he is silent in the car. To cheer him up, I play some music from a channel he has chosen before—some classic rock. We both laugh when we hear the song that's playing: "Light My Fire." Thank God for a little humor.

Each day, I take Jonathan to the nurse to change his bandage. I also have to take him daily to the evaluation at the Department of Rehab. My body, still recovering from Sunday's shock, is feeling the weariness of these added tasks. One of the waiting rooms is especially crowded. People are coughing.

"Can you stay by yourself?" I ask him. "I want to sit in the car. Just go in when they call your name."

He nods, and I go outside, breathing deeply the fresh December air. The climate in San Diego is still mild. In the car, I correct some papers. Half an hour goes by, then an hour. I know that the waiting room was crowded, but he should have been seen by now. I go and check. There are very few people waiting. He says they haven't called him, so I wait. Soon we are the only ones in the waiting room.

A nurse comes out of a different door. "Are you Jonathan Carr?" she asks.

"Yes," we both reply. Finally, I think.

"We called your name earlier, but no one replied. The clinic is closed now."

I panic and beg her to let him in. He needs to change his bandage.

"I am going home, but you can knock on the door," she says.

I knock loudly, and thankfully a nurse lets him in. I am able to go with him, and I ask many questions. They give me lots of bandages and other supplies. Now I know I should never leave him alone.

I finally take Jonathan to his primary care physician to check his progress. We haven't seen this doctor in a long time. Normally we go to the mental health department or to the emergency room. As usual, Jonathan is quiet all the way there. This time I walk, without asking, into the office with him, and he doesn't object. When the doctor comes in, Jonathan doesn't respond. He stares at the walls as if he were in another world. His absent-mindedness has never been so serious. It's as though he wants to shut out everything around him.

The doctor says the burn is healing well. Jonathan can

just care for it at home. He shows me what to do, because it's obvious that Jonathan won't do anything to care for himself.

"I don't understand how he could have been lying in the hammock and burn his whole side," I tell him. "Didn't he feel anything?"

The doctor looks at his papers. "Prolixin can do that. It can take away sensory feelings."

I am appalled. I was already convinced that he is taking too many medications, but his psychiatrist persists in prescribing the same types and dosages.

"Can you tell the psychiatrist to change medications?" I ask the doctor.

"It's not my department," he says. He scribbles something in his papers. Hopefully someone will get the message.

I walk out of the hospital, absorbed in my concerns. Next to me, Jonathan walks peacefully, as if he has no care in this world. His face is relaxed. Under his untidy cascade of brown dreadlocks, his eyes shine contently, almost knowingly. He looks much younger than his age. I probably look much older than mine.

As we approach the exit, one lady asks me, "Is he your son? He is adorable!"

It's not the first time someone has told me this. In fact, it happens everywhere we go. I heartily agree and look at him. He lowers his head and smiles to himself. Did he hear?

"Guess what that person said about you," I tell him while we walk to our car.

"I am adorable?"

Yes, he is adorable—inside and out. Adorable and patient.

Since he can now care for his wounds at home, I check on Jonathan every day and ask if I can help him. He takes off his shirt and lifts his arm in silence. His skin is soft, and he seems relaxed, not resisting my help. It has been a long time since he has let me touch him, and I am grateful for these moments of contact; but my heart quivers at the thought that his mind might have traveled further away from us. At least he seems at peace.

But how much can he care for himself now? It's as though he has given up, surrendering his life to others and retreating to a world of safe thoughts.

He also sleeps more than usual. Yesterday he found out that he will not get his car back for another week and went to bed at 2 p.m. I wish he could learn to lean on the Lord. It's hard for everyone.

His written words continue to express pain. I don't know when he wrote the ones I find next. Maybe they are just songs he is trying to compose, but I am not taking them lightly.

To the end,
these scars don't mend,
rules don't bend.
Not just pretend every instant.

Quickly trying to get to Zion.

I contact the psychiatrist again, relating these new developments and begging them to reevaluate his medications. The nurse says they will review everything with Jonathan, since he is twenty years old. In fact, she suggests that he is not properly cared for at home. This comment pierces me like a sharp sword.

I try hard to think rationally without falling into useless feelings of guilt. Will he be better off in a hospital? I am sure he will be safer in an institution, but is that the best solution for him? From everything I have read, a home environment seems to be ideal. I still think they should take him off the medication that is numbing his feelings and help him to become more independent.

I hang up the phone, but the nurse calls back after a few minutes. The psychiatrist has recommended that Jonathan not drive. I fully agree—but how can we tell him? I regret getting the car repaired. Thankfully, the mechanic has had many delays, but it's supposed to be ready this Saturday.

I talk to my husband. We both think the suggestion should come from the doctor so that it carries some degree of authority, otherwise Jonathan will dismiss it.

I call the nurse again to explain our request. She sounds annoyed, even angry.

"You are the ones who need to tell him," she says. "Why are you afraid to talk to your son?"

I don't do well with provocations. "We are not afraid," I tell her. "We just think it would be better if this came as doctor's orders. Besides, you have been telling us for months that we have no power over him because he is twenty years old. How is this different?"

The nurse pauses. "I will talk to the doctor," she says. "In the meantime, don't let him drive. You don't want to have a deadly accident on your conscience."

Of course not.

"Maybe you can tell the DMV not to let him drive; then it will come from them. You can do that, can't you? For medical reasons?" I insist.

"I don't think so."

I hang up the phone with a heavy heart. I talk to my husband again. We can just postpone picking up the car for another week. If it's actually ready on Saturday, we may have to pay for storage, but it will be worth it until we can decide what to do. Jonathan's court case is coming up soon, and maybe the judge will forbid him to drive.

Change of Doctors

The following week, we go to the hospital for the usual biweekly shot of Prolixin. I feel uneasy, knowing how strongly it's affecting Jonathan's body and mind, but we can't just stop on our own. Any change has to be done under doctor's supervision.

The nurse calls us both into her office. It's strange; she has never before called me in for a shot. She tells me immediately why. Apparently, now that we switched Jonathan's insurance to Medi-Cal, he cannot continue to be seen in this mental health clinic. The change happened a couple of months ago, but they just received notice.

"But he has just been seen at the emergency room and by his primary care physician, and no one told us anything," I say.

"He can still continue to use our medical facilities," she explains, "just not the mental health department."

She doesn't explain why. Maybe she doesn't know. She hands me a paper with numbers to call.

"What about today's injection?"

"It's not covered."

"So he should just go without?"

After a long pause, she leaves the room to talk to a psychiatrist. An abrupt change is not advisable. Jonathan's psychiatrist is not in the office, but another one comes in and authorizes the injection. I'll decide later how we can pay.

I leave the office with my list of numbers. I have always wanted to change doctors, but this is all very sudden.

I call Medi-Cal as soon as we get home. Apparently, the HMO facilities we have been seeing are not equipped to treat serious mental illnesses, so Medi-Cal doesn't approve their care. *Now you tell me*, I think.

I call the numbers on the list, but many of the doctors have stopped taking Medi-Cal. I am left with five options in the whole county of San Diego. One is close to us. I make an appointment just to have something going, but I am determined to keep searching.

This is my chance to get better care for Jonathan. He has never wanted to change doctors, but now he has no choice. I contact Asheka, who writes back immediately. In her opinion, three of the five psychiatrists (including the one in our area) aren't a good match for my son. She doesn't know the other two.

At this point, I am not opposed to paying out of pocket. I start thinking of all the ways I can cut on other expenses. I can get better care for Jonathan. I can make it work.

I start calling friends, and even my own primary care physician, for recommendations. Some of their psychiatrists are not available, and I am not sure about some others. I know Jonathan will never agree to change again. I need to find the best choice now.

I think of a great article I have just read—"Successful and Schizophrenic," by Dr. Elyn Saks, published online by the New York Times.[2] The author, Orrin B. Evans Distinguished Professor of Law and professor of psychology and

2. Elyn R. Saks, "Successful and Schizophrenic," *The New York Times*, January 25, 2013, http://www.nytimes.com/2013/01/27/opinion/sunday /schizophrenic-not-stupid.html?_r=0.

psychiatry and the behavioral sciences at the USC Gould School of Law, has been living with schizophrenia since she was a college student. The article is one of those encouraging stories we all like to read. I have also ordered her book, *The Center Cannot Hold: My Journey through Madness*. If Saks can be successful in spite of her tremendous challenges, maybe Jonathan can too.

I contact her by email, and she replies. "I am sorry your son, and you along with him, is struggling with this illness. I think my story suggests that there is hope." She asks me where we live and warns me that most clinicians she knows have expensive fees.

I explain I am ready to pay anything and willing to go anywhere in San Diego. It's a desperate situation.

Since she works in Los Angeles, she emails some colleagues in San Diego and sends me a referral: Dr. Steven Ornish, MD, past president of the San Diego Psychiatric Society.

I email him and also call him. He picks up the phone. He tells me he gets a lot of clients who are unsatisfied with the psychiatrists who take Medi-Cal or who work for HMOs. He believes he can help Jonathan. Somehow, I think he is my best choice. I can't aim any higher, at least in San Diego.

I balk a little when he tells me his fees. They are higher than I expected. Noticing my reticence, he explains that he spends a full hour with his patients, that he combines psychiatric care with therapy, and that his fees will drop to half the price once the care is established and the visits become routine. I have already decided to pay any price, so I make an appointment for December 30 and cancel the one that I made with the other doctor. We are set!

In the meantime, we gather papers to take to court. Jonathan's public defender gave him a list of documents he should bring to the next hearing—including his marijuana card. The problem is, he can't find it. After a brief search, I decide to drive him to the office, about twenty minutes from home. We find some traffic on the way, but it's not as bad as it will be in a couple of hours. As usual, he sits next to me, absent-minded. Strangely, however, he tells me where to get off the freeway. Apparently there are things that don't escape his attention.

The office is very modern, in one of the best areas in town. I park and ask him if he wants to go inside by himself.

"I forgot my driver's license," he says.

This time I lose it. We have so many appointments, and I really want to get this card today; but it's almost rush hour, and driving back and forth again will be crazy.

"Branch, can't you just check these things before you leave the house?" I blurt out, frustrated.

He sits quietly, avoiding my eyes. No, he can't check these things—not at this point. I should know better than that.

"I am sorry," I tell him, "but do you understand my frustration?"

"No."

"Okay, then, can you forgive me?"

"Yes."

I love how forgiving he continues to be, in spite of my outbursts and blunders. I drive him back home, get the license, and drive back. Traffic isn't so bad. I breathe deeply, calming the contrasting emotions that try to overwhelm me like roaring waves. Thank God that all of our gifts—including Jonathan's forgiveness—come from "from the Father of lights, with whom there is no variation or shadow due to change" (James 1:17).

Family and Friends

The court hearing is just a formality. The judge calls the defender, and they agree on the date of the actual trial: January 23, in front of a jury. I am disappointed because this thing is lasting so long, and especially because I can't rely on the court to forbid Jonathan to drive. My husband has been able to delay picking up the car until January, but we probably can't postpone it until the end of that month. We'll see.

For now, we are busy with Christmas shopping. I take Jonathan out to buy presents for his brothers. He zips through the department store without any hesitation. He knows exactly what to get. I wish I could do the same.

I ask if he wants to wrap the presents, and he says yes, but they stay on his floor for days next to the wrapping paper.

"Do you want me to wrap them for you?" I finally say.

"Yes."

Christmas finally arrives, and it's a happy occasion. We give Jonathan a beanie to keep his head warm (and hide the dreads when needed), two chess sets (we couldn't decide), and a T-shirt that says, "I'm adorable." He smiles, puts on the T-shirt and the beanie, and wears them all day.

I still find occasional messages in his room, and they are still disturbing. I should probably stop looking at his writing, but I want so much to know what's going through his mind. Besides, I need to watch for dangerous signs.

"Satan said, I want you to go to hell," he wrote. "Discipline. I jumped." "For some sins there is no remedy." "I believe in my own mistake over reality."

I think many of us—some more frequently than others—have doubts about our salvation. We all battle against Satan and sin. We just don't write down all our thoughts, and they are probably not as intense.

I talk to Aaron, one of the church elders mentioned earlier, who has visited Jonathan a few times and has been very encouraging to me through the recent trials. "Jonathan has certainly found a spiritual remedy for his sin in Jesus," he says. "The symptoms of the curse are still clinging to the outer man, but they have been removed from the inner man. The Lord will see his son through this momentary affliction, and what seems so difficult will melt away in the face of the glory of God in Jesus Christ at his revelation."

Jonathan comes to church on most Sundays. At home, I try to reassure him with the gospel whenever I have a chance to talk about it in a natural conversation. It's easy to do it after church, when I can ask him about the sermon and reinforce its reassuring message.

A few people from church have visited him occasionally, and I am very grateful, but I still wish he had one Christian friend who could go outside his comfort zone and call him weekly to show that he cares or meet him regularly for coffee or a bite to eat—a friend who encourages him to look to Christ. Jonathan still hears negative voices, so he should hear the gospel just as frequently. Mike used to come over regularly, but now he is married and has new responsibilities. I am praying that the Lord touches someone's heart to take on this ministry.

I share this burden of my heart with Dom, a young man from church with long dreads and a contagious smile—the kind of smile that warms you inside and makes you feel that everything is fine. Jonathan seems to feel comfortable with Dom—maybe because they are dread brothers.

At first, Dom is hesitant. "Jon doesn't talk much."

"I know—but when he opens up he has a lot to say. It might take a couple of times. Other people have come to see him but stopped after a couple of times, so he never got a chance to get close to anyone." I feel like a helicopter parent—but do such parenting rules apply in these cases? It hurts me to see him lonely. Last night he went to sleep hugging a teddy bear.

I tell Dom that normally I get Jonathan talking about easy subjects—"about nothing," Seinfeld would say— without expecting anything in return, and then I interject a deeper question here and there.

Dom comes often and takes Jonathan out. They seem to get along. They have fun, and—from what I hear—Dom is able to share some encouraging words. Once again, Jonathan talks about his frustration with his sin.

"He said he knows that he does things he can't help," Dom tells me. "I told him it's the same for me and every human being who walks this earth and that Christ is the only hope we have for forgiveness. He confirmed that apart from his love we are dust."

It's a comfort for me to hear this. This theme of acting against his will recurs in Jonathan's spoken and written words. Recently he gave me a very confused story that he wrote about a man who starts out very violent but ends up, after a long journey, back home with his mother. At one point in the story, the man says, "I don't know why I keep doing bad things."

I think of the accident, the fire, and many other occasions when my son seemed confused about his actions. I pray that the Lord will continue to reassure him with the unwavering truth that we are safe in Christ in spite of our failures.

The New Psychiatrist

We see the new psychiatrist on December 30. I am very nervous before the visit, not knowing how Jonathan will react. It doesn't help that the GPS is not working properly. I don't do well when I get lost. I remember something a visiting pastor said yesterday in his sermon: "Sometimes we panic to the point of forgetting what we know so well." In my anxiety, I try to focus on what I know—God's loving sovereignty over our lives.

Finally I decide to follow my instincts and arrive at the right address, just when the GPS is telling me to continue ten more miles on a freeway I have never taken.

We are early, so I take Jonathan to a small coffee shop in the same building. He wants a sandwich and a bag of chips. The woman behind the counter greets us with a welcoming smile. I wonder if she's thinking that he is adorable.

The place is impressive: a glass building with wide spaces—the kind of building that makes one walk taller. The small waiting room is empty, and we sit down in silence. I am afraid to say anything, while Jonathan is compliant.

Dr. Ornish arrives soon. He is a small, energetic man with a full head of rebellious grey hair. He looks quickly into our room, as if he has just been walking briskly from the elevator.

"I'll call you soon," he says.

He spends some time in his office, then calls Jonathan. I stay in the waiting room, praying and correcting a translation in order to keep my mind occupied. As promised, he keeps Jonathan for a long time.

After almost an hour, he opens the door of his office. I hear him saying to Jonathan, "I'm going to call your mother—is that okay?" Apparently Jonathan agrees.

I like the direct approach—a statement, not a question. "Do you mind if your mother comes in?" or, even worse, "Do you want your mother to be here?" have never worked in the past.

The office is spacious. Jonathan is sitting on a chair, and I sit on the couch next to him. Dr. Ornish sits on the opposite side of the room, by the window, at a distance from us.

He tells me he has not received any records from the previous clinic and asks me to look into it. He has, instead, received all the documentation I have sent him, and he thanks me for it. Finally, he explains that he has reviewed Jonathan's treatment and doesn't see the need for two different medications for schizophrenia. His plan is to slowly decrease one medication while increasing the other. The goal is to reduce the overall dosage, but the transition has to happen gradually and carefully.

I ask him about the other medications: Ativan, Zoloft, and Trazodone.

"We can decrease those also. One thing at a time."

He decides, however, to substitute Ativan with a milder medication that has a longer-term effect.

He asks if I have other questions, but I don't. I know I can also reach him via email or phone. So far, he has always listened to my concerns and replied quickly. I am heard and respected. I feel he sincerely values my input as mother and caretaker. Finally I can work with a doctor on the same goal: improving my son's health and well-being.

Before we leave, he tells Jonathan not to drive for the time being, while the medications are switched. I have written an email expressing my concern, and he is addressing it promptly. My son agrees. I breathe in relief.

"Will you be able to drive him where he needs to go?" the doctor asks.

"Yes!" I reply promptly. I have already planned to revolve my whole life around my son's needs.

I leave hopeful. For the first time, I feel someone is going to attack this thing. Jonathan seems quite happy too—maybe just from knowing that someone is really on his side. I ask him if he liked the new doctor, and he says yes. I thank God with my whole heart.

There are still a few obstacles. All of a sudden, I receive a call from our HMO saying that now they are taking Medi-Cal patients for mental health. I am not planning to change doctors right now, but if I want to fill a prescription or get tests ordered by Dr. Ornish, Medi-Cal will not pay. I am planning to file a grievance, since the change of doctors was not our fault. In any case, I see God's hand in all this. Jonathan has always refused to see another doctor, and then suddenly he had to; and this doctor—one of the best in San Diego—just happened to have an opening the day before the HMO called back. It's amazing timing.

The fees are high, but staying with this doctor is the right thing to do—at least for a while. I have just received a bonus, for the very first time, from the school where I have been teaching. This paid for the first visit. Then I was assigned a long translation that will pay for the next visit. I feel like Hansel and Gretel following a trail of crumbs. Since the Lord is putting them along my way, they are accompanied by his promises. All these steps forward are answers to prayers. We still have a long way to go, but God is sustaining us one step at a time.

9

Hope for the New Year

I will be with you.
(Exodus 3:12)

In spite of all the struggles, we have a happy New Year's Eve dinner in our backyard (something we are able to do in San Diego). All our kids are with us, except for the two oldest. Christian is still in North Carolina with his family, and Simon works in a restaurant, where this is one of the busiest nights.

We eat lots of Thai food and end the evening around the fire, roasting marshmallows as the sky turns slowly from light blue to dark purple. The air gets chilly, so I grab some blankets. We are not going to stay up until midnight. My husband and I are too old for that.

As we do every year, we go around in a circle sharing what makes us thankful for the past year and what we hope to do in the new one.

Jonathan surprises us. "I am thankful for my mom and dad," he says. "For the new year, I want to do well in school."

I know he means it. He has already ordered books for the new semester. For the first time in years, he is planning to take almost a full semester at the local community college. I am planning to drive him every day. I can take a laptop and work there.

He has been studying the new books so much that we are all joking that he'll finish the semester's curriculum before school even starts. As usual, he fills pages with math problems. In one corner of the paper, he writes what seems like a small conversation:

"You better?"

"Yes, actually I am."

He is better. He is more peaceful, and his mind seems less cluttered. I think it's because we have lowered the medication.

We talk for a while, and he confirms my perceptions. "I still hear voices, but I know they are not real," he tells me, "like in the movie *A Beautiful Mind.*"

That's encouraging.

We go shopping for school supplies and clothes before the new semester begins. Once again, he moves quickly through the store. He knows what he wants. As we leave the store, I say jokingly, "You will look handsome. You're going to steal some hearts."

He smiles widely.

We also buy a new pair of slacks for church. His name has been in the list of ushers for a while, but they have never called him, and he has noticed that. Last Sunday, when the deacon called one of his brothers to be an usher, Jonathan looked at the bulletin and then at me, questioningly. He was right. Jonathan's name was down for duty, probably by mistake, and the deacon hadn't thought he would be able to do it.

"Do you want to be an usher?" I asked him.

"Yes," he said promptly.

After the service, I told the deacon, who agreed to let him do it in a couple of weeks. Now, with the new slacks, he is all set!

What the Future Holds

We still don't know what the future holds, but we are hopeful. Occasional dark clouds will hint at a storm, but the wind is strong enough to dispel them. One of these clouds is the return of Jonathan's car. We predict trouble, in spite of Jonathan's assent to the doctor's orders. My husband asks me to take his keys from his room. As foreseen, he asks us for them.

"We have them. The doctor said you can't drive," my husband says.

"Don't you remember?" I ask.

He shakes his head.

"Do you want to see the email? I'll forward it to you," I continue. Wisely, Dr. Ornish put these orders in writing.

Jonathan doesn't reply and returns quickly to his room.

I go after him, trying to ease his pain. "It's temporary," I add, "while they are changing your meds."

I can't even persuade myself. I remember the doctor's puzzled look when I asked him how long Jonathan would have to refrain from driving. It was a stupid question, because there is no definitive answer, but it's a question a mother would ask. We want to know that there will be an end to our children's suffering.

Another dark cloud is a phone call from Medi-Cal. It's from a unit that specializes in critical cases. Those words ring ominously in my mind, casting doubt on my recent hope of a speedy recovery. Is he a critical case?

The agent on the phone has a long checklist of questions, but before she talks to me she needs to get my son's permission. I take the phone to him. He is playing a video game in our garage. He listens for a few seconds, says yes, and returns the phone to me, totally uninterested. At least he trusts me. It's a huge improvement. He would have never trusted me a year ago.

The agent explains that Jonathan has been classified as critical case and that Medi-Cal requires a closer supervision. She suggests I request to become his legal guardian. I have thought about it in the past. For now he is compliant, so I will see how things progress.

She asks questions about safety, medications, and doctors. Since Jonathan has not seen a dentist in a couple of years, she asks me to set up an appointment. That's the only area where he is lacking. For everything else, we are up to their standards.

I am glad that someone is taking such interest in our case and will supervise my care of my son. I need all the help and supervision I can get. My initial fears are dispelled. I am building a good network.

A Second Visit

I take Jonathan for a second visit to the psychiatrist. Once again, Dr. Ornish talks to Jonathan for a long time, then invites me in at the end. We talk about marijuana.

"I don't want to be the marijuana police," he tells Jonathan, "but the substance competes with your medications so that they are less effective. Can you try to limit it?"

Jonathan nods.

"Is your mother giving you a hard time with it?"

"No."

This time, Jonathan notices how much I am paying and mentions it on our way out. "That's a lot of money."

"I know," I tell him, "but I want the best for you."

In the evening, I find him sitting in the shed in our backyard. I sit with him for a while. I think he has been smoking his daily allotment of pot.

"It's not working anymore," he says.

"Marijuana?"

"Yes. The doctor said the medications are decreasing its potency."

Actually, the doctor mentioned the effect of marijuana on medications, not the other way around, but I am sure it works that way too. "It's better," I tell him. "You'll need a clear head once school starts."

"I don't need medications."

That's scary. Many people with mental illness think they can get off meds when they start feeling better. "Don't you remember how bad it was before?"

"I was fine. You were stupid."

"Now I am not?"

"No."

"I am glad."

"I just take them for you."

"Thank you. I appreciate that." I really do—more than he can imagine.

"I Will Be with You"

At church, Dr. Michael Horton preaches a very encouraging sermon on Exodus 3—one of those sermons that seem to fit our particular situation exactly. "It's sometimes in the specifics where we have trouble really affirming and really believing," he says, "especially in the midst of crises, that God is there for us—that God really is there, not just in general for the world or even in general for the church, but that he is there for us, even in our suffering, even in our pain; that he hears our cry; that he remembers his faithfulness toward us." I agree.

"Are we going to allow the circumstances of our lives—what we see—to determine who we are, or are we going to be determined by the promise that we hear?" he continues. "That's really at the heart of the text before us."[1]

I know that all too often I become so absorbed in my circumstances that I can't distinguish the forest from the trees, so this reminder to fix my eyes on God's promises is a balm to my soul.

I follow the story attentively. The challenge before me—caring for my son with schizophrenia—may not be as monumental as Moses's challenge to face Pharaoh, but it feels equally overwhelming. "Who am I?" I say with Moses. Who am I to deal with this unexplainable force that seems to be ransacking Jonathan's brain? Who am I to lead him, when I daily struggle—and often fail—to make wise decisions?

I have learned enough theology not to ask, "Why him?" God's ways are above our ways. Even Jonathan knows this. But I still wonder why God is placing so much responsibility on my weak and unstable shoulders. The prospects of failure are terrifying. I already blame myself for so many things in Jonathan's life, and, apart from God's grace, I will probably continue to do so. "Who am I?" asked Moses.

1. Michael Horton, "The Eternal Flame" (sermon, Christ United Reformed Church, Santee, CA, January 12, 2014), available online at http://www.christurc .org/sermons/the-eternal-flame?rq=exodus%203.

"But I will be with you," God answered (Ex. 3:12). That's probably all Moses needed to hear. That's all I need, because this is the great God Yahweh, the Creator and Sustainer of the universe—the great "I Am," who is ever faithful.

"I have surely seen the affliction of my people who are in Egypt and have heard their cry because of their task-masters. I know their sufferings, and I have come down to deliver them out of the hand of the Egyptians and to bring them up out of that land to a good and broad land, a land flowing with milk and honey," God said (Ex. 3:7–8). I feel comforted. God sees, hears, knows, and delivers my cry and Jonathan's. He remembered his covenant with his people, and that covenant is not broken.

He will be with us.

10

The Last Enemy, Death

He is my strongest reason.
(Jonathan Carr)

The week has gone by quietly and without incidents. Jonathan has been getting ready for school and exercising daily. His mind has been much clearer, too.

Today, Tom leaves early to get some natural fertilizer for our vegetable garden. He does this every year. Dustin and Raphy go with him. Later, they will all dig in our backyard, mix the fertilizer with the soil, and prepare the vegetable beds. He will pay them for their work. He has offered the same deal to Jonathan, but when he left this morning Jonathan didn't answer his door.

I work on a translation for a while—"Exodus and Conquest," a chapter from Michael Horton's *The Gospel Commission.* I am translating it into Italian for the pastor of our sister church in Italy, Chiesa Evangelica Riformata Filadelfia. It's an edifying chapter, and it's hard to stop working.

I get off the computer a little after 10 to do some grocery shopping. Before leaving, I try to open Jonathan's room, but the door is locked. It's strange. He doesn't usually lock it. I am not too concerned, because he has been doing so well. The television is playing loudly. That doesn't mean he is awake. He often sleeps through noise.

As I walk to my car, I notice that Jonathan's window is open, so I move the curtains to make sure he is okay. He is kneeling with his hands resting peacefully on the bed. A laptop is open in front of him, and his eyes are closed. Is he praying?

I notice something strange. Is that a belt? Yes! It's a belt, wrapped around his neck and attached to a cabinet doorknob.

My heart starts racing. "Branch! What did you do?"

I run back into the house and try to bust down the door with my shoulder. Given my size, it's as absurd as expecting a mouse to carry an elephant, but never mind. I run to my room and grab the home phone to call 911.

"My son is dead! He hung himself."

The receptionist is calm. "Are you with him?"

"No, I saw him through the window. He hung a belt from a cabinet to his neck."

"You need to get into the room and see if he is breathing. You need to cut the belt. Can you get into the room?"

"I don't know . . . maybe through the window."

"Can someone help you? Get someone to help you."

Everyone is out except for my fifteen-year-old daughter, and she can't help. There is a student staying with us for a while. I don't see how he can help either, but I call him. At this point, if the receptionist told me to stand on my head, I would do it.

We run together to the window. By this time, my daughter follows me. I send her away. Pressing my foot on an outdoor faucet, I manage to jump through the window.

"I'm in the room," I tell the receptionist.

"Cut the belt," she says, "first around his neck, and then the portion that's attached to the cabinet."

I move Jonathan's dreadlocks carefully. Even now, I don't want to damage them. I cut the belt and feel Jonathan's skin under my hand. It's cold.

I cut the rest of the belt, and Jonathan remains in the same position, completely stiff.

"It's finished," I whisper.

"The ambulance is at your door," the receptionist tells me. They are actually in the house. I walk out of Jonathan's room and direct them inside.

I recognize one of the policemen. He's the same one who came when Jonathan refused to leave his room.

"He was doing much better," I tell him. "He had been hospitalized and was taking his meds."

A young policewoman stays in the living room with me while the others buzz around Jonathan's room. It's not long before one of them comes out to give me the news.

"I am sorry, ma'am. He has been dead for some time. There was nothing we could do."

I nod and turn to look at the policewoman, who seems totally emotionless. Then I walk outside and call my husband. "Branch is dead. He killed himself."

Tom asks me a few questions. "Did you call the police?"

"Yes; they are here."

"I'll be right back."

I am back in the living room with the same policewoman. I don't think she has moved a muscle. Another policeman asks me for Jonathan's information—social security number, date of birth. He also wants to collect his meds.

I go to my room to get the meds and all his legal papers. I don't feel like talking. He can sort them out by himself.

"Can I sit down?" I ask the policewoman. She nods.

I don't know where my daughter went, but my legs have lost every ounce of strength. My mind, initially dumb, suddenly starts spinning. What happened? What went wrong? The television in Jonathan's room is still on. He was watching a Scooby-Doo video. It probably kept playing all night.

"When did he die?" I ask one of the men as he passes by the couch. I don't know what his job is.

"It's hard to say. He's been dead at least four or five hours."

Four or five hours? That would be early morning. Could we have done anything to prevent it? If I had only come downstairs to check on him earlier! Normally I check on him every night before he goes to bed, but last night I didn't.

My thoughts stretch back further. Yesterday I translated a death certificate from English to Italian. I do this sort of work all the time, but this document was different. It certified the death of a man who had hanged himself. I remember talking to Dustin about it. I told him it was the first time I had ever translated a document related to a suicide. I felt so sorry for his wife.

A cold shudder runs down my spine. After I talked about this man, I turned around and Jonathan was there. He heard me. I tried to remedy the situation by adding how awful the man's death was, but what if the thought got stuck in his mind?

My husband arrives within minutes and talks to the coroner. Dustin comes straight to me and hugs me, releasing a flood of emotions. I start to cry uncontrollably. Dustin keeps quiet. The policewoman watches.

I walk to another room of the house, where my husband and my daughter are sitting, hugging each other.

He motions for me to join them, and we all melt in one embrace.

The coroner asks if we want to see the body. I say no. I have seen him already. That's enough. Dustin says yes and goes into the room. He returns quietly and bangs his hand on the wall.

Making Some Sense

Days go by, and then weeks. We are still aching, but it's getting better. Each night we sleep a little longer; at each meal we manage to eat a little more. The emotions come in billowing waves. In my case they are mostly guilt—an unbearable yearning to leave this world and join Jonathan— and a great feeling of loss—not just loss of my son but loss of purpose. I have taken care of him for so long, and my daily prayers have been for his recovery, for his safety, and mostly for his salvation. Then God said, "It's over." He answered my prayers in an unexpected and abrupt way, and I find it difficult to adjust.

I manage better during the day, with a semi-normality that is interspersed by tears—but nights are difficult, because I keep dreaming about Jonathan and can't control my dreams. Tom likes to dream about him. He feels grateful to have some extra time to spend with Jonathan, even if it's just in a dream. For me, it's harder to have to let go again every morning. Sometimes I wish I could unscrew my head at night and place it by my bed.

Talking helps to make some sense of things. The coroner told my husband that Jonathan could have died any time during the night. He also mentioned that some kids play something they call the "choking game." They put pressure on their neck arteries, usually with a belt, until they doze off and get a short high. He believes this could possibly have been the cause of Jonathan's death, although there is no way of knowing for sure.

This makes much sense. When the voices bothered him, Jonathan often looked for relief in marijuana or medications, but we kept medications locked and restricted his use of marijuana. Now I almost feel guilty for doing it, because no one dies from marijuana—but it's a pointless regret.

I remember seeing red marks on Jonathan's neck twice before. Each time, I attributed it to other causes. So maybe he had done this multiple times. It could also explain his slow mental decline, in spite of his medications. Oxygen deprivation, however short-lived it is, causes the death of brain cells.

Later, as my husband cleans out Jonathan's drawer, he finds two of my belts hidden under my son's clothes. They were soft leather belts. This time, he used a cloth belt that he and his brothers had used when they were younger— the kind with teeth that grab the material and prevent it from moving. So, maybe in the past he was always able to move back just in time. This time, because of the type of belt and the evening medications he had just taken, he probably passed out.

This also explains Jonathan's position, kneeling with his hands on the bed. He probably meant to push himself up. Our pain is still here, but we know that he didn't intend to die.

Dr. Ornish also returns my call and expresses his sorrow and surprise. "Jonathan never gave any indication of being suicidal," he tells me. I know that the doctor was very careful as he adjusted Jonathan's medications. If Jonathan had been suicidal, he would have noticed.

I tell him about my mention of the death certificate the day before Jonathan died, and how he had heard me talking about a man who hung himself. "And this is related how?" Dr. Ornish asks. I thank God for common sense.

Even my husband thinks the incident is unrelated. "He could hear about suicide on TV or read about it in any paper," he says.

Most of all, I realize I need to stop finding a reason to blame myself. It was Jonathan's time to go. It was part of God's plan—as hard as it is to accept.

The Only Comfort

"Remember the good times you had together," people tell me. "You did all you could." "He lives inside of you." They are well-meaning remarks, and I appreciate them deeply. I have read countless articles on what not to tell a person in grief, but I can honestly say that at this point I appreciate any caring word. Just the fact that others are reaching out to me is heartening and deeply treasured. In the dark hours of the night, however, the same words provide flimsy comfort.

The Heidelberg Catechism we use in our church starts with a very pastoral question: "What is your only comfort in life and in death?" The answer reads,

> That I, with body and soul, both in life and in death, am not my own, but belong to my faithful Savior Jesus Christ, who with His precious blood has fully satisfied for all my sins, and redeemed me from all the power of the devil; and so preserves me, that without the will of my Father in heaven not a hair can fall from my head; yea, that all

things must work together for my salvation. Wherefore, by His Holy Spirit, He also assures me of eternal life, and makes me heartily willing and ready henceforth to live unto Him.[1]

It's easy to see God's hand on my son's life. Jonathan could have died so many times before—when he overdosed on Ativan, when he burned the leaves under his hammock, when he crashed on the freeway. I could go on and on. Instead, God preserved his life until now. I don't know why, but I do know that, if Jonathan had died before, my feelings of guilt would have been heavier. He lived long enough to show that he had forgiven any hurt I had caused him. More importantly, he lived long enough to reaffirm his faith in Christ and his trust in him alone for his salvation—and that is to me the greatest comfort.

Knowing that God is so much in control that not one hair can fall from our heads is comforting only if we know that we have a Savior and Mediator to stand between us and a perfectly holy God, and Jonathan had professed faith in this Savior. At the funeral, our pastor confirms this faith.

Jonathan believed these things. I know that. The elders of this church know that. And, like the rest of us, faith surely was up here some times and down here at other times—and yet, looking away, as faith does, from ourselves to Jesus—there in the Word, there in the Supper, and saying, "I believe."

As Jonathan's pastor, I saw him struggle in faith over some years, which is of course always heartbreaking to a

1. Heidelberg Catechism, question and answer 1.

pastor. I was also his catechism teacher. He was so bright, so clear in his understanding of the Bible and Christian doctrine. He was able to always give the right answer and reason. Then I saw him struggle, then the mental illness . . . and then I had the joy by God's grace—the elders had the joy—of hearing a good and strong confession by Jonathan. He wanted to meet with us and tell us what he believed in, even with all his struggles with mental illness. "Pastor, this is what I believe. I believe Jesus is the Christ, the Son of God who is coming into the world."

What a joy it was for us to see those dreadlocks showing up every Sunday morning as I would look out into the audience. Jonathan was hard to miss, and seeing that face smile, even once in a while, and that crazy hair, brought me such joy—seeing him not only coming to hear the gospel, to hear again the promises, to hear again that Christ had died for him, to hear again that there is a resurrection, but also seeing him get up and get in the line that was formed and come forward to receive a tiny foretaste of that great feast yet to come: the Lord's Supper—a little bread, a little wine each week, coming down that line, believing, trusting.

And yet, even with such strong confirmation, I find myself assailed by occasional doubts. At the funeral, our pastor reminds us that faith is not easy. He reminds us not to expect our faith to always feel strong—not any stronger than Mary's and Martha's, Abraham's, Elijah's, and even David's, who cried repeatedly in the Psalms, "How long, O God? Will you forget me forever?"

God receives us because of the merits of his Son, not because of our own. As sixteenth-century Reformers clearly laid out, our salvation is by grace alone, through faith alone in Christ alone. I know my eyes should be fixed on Christ, but they often fall on Jonathan's actions, as if they could provide a stronger certainty than God's promises.

As much as I am convinced that salvation is not by works, I think of Jonathan's addiction to drugs and his search for comfort in something other than Christ. His mind was so tormented that he often wavered, going from great heights to deep lows—deeper than I could ever conceive. Looking at his actions is a slippery slope that leads to a terrifying pit.

In spite of my strong religious convictions, it's easy for me to look for "signs" of his salvation. I would like to see him now in heaven and put my heart at rest. As I walk by the Roman Catholic church in Little Italy, near the school where I normally teach Italian, I understand the attraction of votive candles and plaques to the saints—the attempts to continue to do something for someone even when the last page has closed. I understand the people's reticence, during the Protestant Reformation, to let go of sights and sounds—bells, incense, and relics—in order to hold on to the pure Word of God.

It's the same temptation that prompted the Letter to the Hebrews in the New Testament, when Jewish Christians were tempted to go back to their traditions. And it's the Letter to the Hebrews that gives the well-known definition of faith as "the assurance of things hoped for, the conviction of things not seen" (Heb. 11:1). Our faith has not yet become sight, but it will. As our pastor reminded us at the funeral, "Faith is not defined by our feelings. What we feel doesn't change what's objective."

I share some of these feelings with Dr. Michael Horton.

In reply, he sends me a quote from a message he will deliver on Sunday: "All things around us are in opposition to the promises of God: He promises immortality; we are surrounded with mortality and corruption: He declares that he counts us just; we are covered with sins: He testifies that he is propitious and kind to us; outward judgments threaten his wrath. What then is to be done? We must with closed eyes pass by ourselves and all things connected with us, that nothing may hinder or prevent us from believing that God is true."[2]

And so I continue, day after day, to divert my mind from all the many things that pull me away from God's promises.

Leaving the battlefield is one of the hardest things to do. For two years, I have been intensely involved in my son's life—sometimes too much, and always with a feeling of urgency and a silent desire to do the impossible, to ease his mind or take away his pain. Adrenaline and sheer will have kept me going, pushing me to the limit and driving me to unknown and frightening territories. Then, all a sudden, this is gone.

A song comes to mind: "Non Nobis, Domine," from the movie *Henry V*, directed by and starring Kenneth Branagh.[3] I watch the scene again. It comes at the end of the battle of Agincourt, when Henry and his surviving men, frayed, limping, and covered in blood and mud, walk wearily back

2. John Calvin, *Commentaries on the Epistle of Paul the Apostle to the Romans*, trans. and ed. John Owen (Edinburgh, 1849), 180; available online at https://ia801902.us.archive.org/17/items/commentariesonep00/commentariesonep00.pdf.

3. *Henry V*, directed by Kenneth Branagh (1989; Los Angeles: MGM Home Entertainment, 2000), DVD.

to their camp, picking up their wounded among rows of fresh corpses. The chant, which is from Psalm 115:1, starts softly and grows in a powerful crescendo:

> *Non nobis, Domine, non nobis,*
> *sed nomini tuo da gloriam.*
> (Not to us, O Lord, not to us,
> but to your name give glory.)

It's not the typical victory song. In fact, it scarcely seems like a victory. The rush of danger, the mortal blows, and the death of loved ones are still too close. The dust and smoke of combat still mingle with the morning fog. The battle against a numerically superior French army has been won, but the victory can hardly be tasted.

Almost mindlessly, the fatigued soldiers follow their king, step after step, their eyes still low. The fight is over, but walking back is still an arduous task. And yet it's a task they can take on, step after step, as they remember that everything—the battle, the victory, the journey back and the prospects ahead—is not about them. Everything is for God's glory. There is a larger story, much larger than any human plan and conjecture, as gripping and absorbing as these may be.

So I do the same. As impossible as letting go seems at this moment, I walk on, doing what I know God wants me to do right now—what he has always wanted me to do: trust him, worship him, and help others in the limited sphere of my ordinary life. And it's there, in the ordinary steps of daily living, that I feel sustained. Doing dishes, cleaning floors, giving rides, teaching and translating, singing and worshiping with other believers on Sundays. This is all God is asking right now, and, by his grace, this I can do.

My Strongest Reason

It's Jonathan's birthday, and we go to the cemetery. He would have been twenty-one today. He probably would have wanted to celebrate with a drink, and who knows whether that would have opened a whole new addiction?

I come home with a heavy heart and check his Facebook page to see if anyone has posted some wishes. Many friends did. Their expressions of love bring new tears to my eyes.

I decide to scroll down further. I have never wanted to read all of Jonathan's posts, because some were disturbing to me. Today, however, a poem catches my eye. It dates back to only two weeks before his death. I have never noticed it before.

> Oh, how I love blessed Jesus
> the one who died to save us
> He makes me laugh like I was Beavis.
> He is my strongest reason,
> the only one who stays through the seasons.
> He picks up my broken pieces.
> He's there in every stroke of genius.
> He forgives me for my constant treason.
> Been watching since I was a fetus.

I can hardly believe my eyes. Since he has been sick, his poetry has been mostly short fragments—often confused or difficult to interpret. This one, instead, is absolutely clear. Did he really write it? I Google it to make sure it's not copied, and it's not. Tears well up in my eyes again, but this time they are tears of joy. God allowed me to find this on Jonathan's birthday—a birthday present for me!

Excited, I send it to my pastors and other friends. "And that's why you're assured you'll see him in Paradise, dear sister," replies Dr. Horton.

The True Happy Ending

This is not how I would have liked to end this story. Like most people, I like success stories and happy endings, and, at first sight, this doesn't sound like one. Or is it? What are, in the long run, happiness and success? I am reminded that our lives are not our stories. They are planned by God and brought about carefully by his hand.

Oddly enough, I have emerged from the agony and struggle with a new, stronger sense of God's goodness. It's not something I tried to muster up. It just happened. God is faithful in pulling us through trials.

In a way, no event in this life can be a true happy ending. That will arrive on the last day, when our salvation is complete. Jonathan is now completely happy, yet still yearning for the final victory, the death of death, the new heaven and new earth, and the bodily resurrection.

To use the classical terminology that the church has adopted for centuries, Jonathan has joined the church triumphant, while I am still here in the church militant, as the church has traditionally called the body of believers on earth. His struggle is over and mine continues, but we both look forward to the same ultimate and complete victory—the true happy ending.

Jonathan ready for prom, about a year
before this story started

PART 2

LOVE AND COURAGE

SUPPORT FOR HELPERS

11

The Unknown and Unexplainable

O thou who changest not, abide with me.
(Henry Francis Lyte)[1]

During Jonathan's illness, I did everything I could to educate myself about schizophrenia. Soon after his death, I continued my research. Reading books on mental illness—especially success stories like Elyn Saks's *The Center Cannot Hold*—was difficult, as they often reminded me how I could have done better. But they were also helpful—not only in helping to make sense of what had happened, but also in reassuring me that I had done what I thought was right under the circumstances and with my limited knowledge.

Eventually I began to write this book, gathering the wisdom of many sources, in the hope that it would be helpful to others. Unexpectedly, but in God's wise providence, I found myself in the situation of helping another person with mental illness, and the lessons that I planned to share with others became useful reminders for me.

1. Henry F. Lyte, "Abide with Me," 1847.

Saks's book is particularly useful for anyone who wants
to understand the illness and what it means for those who
live with it. Drawing from her personal experience, she has
an incomparable way of explaining the onset of the illness:
"I think I am dissolving. I feel—my mind feels—like a sand
castle with all the sand sliding away in the receding surf."
She continues:

> This experience is much harder, and weirder, to describe
> than extreme fear or terror. Most people know what it is
> like to be seriously afraid. . . . But explaining what I've
> come to call "disorganization" is a different challenge alto-
> gether. Consciousness gradually loses its coherence. One's
> center gives way. The center cannot hold. The "me" becomes
> a haze, and the solid center from which one experiences
> reality breaks up like a bad radio signal. There is no longer
> a sturdy vantage point from which to look out, take things
> in, assess what's happening. No core holds things together,
> providing the lens through which to see the world, to
> make judgments and comprehend risk. Random moments
> of time follow one another. Sights, sounds, thoughts, and
> feelings don't go together. No organizing principle takes
> successive moments in time and puts them together in a
> coherent way from which sense can be made. And it's all
> taking place in slow motion.[2]

While this and other books and resources help us to
catch a glimpse of the struggle of a schizophrenic mind,
we who have never lived it in person will never understand

2. Elyn R. Saks, *The Center Cannot Hold: My Journey through Madness* (New
York: Hyperion, 2007), 13.

it completely. And that's frightening. The whole experience of schizophrenia frightens everyone involved. We fear the unknown and unexplainable, and with this disease, some uncontrollable and impenetrable force seems to have taken hold of the mind. It's what my son initially tried to explain as an "extension of life."

Demon, Saint, or Patient

In the course of history, people have tried to make sense of mental illness by giving it a logical explanation. Some think of it as demon possession. Others consider it a sign of a highly spiritual mind. For many, especially in recent times, it is nothing more than a faulty mechanism in the brain.

Demon

The first explanation is easy to understand because people with schizophrenia often act in an irrational and alarming manner. Often relatives and friends agree that there is an occasional look in their loved one's eye that is simply terrifying.

Today, many people—regardless of their religious convictions—describe troubling mental and emotional experiences in terms of demons, since the word has been accepted to have a secondary meaning of "a source or agent of evil, harm, distress, or ruin."[3] In fact, the demons of schizophrenia seem palpable and much more real than simple inner sources of distress. My son drew dark images and wrote frightening sentences, talking about Satan's lullaby and "running on fear."

3. *Merriam-Webster*, s.v. "demon," last updated August 31, 2018, https://www.merriam-webster.com/dictionary/demon.

"My psychosis is a walking nightmare," says Saks, "in which my demons are so terrifying that all my angels have already fled."[4]

In the strict sense of the word, Christians understand that demons are actual spiritual beings who are actively working in constant rebellion against God. Serious problems arise when we extrapolate this basic concept from its biblical context and mingle it with folklore, which has traditionally connected mental disorders to demonic activity. According to a 2008 Baylor study of 293 Christians who approached their local church for assistance with mental illness, in approximately 30 percent of the cases the reaction was negative, involving either "abandonment or shunning by the church because of the mental disorder" or suggestions that "the mental disorder was the work of Satan or demons" or "the result of personal sin."[5]

This situation begs for some clarity. When tempted to associate mental illness with demonic activity, we must first remember that Christians cannot be demon possessed. In answer to the question "What is your only comfort in life and death?" the Heidelberg Catechism replies, "That I, with body and soul, both in life and in death, am not my own, but belong to my faithful Savior Jesus Christ, who with His precious blood has fully satisfied for all my sins, and redeemed me from *all* the power of the devil."[6] "Whether we live or whether we die, we are the Lord's" (Rom. 14:8).

---

4. Saks, *The Center Cannot Hold*, 336.

5. Matthew S. Stanford, "Demon or Disorder: A Survey of Attitudes toward Mental Illness in the Christian Church," *Mental Health, Religion & Culture* 10, no. 5 (Sept. 2007): 446, available online at https://pdfs.semanticscholar.org/6e41/97b555ac4422ac187574efee43ce33a340ed.pdf.

6. Heidelberg Catechism, question and answer 1, emphasis added.

We are bought with a price, and our "body is a temple of the Holy Spirit" (1 Cor. 6:19; see also v. 20).

As in every other aspect of our lives, God's promises trump our experiences. A young woman with occasional psychosis triggered by stress told me how her sister had found her in their living room performing some sort of "Lord's Supper" with cookies and coffee. Until her sister told her, this woman had no idea that she had ever done such a thing. It was obviously frightening and understandably raised the question, "Am I demon possessed?" Her pastor, however, encouraged her to keep her mind on God's promises, knowing that Christ "has delivered us from the domain of darkness and transferred us to the kingdom of his beloved Son, in whom we have redemption, the forgiveness of sins" (Col. 1:13–14).

While the Bible doesn't offer the same promises to unbelievers, it's also important to remember that demonic activity in today's world is different than it was while Jesus was on earth. That was a time of unmatched demonic concentration, because Jesus was about to defeat Satan and his forces.

In the gospel accounts, the demons knew exactly who Jesus was and knew that his arrival had already marked their destruction, which was to be fully realized in the end. That's why the group of demons in Matthew 8:29 asked him blatantly, "What have you to do with us, O Son of God? Have you come here to torment us *before the time?*" Christ's casting out demons showed that his kingdom had been officially inaugurated (see Matt. 12:28; Luke 11:20), and his death, resurrection, and ascension effectively opened it to anyone who repents and believes.

Today, the demons' main activity seems to be to mislead

and deceive, oppose the gospel, spread false doctrine, and encourage sin. From the book of Revelation we learn that Satan is also busy inspiring governments and rulers to blaspheme Christ and persecute his followers (see Rev. 13:6–7).

While the Bible doesn't rule out the demons' ability to afflict in other ways (see Job 2:7), it's important to remember they can do so only with God's permission and under his restrictions (see Job 1:12; 2:6; Matt. 10:29–31) and are not to be feared. "They are lost and hopeless spirits. They are even now chained to hell and pits of darkness, and though not yet limited to one place, yet, as [John] Calvin says, drag their chains with them wherever they go, II Pet. 2:4; Jude 6."[7]

It's equally important to remember that, unlike Jesus and his apostles, we don't have the ability to recognize demonic activity. Labeling mentally ill persons as demon possessed or under demonic assault will serve only to aggravate their agony and marginalization. Instead we should do what the Bible tells us to do: proclaim the good news of what Christ has accomplished for us in his life, death, and resurrection as well as the promises that are contained in his Word.

Saint

Traditionally, many cultures have seen mental conditions such as schizophrenia as signs of spiritual awakening or an advanced spiritual state, and this belief is not uncommon today, even in the spiritual smorgasbord of our Western society. Author and artist Henry Cockburn describes his

---

7. Louis Berkhof, *Systematic Theology* (repr., Grand Rapids: Eerdmans, 1996), 149.

first reaction to his diagnosis of schizophrenia this way: "I didn't think of it as an illness but as an awakening, a spiritual awakening. I thought there was another side to the world I hadn't seen before."[8]

When that is the main experience, it's understandable that a person with schizophrenia might initially want to hold on to the illness and refuse medical help. "I was convinced that my visions were a spiritual awakening and not symptomatic of any illness," said pharmacist Mark Lawrence. "Compare it to a wild love affair, and you might begin to appreciate the sense of deep enchantment and motivation I felt." He eventually realized that he had a mental disorder, but that was only after succumbing to the conviction that if he "didn't walk to Bosham Harbour and perform a ritual by four P.M., the world was going to end."[9]

According to Michael Foster Green, professor of psychiatry and behavioral science, "Schizophrenia is shrouded in an overpowering sense of mystery—which is a wonderful quality for a romance or a novel but not for an illness. When an illness is viewed as inexplicable and impenetrable, people tend to react to it with one of two extremes: either they *stigmatize* the illness or they *romanticize* it. It's hard to know which is worse."[10] Green believes the solution is education.

In the meantime, however, what do we do when our loved ones seem to cling—whether with fondness or with terror—to their hallucinations? I learned that it is important

8. Patrick Cockburn and Henry Cockburn, *Henry's Demons: A Father and Son's Journey Out of Madness* (New York: Scribner, 2011), 31.

9. Quoted in Cockburn and Cockburn, 106.

10. Michael Foster Green, *Schizophrenia Revealed: From Neurons to Social Interactions* (New York: W. W. Norton, 2003), 1.

not to flatly dismiss what they are saying. As odd and absurd as their perspective might seem to us, it is absolutely real to them. As acclaimed clinical psychologist Xavier Amador explains, "The first step . . . is to stop arguing and start listening to your loved one in a way that leaves him feeling that his point of view—including his delusional ideas and the belief that he is not sick—is being respected."[11]

"Try not to fight them mentally," adds Britton, the young man at my church who has been in and out of several hospitals and recovery centers. "Confrontation never works." In fact, it can even reinforce and validate their beliefs and make them fight all the harder.

Yet it's also true that we don't need to concur, as Saks pointed out to me in a recent phone interview. We don't need to start doubting our own sense of reality. There is a difference between respecting what people are saying and agreeing with them.

Being in a church that upholds the historical, confessional Christian faith (meaning that it's a faith that has been expressed in well-thought-out, Bible-based creeds and confessions) benefitted my son during his illness. It gave him a solid ground to stand on and return to when, as did Icarus of old, his mind attempted to fly close to the sun.

Christianity is hinged on one foundational historical fact: Christ's resurrection—something that, in my view, is easier to prove than to disprove. Without this single fact, Christianity would crumble. The historicity of this fact and its position outside our minds gives it a solidity that inner perceptions and feelings cannot possess. Britton makes a

---

11. Xavier Amador, *I Am Not Sick, I Don't Need Help!: How to Help Someone with Mental Illness Accept Treatment*, 10th anniversary ed. (New York: Vida Press, 2011), 61.

clear distinction between what's outside and what's inside. "I deal with internal stimuli that cause me to lose every fabric of sanity on a daily basis. That does not, however, change the gospel promises for all."

The search for secret spiritual knowledge is as old as time, from the temptation in the garden of Eden to first-century Gnosticism to various forms of mysticism. The long response given to the Gnostics by second-century theologian Irenaeus can be summed up in these words: "If . . . we cannot discover explanations of all those things in Scripture which are made the subject of investigation, yet let us not on that account seek after any other God besides Him who really exists."[12] The French Reformer John Calvin echoes this statement with a warning: "Let us then learn to make no searchings respecting the Lord, except as far as he has revealed himself in the Scriptures; for otherwise we shall enter a labyrinth, from which the retreat is not easy."[13]

Deuteronomy 29:29 gives us an invaluable sense of balance: "The secret things belong to the LORD our God, but the things that are revealed belong to us and to our children forever, that we may do all the words of this law." This is safe advice for every Christian. For Christians battling with schizophrenia, it's also a valuable protection against a subtype of delusion that psychiatrists call *grandiose*—a belief that one possesses superior qualities or the ability to know

12. Irenaeus, "Against Heresies," in Alexander Roberts and James Donaldson, eds., *Ante-Nicene Fathers: Translations of the Writings of the Fathers down to A.D. 325*, vol. 1, *The Apostolic Fathers—Justin Martyr—Irenaeus*, ed. A. Cleveland Coxe (1885; repr., New York: Charles Scribner's Sons, 1903), 399.

13. John Calvin, *Commentaries on the Epistle of Paul the Apostle to the Romans*, trans. and ed. John Owen (Edinburgh, 1849), 445; available online at https://ia801902.us.archive.org/17/items/commentariesonep00/commentaries onep00.pdf.

more than others (or to be more than others, as in messianic delusions).

Patient

Today, schizophrenia is most commonly seen as a physical dysfunction involving the brain. Science has a long way to go in pinpointing its causes and therapies, but this is the current medical definition of the illness, and many Christians have come to accept it. Others are still unconvinced, especially since schizophrenia can't usually be diagnosed by tests. After having being caught for three years in the whirlwind of this illness and having spent three more years in quiet reflection, I believe that the answer lies somewhere in the middle.

The main danger in seeing a person with schizophrenia as merely a patient is the temptation to reduce all treatment to medications—chemical substances to combat a chemical imbalance. Many doctors and nurses still convey the idea that this is all one can do. As I mentioned in the first part of this book, I thought Jonathan's first doctor's prescription was as simple as "Take two aspirins and call in the morning."

From a theological point of view, however, there is much more to it. Mental illness, even in its most damaging forms, cannot erase the image of God in a person. For a Christian, it cannot deny his or her union with Christ and the work of the Spirit in conforming him or her to Christ's image (see Rom. 8:29).

This view was strongly advocated by Pope John Paul II at a 1996 conference, when he said, "Whoever suffers from mental illness 'always' bears God's image and likeness in himself, as does every human being. In addition, he 'always' has the inalienable right not only to be considered as an image of God and therefore as a person, but also to be treated as such."[14]

Most physicians today recognize the danger of compartmentalizing their patients' care by creating a division between body and soul, which are deeply interconnected. Departing from the views of Sigmund Freud, who linked religion with neurosis, today's psychiatrists widely acknowledge the importance of a person's faith, even if most of them define it as a form of "spirituality" that helps believers to cope.

For Christians, faith is much more. Contrary to common perceptions, it's not a subjective feeling or a leap in the dark that is separated from facts, but a hearty trust in Christ, which rests on certain historical facts that are acknowledged to be true. As such, it must be respected, along with the work of the pastor who nourishes it with the gospel.

Fear of the Unknown

"Losing control over one's body is a frightening thought," a friend told me recently. "What happens when one's own mind is the enemy? How does one escape?"

If, as Saks explained, the experience of people with schizophrenia can exceed fear and terror, these heightened feelings are often shared by those who care for them, as well. In fact, many caretakers describe the first signs of the illness or the initial diagnosis as times of fear—fear of the unknown; the overwhelming realization that something

---

14. Pope John Paul II, "Mentally Ill Are Also Made in God's Image (address, XI International Conference of the Pontifical Council for Pastoral Assistance to Health-Care Workers, November 30, 1996), available online at https://www .ewtn.com/library/PAPALDOC/JP96N30.htm.

higher than their comprehension and absolutely alien to their logical thinking has overtaken their loved ones.

What's worse, even with the common definition of schizophrenia as a chemical imbalance, the medical community is often unsure about its causes and cures. Any sense of security provided by our rationalistic frame of mind goes out the window in the face of this bewildering illness, and we are left with the same sense of awe that the ancients felt when facing a storm. Maybe that's why, since the eighteenth-century Enlightenment, people with mental illness have often been abandoned by their families and excluded from society, shut up in some institution where they can be out of sight.

"Schizophrenia, like any other disease, is a result of sin in this broken world," my friend Jody told me, referring to the biblical account of the first entrance of sin into God's original, perfect universe—the scriptural explanation of the pervasive misery that afflicts this world, often doing so without an identifiable correlation to personal sins. Tragically, Jody's son Matt was killed in 2013 after living with schizophrenia for at least ten years.

Our society has become very skilled at denying human weakness. People talk about "beating cancer" and "defying aging," and scientific progress is supporting some optimistic feelings of invincibility. Schizophrenia, however, is too puzzling. "A man's spirit will endure sickness, but a crushed spirit who can bear?" says Proverbs 18:14.

In some ways, this verse can apply to most cases of mental illness, when the mind fails. In schizophrenia, this failure is particularly bewildering because it creates a new reality with persuasive delusions that are hard to recognize as illusory. Apart from the biblical account of a whole creation that is groaning to be delivered from the consequences of sin (see Rom. 8:22), it's hard to give it a philosophical explanation. Unlike the Gnostics, who had to imagine an evil god as the creator of an imperfect world, Christians acknowledge the responsibility they bear themselves as heirs of a debt of sin that they all too clearly recognize as their own. "For the rest," Jody continues, "I do have a struggle trying to explain it, and it seems unfair that the delusions are never kind."

One of Matt's delusions was that his father was a member of the Dutch Mafia, so he would call and tell him to hold off his spies. "Matt was really scared and certain he was being watched," Jody explained—so scared that once he threatened to kill his father.

"We weren't the only ones who received threatening phone calls," she continued. "Some of Matt's friends from high school, who had been really good friends at one time, were also getting bizarre calls from Matt. They became afraid of him, and even after he was on medication and could carry on a normal conversation, they wanted nothing to do with him. That was so painful it made my skin hurt."

Fear can be paralyzing, causing us to retreat in caution and perceive others as potential enemies. When dealing with my son's unpredictable behavior, especially when he refused to take medications, I found it useful to believe the best, giving him the benefit of the doubt while preparing for the worst. Countless times I failed in this attempt, going overboard with my suspicions while Jonathan struggled with his own wariness and paranoid apprehension. Eventually, by God's grace, after a long time of trial and error, a mutual trust began to build up between us.

Once again, as Britton said, the promises of the gospel sustain us in the struggle. As impossible as it might seem to us in our most frightful moments, we know that in Christ "God gave us a spirit not of fear but of power and love and self-control" (2 Tim. 1:7). In the middle of the battle, my pastor, Rev. Michael Brown, reminded me that even if "the secret things belong to the LORD our God," including the apparent chaos and unpredictability of a schizophrenic mind, "the things that are revealed" (Deut. 29:29) are sufficient to show us that "his steadfast love endures forever" (see Ps. 118).

At times my own fears were so overwhelming that I could only admit my weakness to the Lord and pray, like King Jehoshaphat of old, "We are powerless against this great horde that is coming against us. We do not know what to do, but our eyes are on you" (2 Chron. 20:12). And that's really the best prayer. Once we recognize our powerlessness and fix our eyes on God, we can understand why his Word constantly reminds us not to fear. "Do not be afraid and do not be dismayed at this great horde," God answered the frightful king, *"for the battle is not yours but God's. . . .* Tomorrow go out against them, and the LORD will be with you" (2 Chron. 20:15, 17).

Ultimately, this battle is God's, and he is not overtaken by chaos. Everything, even the apparent randomness of our earthly realities, is part of his plan and follows an order that escapes our finite minds. He is greater than our minds, our circumstances, and our fears. Things are often not what they seem, as the book of Revelation points out. We can't see the full reality, but God does; and this is a great comfort for those who, through faith in Christ, know God as their loving Father.

Equally reassuring is knowing that God and his promises are unmovable. When, as Saks puts it, our inner "center cannot hold," we can look outside us to a reality that's objective and unvarying. We can run "to the rock that is higher than" us (Ps. 61:2) and point our loved ones in that direction.

I often found comfort from question and answer 4 of the Westminster Shorter Catechism. "What is God? God is a Spirit, infinite, eternal, and unchangeable, in his being, wisdom, power, holiness, justice, goodness, and truth." Not only is God unchangeable, but, because he is unchangeable in *all* his attributes, they *all* stand true for me at any moment (see Mal. 3:6; Heb. 13:8; James 1:17).

As Henry Francis Lyte wrote on his deathbed as he struggled with tuberculosis, "Change and decay in all around I see; o thou who changest not, abide with me."[15]

---

15. Lyte, "Abide with Me."

12

The Medical Dilemma

If any of you lacks wisdom, let him ask God, who gives generously to all without reproach, and it will be given him.

(James 1:5)

Schizophrenia is such a dangerous condition that the choice of treatment cannot be taken lightly. In this chapter, I only briefly mention some of the different options. There are several helpful books and resources (some of which are mentioned at the end of this book), but it takes much wisdom, prayer, and counseling to compare them and determine whether they are appropriate in any particular situation (see chapter 3).

Early Detection

If you are reading this book because your loved one has exhibited some strange behavior and you are wondering if it could be schizophrenia, you are at a definite advantage over those who are dealing with advanced cases. The earlier schizophrenia is addressed, the less brain damage the sufferer sustains.

Early detection, however, can be difficult because the symptoms are not always obvious. They can be dismissed as simple teenage behavior. Since some can also be caused by the consumption of street drugs such as marijuana, hashish, mushrooms, acid, and PCP, it's also easy to assume that a person has taken these substances or, if the consumption is an established fact, that these are the only reason for the strange behavior.

Quite often, the person with schizophrenia is also afraid (or, in some cases, ashamed) to discuss these symptoms. Many think the condition is their fault. Besides, they usually lack the vocabulary to explain what is happening in their mind. It's all very confusing.

"Even for me, these symptoms are hard to put into words," explained my friend Amy. Her daughter has been diagnosed with depression and schizoaffective disorder. "And I'm a calm adult who has been writing for years, not a person in terror and disorganization and disintegration. It takes a lot of time, energy, and creativity to express these things, and a person in such distress doesn't have those resources. Then, when the distress is over, they try to push it away, not analyze it. How can you explain something like 'Everything is too slow' or 'It's all tangled,' until you have had a long time to mull it over without being panicked?

"They look for someone they can trust," Amy continued, "but most of the people they trust (family and close friends) are also people who they wouldn't want to hurt or with whom they most feel ashamed, and they don't want to ask their parents to pay for a therapist. This makes it all very difficult." For this reason, it's good for parents to establish a relationship of mutual trust and openness with their children from an early age, encouraging them to talk about their problems without fear of being rejected or misunderstood.

At the same time, parents are often caught off guard. They don't understand what's happening or how to deal with the new situation. Some are in denial, refusing to believe that the symptoms could be signs of mental illness—mostly due to the stigma attached to it. My friend Dave, who has emerged from a long and traumatic struggle with depression, calls it a catch-22. "You want to help your child, or get him to a form of help, but you don't want to push or add more stress to the situation (and maybe you were not sure what help would be or what it would entail and whether that might make things worse anyways). That dynamic plays out all the time, and it played out heavily in my case. My parents didn't want to push me, and I didn't want to do anything since I couldn't think straight."

Since most cases of schizophrenia show up in the late teenage years or early adulthood, they often surprise young people while they are in college away from home. It would be good if qualified personnel could visit high schools and colleges to educate young people on schizophrenia and if parents could at least be alerted of the possibility, just as they are alerted about meningitis and other diseases that are frequent in early adulthood.

Britton first noticed something strange when he was seventeen. He started to feel that people were either following him or looking for him. By the time he was twenty-three, he could no longer distinguish fiction from reality. Fixating on a few episodes in his past when he had behaved strangely, he concluded that he was the Antichrist.

In my son's case, I recognized unusual feelings of frustration, social withdrawal, and avoidance of common social situations such as going to the bank or a shop. I also noticed a greater physical neglect of his person, room, and belongings along with an increased absentmindedness. I had the feeling there was cause for concern, but I dismissed it because Jonathan had always been a little distracted. I also blamed it on the fact that he was preoccupied with college and adjusting to a new situation. This is a natural reaction, because these are not in themselves definite signs of schizophrenia. However, it's good to be aware of them—especially if there is a family history of this illness.

In San Diego, there is an early psychosis treatment program at UC San Diego Health, a center that has received several awards for its research with schizophrenia. The program "is designed for adolescents and young adults who are experiencing changes in their thoughts, behavior or emotions that might be associated with serious mental health issues."[1] Its medical team is trained to recognize early signs and to determine whether they are caused by schizophrenia or by another mental, medical, or neurological condition. I wish I had known about it when my son first started to talk about his symptoms. There may be a similar program where you live. You may also be able to contact UCSD and ask for referrals in other parts of the country.

Diagnosis

Psychiatric diagnoses are normally made through a careful examination of the patient and his or her medical and psychiatric history, in accordance with the criteria outlined

---

1. "Early Psychosis in Adolescents and Young Adults," UC San Diego Health, accessed September 5, 2018, https://health.ucsd.edu/specialties/psych/clinic-based/early-psychosis/pages/default.aspx.

in the *Diagnostic and Statistical Manual of Mental Disorders* (DSM-5).

Brain scans such as MRI, fMRI, and PET can be useful for showing abnormalities within the brain. They are not always accurate in determining a specific diagnosis, because the way a condition alters the brain can be different across individuals. Conversely, different types of conditions can have similar effects on the brain structure. For example, low activity in parts of the frontal lobe has been associated with schizophrenia, but it can also be present in cases of anxiety, PTSD, and simple sleep deprivation.

I have discussed this issue with two psychiatrists, who have given me the same answer: brain scans are not necessary because, no matter what they might show, the best diagnosis comes from observing a patient over a period of time when the medications for his condition will remain the same.

A growing number of psychiatrists, psychologists, and neurologists are optimistic about the efficacy of brain scans in determining the best treatment and avoiding the frustrating period of trial and error that typically follows an initial diagnosis. Brain imaging can also rule out a physical cause such as a tumor or a brain bleed. And seeing an abnormality in the brain can motivate an individual to comply with treatment.

Typical brain scans can be prescribed by a neurologist. In the case of schizophrenia, the scan of choice is fMRI (Functional Magnetic Resonance Imaging). The main problem with this type of scan is the environment in which it is performed. The patient is forced to lie still inside a dark tube with intermittent banging noises, which can be frightening for people who are already having auditory hallucinations or are paranoid and frightened by the reality around them.

To obviate this problem, some centers offer antianxiety medications or bring the patients into the tube ahead of the procedure to familiarize them with the place and its sounds. The Center for Functional MRI at the UCSD offers a compensation of $20 per hour to those who are willing to participate in the research.

If money is not an issue, a more comprehensive type of imaging called SPECT (Single Photon Emission Computed Tomography) has been developed by Dr. Daniel Amen. While many psychiatrists downplay the usefulness of his prohibitively expensive tests, his work has opened new avenues and raised new questions that could potentially improve mental health care.

David A. Peters, a licensed marriage and family psychotherapist in San Diego, uses samples of Amen's SPECT images "to help clients understand the importance of protecting the brain from drug and alcohol abuse. Somehow, seeing the images helps my clients understand the risks," he wrote.

Clinical Remedies

Finding a Good Doctor

Anosognosia, or the mental inability to recognize one's own illness, is so prevalent in cases of schizophrenia (and particularly its paranoid form) that any time you as a parent or relative have the opportunity to take your loved one to a doctor, you should seize it as if it were your last chance—because it may very well be. This doesn't always mean rushing to the *first* doctor you can find, however.

If I could press a rewind button and do it all over again, I would pause to reflect on the advice that my pastor friend

Alex gave me and spend more time and energy on finding a good doctor, instead of going down the rabbit hole of inadequate medical care. Besides, in some cases the illness is progressing too fast to allow caregivers to learn from the bewildering number of sometimes contradictory books on the market.

If I could go back to the start, I would do what I did at the very end: contact experts to find recommendations for doctors. Your local branch of the American Psychiatric Association (APA), or widespread organizations such as the Schizophrenia International Research Society, may help. Some local universities may also be conducting important studies in this field.

Do your research, and don't settle for easy choices. It was only after my son's death that I learned that the HMO I had been using had actually been sued due to some psychiatrists' dangerous practice of prescribing medication based solely on a therapist's or social worker's recommendations, without first examining the patient themselves. The practice was strongly condemned by the APA and other organizations and was finally retracted—although, looking back, I think the therapist who allowed my son to get off medications was probably overstepping her boundaries, as the matter should have been referred to the prescribing physician.

A qualified psychiatrist's fees may be high, but in my case, after two years of painful trial and error, money had lost all value. I was prepared to drastically cut expenses and find new ways of income.

Dr. Steve A. Ornish, the psychiatrist who my son and I finally consulted, defines a "good" psychiatrist as "one who is well-trained and board-certified. He or she should be well-grounded in medicine and psychopharmacology, but is also psychologically minded and able to think psychodynamically. Personal qualities include good judgment, warmth, intelligence, caring, sensitivity, compassion, and good communication skills."

I would add to this list years of experience in treating schizophrenia and a willingness to listen to the family and to discuss alternative options in order to work together toward the best treatment. If your loved one is over the age of eighteen, the doctor should calmly encourage him or her to sign a form that allows you to be informed of his or her progress, therapies, and so on. In my experience, this is best done when it is presented matter-of-factly, without feeding in any way the paranoia that often accompanies the illness.

A combination of all these qualities is extremely rare, and the doctors who possess them are worth their weight in gold.

Medications

The use of medications for mental illness is controversial in some circles. Some of this resistance is justified, because psychiatric medications are often over-prescribed and carry the risk of harmful side effects. Many describe them as a crutch that can detract from the person's efforts to solve his or her problems.

As of this writing, however, antipsychotic medications seem indispensable in treating most cases of schizophrenia, because of the seriousness of the condition and because no other method has proved to be effective in the majority of cases. I recommend consulting experts and not taking this decision lightly.

As in most situations, it's best to avoid extremes. Dr. D. J. Jaffe, adjunct fellow at the Manhattan Institute and executive director of Mental Illness Policy Org, has excellent advice on finding a healthy balance: "The mental illness narrative in America falls into two main storylines, psychiatry and antipsychiatry. Antipsychiatry groups deny mental illness exists. And whatever does exist, is not medical in nature. Psychiatry groups represent the other extreme: they believe almost everything is a mental illness and up to 50% of people had a 'diagnosable' mental disorder during their life. What's needed is a middle ground that accepts the antipsychiatry mantra that we have medicalized everything, and their devotion to confronting abuse, but rejects their position that mental illness does not exist."[2]

Jonathan went almost a year without medications, and his condition noticeably worsened. Even the low dosage of antipsychotics that were initially prescribed by our first psychiatrist brought no visible improvement. A breakthrough happened when he was hospitalized and given a larger amount of medications, but I believe that this dosage represented a drastic swing in the opposite direction, which needed to be tapered off. This reduction didn't happen until we saw Dr. Ornish, who worked with Jonathan to establish the correct prescription for his case (see p. 171). That was at the very end of Jonathan's life, but even in the short remaining time I noticed a tremendous improvement.

Dr. Ornish sees psychopharmacology as "both an art and a science." In some ways this can be said of medicine in general, which is an applied—rather than exact—science and can't always proceed by a strict adherence to scientific

2. DJ Jaffe, review of *Anatomy of an Epidemic: Magic Bullets, Psychiatric Drugs, and the Astonishing Rise of Mental Illness in America*, by Robert Whitaker, Mental Illness Policy Org, accessed September 5, 2018, https://mentalillnesspolicy.org/myths/mad-in-america.html.

rules. This is, however, particularly true when psychiatric illness cannot be monitored by tests.

It's refreshing to find a doctor who admits that there is much to be learned and who spends the necessary time to listen both to the patient and to family members. Before becoming increasingly science- and technology-based in the twentieth century, the practice of medicine was considered an art (*ars medica*). It's time that we recover that aspect of personalized treatment without forsaking its scientific foundations.

Regarding the need for medications, Dr. Ornish believes that "the majority of patients who suffer from schizophrenia, especially those with active psychotic symptoms (e.g., all types of hallucinations, paranoia, disorganized thinking), will benefit from antipsychotic medications, both during the active phase of their illness and to prevent relapse of the psychotic symptoms."

He agrees that "there is a subset of patients who do not seem to benefit from antipsychotic medications." In his view, "the only way to identify who those might be is to first systematically try different antipsychotics and dosages, since a patient who does not respond, or only partially responds to one antipsychotic, may show improvement with a different one."

David Peters compares medication adjustments to trying on different pairs of shoes. A pair of shoes may fit on the first try, but most of the time there is a period of trial and error. Some shoes will have to be returned, while others may produce some small blisters that can easily be corrected by the temporary use of Band-Aids. It's the same with medications. It might take a while to find the correct prescription and dosage for each individual.

Overall, antipsychotic medications have to be taken carefully, even if some doctors promote them as the *only* cure. It's important to take the necessary time to consider both the seriousness of the illness and the side effects of the medication. A good doctor is trained to make this evaluation. In early cases of psychosis, medication is usually given sparingly (if at all) while the doctor determines its nature.

Decreasing or discontinuing medications requires equal care. "There are patients with schizophrenia who have an acute psychotic episode, take antipsychotic medications, go into relative remission, and are able to go off their medications and still remain in remission for months or years," Dr. Ornish explains, "but such patients are in the minority and at greater risk for relapse."

Dr. Richard Warner lists some recommendations that may be useful under medical supervision.

If an antipsychotic medication is ineffective, do not keep increasing the dosage; consider stopping or decreasing it or trying another type of antipsychotic medication. . . . Be cautious about concluding that every exacerbation of the person's condition is due to the schizophrenic illness. . . . When a patient is in an acute psychotic episode use minor tranquilizers, not heavy doses of antipsychotic medication, to reduce agitation and other acute symptoms. . . . Try and establish the lowest dose of medication that keeps the worst aspects of the illness at bay without causing intolerable side effects.[3]

3. Richard Warner, *Recovery from Schizophrenia: Psychiatry and Political Economy*, 3rd ed. (2004; repr., Hove, UK: Brunner-Routledge, 2013), 253–54.

In any case, caregivers should be very careful when doctors switch medications or change doses, because the transition may take time and cause different reactions. Some medications can actually exacerbate what are called "negative symptoms" of schizophrenia, which can range from lack of motivation to actual depression. Don't hesitate to speak out if you have concerns.

Psychosocial Interventions

While antipsychotics might be necessary to suppress what are called "positive" symptoms (delusions, hallucinations, illogical and disorganized thinking, and unfitting behavior), the "negative" symptoms (withdrawal from society, blunted emotions, and loss of drive) require a different approach. In some cases, negative symptoms are treated with antidepressants, since they may be due in part to a coexisting major depression. Psychosocial interventions have been particularly useful—these include counseling as well as cognitive behavioral therapy (CBT), a training of the mind to recognize its thoughts and their relationship to behavior.

Don't let these technical words scare you. The concept, in reality, is quite simple. Psychosocial interventions are meant to help people to understand their illness, participate in their recovery, and develop sufficient social and working skills to become integrated in a community, which is in itself a great tool to recovery.

Amy told me that her daughter has benefited greatly from a form of CBT aimed specifically at psychosis, while the doctors worked carefully with their family to reduce her daughter's antipsychotic medications. In fact, Amy is studying this form of CBT while her daughter undergoes the therapy, in order to gain a better awareness of her progress. Courses on CBT are available for caregivers and can be found through an online search.

Christian Counselors

Some Christians believe they should consult exclusively Christian counselors. They may be willing to see a non-Christian psychiatrist if his or her practice is limited to dispensing medications (just as they will see a non-Christian doctor), but when it comes to choosing a psychologist or therapist, they are afraid these people may impart different theological and social beliefs.

I have found that most professionals today are considerate of their patients' religious convictions. In fact, most people today will respect whatever you believe—if nothing else, for fear of being accused of intolerance or being sued. It is, however, wise to stay watchful.

Conversely, there could be problems even with Christian counselors. In fact, choosing a Christian counselor may actually require greater caution. First of all, when it comes to matters that demand specific knowledge, experience, and skill, the adjective *Christian* cannot be a substitute for proper qualifications. Second, the word *Christian* embraces such a wide range of beliefs today that a Christian counselor's convictions may be more distant from biblical teachings (and more potentially damaging) than those of a non-Christian.

For example, what if a Christian counselor insists that God is inside you and that all you have to do is unleash his power in order to be healed? Or, on the contrary, that God is completely distant and unaffected by human suffering? Or that your mental illness is solely a result of some personal sins you have to recognize and defeat—without either giving room to the gospel or allowing the use of common means such as medications?

A third potential danger comes when a Christian counselor disparages or tries to take the place of a well-taught local church, with its properly appointed leadership. There are of course many Christian counselors who are qualified, theologically sound, and respectful of local churches, but they need to be carefully sought out. Your local pastor might have some recommendations.

Hospitalization

Hospitalization can be an option when the illness becomes hard to manage in other ways, and it can be voluntary or involuntary. Voluntary patients are free to leave whenever they wish. They are also frequently placed in relatively pleasant wards, as opposed to loud and depressing Intensive Care Units, and are awarded more privileges.

Involuntary admission can occur when a person refuses treatment. Normally the criterion is if the patient is perceived as being likely to harm self or others or is gravely disabled (which is defined as an incapacity to provide food, clothing, or shelter for oneself). In this case, a doctor can place the patient on a 24-hour hold, which can be extended to 72 hours—or even longer, with the approval of a court. Voluntary hospitalizations may become involuntary in some cases, when a psychiatrist believes that, by leaving the hospital, a patient will place self or others in danger.

The criterion of danger to self or others is however vague and subjective, forcing some parents and caregivers to watch helplessly as their loved ones' mental or physical state deteriorates. Some individuals, for example, are able to converse rationally and comfortably for limited periods of time and can thereby convince a peace officer or psychiatrist that hospitalization is not necessary.

In some states, a psychiatrist or primary care physician who is acquainted with the patient's history can sign a form requesting forced admission, but they hesitate to do so because, if a hospital refuses admission after an initial evaluation, the trust between doctor and patient will be broken.

As an alternative, caregivers can make a list of problems that come up over time. Jody listed episodes when her son screamed and threw soda cans at people across the street, guarded the door with a hammer in his hand, slept on the cement floor in the basement, and dug a hole through a wall (ending up in the apartment next door) because he heard voices on the other side. When caregivers have enough evidence, they can bring the list to a judge, who may order forced admission and/or guardianship. You may find some information online about this process.[4]

If your loved one definitely poses a danger to self or others, you should call 911 and request a visit by the Psychiatric Emergency Response Team (PERT) or similar intervention squads. These teams are trained to deal with people with mental illness in a respectful and efficient manner. In rare cases, however, their intervention may turn into an extremely traumatic experience for everyone involved, as it was when we first contacted them (see p. 69). Also, the use of force may damage the person's trust in the caregivers and make the familial environment even more difficult. However, the media is quick to remind us of tragic

---

4. See "Learn about Guardianship," Treatment Advocacy Center, accessed October 11, 2018, http://www.treatmentadvocacycenter.org/component/content /article/183-in-a-crisis/2615-learn-about-guardianship.

situations when families waited too long to act. Much wisdom is required, but most experts' advice is to err on the side of prudence.

The ideal course of action is obviously to help the person with schizophrenia to voluntarily accept treatment—in whichever form may be most advantageous. "A bunch of my work has been on the capacity to consent to or refuse treatment," Elyn Saks says, "and that to me is the line: whether the person lacks or has capacity. And it's a fine line."[5]

Saks is not completely opposed to force.

> I think there are cases where force is needed. For example, if someone's imminently dangerous, or if they cannot understand their situation and make a competent choice. If my loved one said, "This anti-psychotic medication has really helped me in the past, but I cannot take it now because I've been told it will cause a nuclear explosion," I would want to step in and say, "Give her the meds."
>
> I'd also like to say that I think force is not good. It causes humiliation and shame. And it's a very unstable solution because once you stop administering the force the person has no incentive to go back. We should use it as little as possible. What I propose is studying ways to get people to want treatment, so we don't have to use force. I think that should be a big research focus of psychiatrists and psychologists.[6]

5. Patt Morrison, "Elyn R. Saks: Mind Matters," *Los Angeles Times*, January 29, 2011, http://articles.latimes.com/2011/jan/29/opinion/la-oe-morrison-saks -112911.

6. April Kilcrease, "The Scholar with Schizophrenia," *Folks*, August 24, https://folks.pillpack.com/the-scholar-and-the-schizophrenic/.

The Treatment Advocacy Center, which is "dedicated to eliminating legal and other barriers to the timely and effective treatment of severe mental illness,"[7] is a useful resource in this area. A visit to their website will help you to learn to navigate the legal system in order to provide the best treatment for your loved one.

A rare alternative to hospitalization is to find a psychiatrist or therapist who is willing to make house calls. My HMO was unsurprisingly astonished when I suggested this, but you may be able to find someone who is willing to go this route, as long as the visit doesn't put him or her in danger. This option is apparently more frequent in Canada and European countries, but I have found one therapist who is willing to embrace it in the United States, and there are certainly more. It may be expensive, but it's worth the price. Likewise, some recovery centers provide environments that are healthier and friendlier than most mental hospitals.

Also valuable are behavioral health programs for outpatient care. I have often thought that if I had waited a little longer before calling 911, the In-Home Outreach Team—the program that became exceptionally helpful to our family—would have called me back soon after. We were on their waiting list. In fact, they called soon after my son was released from the hospital (see p. 106). Possibly, with their help, we could have achieved a positive outcome without the forced hospitalization.

That said, the fact that the hospital kept Jonathan for a whole month shows the gravity of his condition (see p. 86).

---

7. "Our History," Treatment Advocacy Center, accessed September 5, 2018, http://www.treatmentadvocacycenter.org/about-us/our-history.

In any case, God used this hospitalization to bring clarity to his mind, which in turn allowed him to embrace once again a course of study, work, and integration into society, including family and church.

Alternative Therapies

A simple online search brings up many recommendations for alternative therapies—from diet to music therapy. These should be evaluated with research, counseling, and wisdom. My son tried acupuncture, which helped him to relax and ease his mind. It didn't seem to help to combat his psychosis, but most people with schizophrenia agree that any calming influence brings some level of peace and clarity to a mind that is overwhelmed by conflicting thoughts. In most cases, however, acupuncture seems to offer only temporary relief.

Involvement in creative or nurturing activities such as art, music, poetry, animal care, gardening, and so on is also helpful. A therapist once suggested video games as a way to keep my son's mind sharp, but there are many less addictive substitutes, such as board games or interesting work projects. Sports are beneficial, as well as simple walks in nature.

Good nutrition and exercise are essential for general well-being, whether or not you have a mental illness. David Peters adds to this list "daylight, regular sleep, creative stimulation, and regular social activity." Researchers have also been studying individual nutrients (such as omega-3) for their positive effects, as well as the impact of allergies on mental illness. Other natural means, such as music therapy, sound promising and are used in many health centers, especially in Europe. These are all important areas of research that confirm the fact that treating schizophrenia has to go beyond the simplistic formula of relying on chemical substances to combat a chemical imbalance.

It's also important to get regular health checkups. Once a loved one is diagnosed with schizophrenia, you may tend to regard other issues (such as tiredness or lack of appetite) as being related to the illness, when they could very well have other causes. A malfunctioning thyroid, for example, could make a person feel lethargic and in turn generate or increase feelings of despondency or lower motivation. A good doctor should be able to detect these problems.

In any case, if your loved one is on medications, don't stop them even if you have read glowing reports about some alternative therapy. Talk to your doctor.

God's Gift of Work

For a Christian, work is an expression of our human nature as image-bearers of God—a participation in his work of creating and serving others. A true appreciation of this biblical view of the nobility of work—as opposed to the culture's view of "working for the weekend," mourning Mondays and celebrating Fridays—makes any appropriate occupation more meaningful and essential for whoever works in it.

For a person with schizophrenia, work is particularly helpful. Eugene Bleuer, the Swiss psychiatrist who coined the word *schizophrenia* in 1908, stressed the importance of an appropriate occupation: "Idleness facilitates the predomination by the complexes over the personality, whereas regulated work maintains the activity of normal thinking." He discouraged, however, "ambitious plans," urging patients to stick to "lighter tasks" such as farm work and gardening.[8]

This way of thinking lasted for much of last century. Recently, psychiatrists started to recognize the danger of imposing limitations on someone's career. They now focus on recovery in all the different aspects of one's life (physical health, social relationships, economic stability, and appropriate employment) and try as much as possible to address them at the same time. A fulfilling employment (or vocational rehabilitation that moves toward that goal) is a powerful element of recovery, and many accomplished people with schizophrenia stand as a testimony to this approach. In fact, some of them are actively involved in helping others who face the same challenges.

There is, once again, a balance. "I think it is a mistake when mental health professionals tell people with schizophrenia to drastically lower their expectations," Elyn Saks told me. "I think with appropriate resources, hard work, and a goodly amount of luck many people can live up to their pre-illness potential." She admits that, because of the illness, some people may lack motivation or find many jobs too stressful. My son looked exclusively for jobs he perceived as simple, such as shelving products in a department store. "You don't want to set people up for failure," Saks added. "So it's a fine line to walk."

On the other hand, she advised me to encourage my son to do what he enjoyed doing. "Maybe he likes sports, or

---

8. Thomas H. McGlashan, "Eugen Bleuler: Centennial Anniversary of His 1911 Publication of Dementia Praecox or the Group of Schizophrenias," *Schizophrenia Bulletin* 37, no. 6 (November 2011): 1101–03, available online at https://www.ncbi.nlm.nih.gov/pmc/articles/PMC3196955/.

maybe coaching kids, or maybe volunteering at a hospital, or maybe doing art, or maybe being a student," she said. "He could start slow—one or two classes instead of four. I do think not only that people can do more than many clinicians believe, but also that work, as well as other engaging activities, provides structure and well-being itself."

The Patient's Opposition

Any type of treatment becomes difficult when a person refuses to recognize a condition that is evident to everyone else and consequently refuses treatment or intervention.

A person may resist getting medical help for a mental illness for several reasons. She may be opposed to medications or afraid of their (all-too-real) side effects. For some who have been brought up to believe in the power of the mind over emotions, admitting to a mental disorder is a sign of weakness. The all-pervasive stigma toward mental health doesn't help. Even the depression that often accompanies schizophrenia may discourage a person from seeking treatment. "I doubted anything would help, since my brain was tinted with negativity," said Dave, my friend who had struggled with severe depression.

This resistance to medical help is aggravated by the feelings of paranoia that are common in many cases of schizophrenia. Jody once had to witness an actual chase through a hospital as her son tried to escape treatment, screaming and banging on the doors. He later told her that he thought the nurse wanted to "put him down like a dog." Based on his perception, the choice to run was perfectly logical.

Saks talks of her own struggle with this awareness.

In spite of my intelligence and education, in spite of all the doctors and the psychotic breaks and the hospitalizations and the lessons so searingly learned, I'd nevertheless managed to hold on to the belief that basically, there was nothing unusual about my thoughts. Everyone's mind contained the chaos that mine did, it's just that others were all much better at managing it than I was. All people believed there were malevolent forces controlling them, putting thoughts into their heads, taking thoughts out, and using their brains to kill whole populations—it's just that other people didn't *say* so. My problem, I thought, had less to do with my mind than it had to do with my lack of social graces. I wasn't mentally ill. I was socially maladroit.

Of course, that wasn't true. Most other people did not have thoughts like mine. They weren't more disciplined about hushing their demons, they simply didn't have any (or at least none that might lead to a diagnosis of psychosis). Thanks to the new chemicals coursing through my body, I experienced long periods of time in which I lived as other people did—with no psychotic thinking at all.[9]

In her case, the right medication convinced her to continue her treatment. "The most profound effect of the new drug was to convince me, once and for all, that I actually had a real illness. For twenty years, I'd struggled with that acceptance, coming right up to it on some days, backing away from it on most others. The clarity that Zyprexa gave me knocked down my last remaining argument."[10]

Xavier Amador's book has many valuable suggestions

9. Elyn R. Saks, *The Center Cannot Hold: My Journey through Madness* (New York: Hyperion, 2007), 304.
10. Saks, 304.

for how to deal with this common form of denial (anosognosia) through honest listening, compassionate understanding, and sincere efforts to win the person's trust.[11]

Self-medicating

Some people with schizophrenia understand that they need help but don't trust doctors and try instead to self-medicate. My son was attracted to anything that would calm his mind or help him to sleep. I was concerned but initially didn't understand that his problem was more than simple insomnia.

Many others try to self-medicate with tobacco, alcohol, or street drugs like marijuana, which has a calming effect. The frequent use of these substances by people with schizophrenia makes it difficult to determine whether they precipitate the onset of the illness or whether users take them to alleviate symptoms that are already present. Drugs can also mask or worsen other problems, which increases the complexity of diagnosing the underlining issues and finding an appropriate treatment.

In the case of schizophrenia, experts generally discourage the use of marijuana, hashish, and even CBD oil, given the evidence that some cases of psychosis have been triggered by the use of cannabis in all its forms and by hallucinogenic mushrooms. Cannabis is now easily available in many states. Even in states where it is not legal, many "medical marijuana doctors" (who can easily be found in an online search) prescribe marijuana in exchange for a

11. See Xavier Amador, *I Am Not Sick, I Don't Need Help!: How to Help Someone with Mental Illness Accept Treatment*, 10th anniversary ed. (New York: Vida Press, 2011).

small fee, often without indicating a dosage and leaving the terms of prescription to the buyer.

In some cases, the addiction to either drugs or alcohol becomes a serious problem on its own merits, which needs to be addressed at the same time as the mental illness. Most qualified psychiatrists are aware of the difficulties connected with this double task and are trained to prescribe an appropriate course of action. The greatest challenge is usually persuading the user that a substance can *feel* beneficial and yet harm an impaired brain and impede treatment and recovery.

Biblically speaking, while the Scriptures indicate that moderate use of wine is permissible, to be enjoyed as a gift from God to man (see Deut. 14:26; Ps. 104:15; Isa. 25:6; John 2:1–11), many things are permissible but not expedient (see 1 Cor. 6:12; 10:23–24). For example, alcohol may cause a negative reaction if taken alongside medications. Besides, since some types of mental illness (such as schizophrenia) cause poor judgment, one glass of wine may quickly lead to abuse (as it may do for people with a history of alcohol addiction). This is particularly true if a person considers alcohol a form of self-medication.

From a purely logical point of view, the same reasoning can be used for other substances, including marijuana. As far as Scripture is concerned, however, marijuana (or any mind-altering drug, for that matter) is not expressly mentioned in the Bible, and Christians have different opinions on the parallel between these substances and alcohol. In any case, drunkenness (from any substance) is expressly forbidden by the Scriptures (see Eph. 5:18), and deliberately risking the well-documented dangers that stem from an abuse of mind-altering substances is foolish and in itself sinful.

13

All in the Family

The greatest of these is love.
(1 Cor. 13:13)

"In a realm where the relation of mind to body remains
so complex and mysterious . . . why, again, such a fierce
belief in an *exclusively* neurobiological view of mental illness, and why so much time and money spent in the search
for chemical and organic causes and cures, while back on
the ward patients languish and die for the simple lack of
human attention to their ordinary, daily needs?"[1] This frustrated and heartbreaking cry from author Jay Neugeboren
as he watched his brother deteriorate in a mental hospital
makes me thankful that I had the privilege of caring for
my son at home—the place where ordinary, daily needs
are met.

Studies show that people with schizophrenia have
a better chance of lasting recovery when they are able to
stay home with their families or at least to receive strong

1. Jay Neugeboren, *Imagining Robert: My Brother, Madness and Survival; A
Memoir* (1997; repr., New Brunswick, NJ: Rutgers University Press, 2003), 21.

family support. Home is the natural place for nurture. But with schizophrenia home care can be very difficult, because the illness is ever present, ever painful, and, in some rare cases, dangerous—particularly when the person exhibits an aggressive behavior.

As with the choice of treatment, the decision of whether to keep a loved one with schizophrenia in the home requires much wisdom and love.

Wisdom

Wisdom is one of the most valuable qualities for dealing with the unpredictable and often puzzling situations that arise from caring for a person with mental illness.

Generally speaking, we don't like the unpredictable and puzzling. We dislike gray areas and want clear and simple answers. Christians often wish that Paul had written detailed, step-by-step instructions on how to maintain healthy relationships, how to raise our children, and—why not?—how to deal with mental illness. Instead, while we can find in the Bible many instructions on what is advisable or sinful, most of the time we are faced with situations that have no clear right or wrong answer from either a biblical or a more broadly ethical point of view.

This is where wisdom comes into play, helping us to apply our knowledge and moral rules to life. The Bible spends much time emphasizing wisdom's importance—not as a substitute to God's law when Scripture seems silent, but as an ability to apply God's general law to specific, but unspecified, situations. It tells us to pray for wisdom (see James 1:5)—but, in most cases, wisdom doesn't come as a sudden flash of light. It's a quality to cultivate, usually through common means—knowledge, counsel, prayer, and careful consideration.

Knowledge

Wisdom and knowledge are interdependent. There is no true wisdom without knowledge, and knowledge without wisdom is sterile.

For a Christian, the most important knowledge is the *knowledge of the triune God*—which, according to the Bible, is the beginning of wisdom (see Ps. 111:10). While wisdom in a general sense is not exclusive to Christians, biblical wisdom has a deeper component because it is rooted in something other than abstract moral principles. It is based on the story of a God who became man to redeem his people—a story that colors everything we know about ourselves, the world around us, our joys and our pain, our battles, and our ultimate end.

This knowledge of God through his written word allows us to make decisions that are based not only on some specific rules but on the general revelation God has given to us about himself and his will.

Practical knowledge is also important. In the case of schizophrenia, this type of knowledge is largely in the hands of professionals, but it's important for families to learn about the illness for themselves.

I have often mourned the apparent chasm between the family and most professionals in the psychiatric field. Medical professionals have a treasury of knowledge and experience at their disposal but don't know much about patients and their families, and their time is limited. Conversely, family members have a much greater knowledge of their loved ones and their history, and have the inherent ability to create an environment that is conducive to healing, but usually know little about the mechanisms and treatment of schizophrenia—particularly if the illness starts suddenly with little or no warning.

My friend Dave shares my impressions. "My family did not have the knowledge to 'help' me at the time when all was falling apart," he said, "and their 'love' and 'care' for me blinded them to the hard realities of the situation at hand. The doctors and various medical professionals did not have the 'love' to help me and were equally blinded by their knowledge and jaded bureaucratic outlook. This jaded bureaucratic juggle, and the interplay of family and medical blind spots, is not all that dissimilar from the confusing whirl of voices within the psychotic state that the individual at hand is experiencing. Navigating the schizophrenic-like State while in a psychotic state is incredibly difficult. Nevertheless, it needs to be done, and I needed the State's help and my family's help together."

I learned much by trial and error that I could have avoided if I had known more about the illness before it started. If only families and professionals could find better ways of working together! This is sometimes achieved through family therapy, in the rare cases when it is offered in the United States. Personally, I have found it useful to do much private study and to ask as many questions as possible.

"All of this, of course, is very difficult for those without scientific background," said my friend Amy, "but it should be a priority, even if it means dropping income-producing opportunities and other ministries in order to find the time. In one sense, I think that investing time now may well reduce the amount of time we need to spend later, since family support and involvement are a crucial factor in 'recovery' and reintegration."

At the same time, don't dismiss the importance of your *knowledge of your loved one*, especially when you are considering other people's opinions (even medical opinions). It's true that schizophrenia can obscure much of a person's personality, but much of it also stays the same. I could often tell if Jonathan was feeling uncomfortable or fearful. I knew when I could trust his words. I could tell the difference between a burst of ordinary frustration (of which I have equally been guilty at times) and a dangerous sign.

Sadly, I didn't always give this knowledge enough importance. I was often so frightened and confused that I did whatever doctors, elders, books, friends, and even total strangers told me to do, mostly because I was scared of making the wrong decision, especially in view of the alarming warnings that the medical system is obliged to routinely issue. Yes, schizophrenia is scary and dangerous, but before assuming the worst, take a minute to breathe, pray, observe the situation, and consider what you know about your child. As Amy reminded me, "It is so easy to forget that this is about our children, whom we love and know and who have human feelings as well as mental illness."

Amy, who has seen an extraordinary progress in her daughter, believes that letting her control her treatment to some extent (and even allowing her to refuse a program that had been recommended for her and that people had worked hard to get for her) was an important factor in her recovery. Amy found support for this course of action in her research and in the example of medical professionals who modeled the importance of listening to her daughter's wishes. A large part of her decision, however, was based on her knowledge of her daughter. "At times, the doctors forced medications on other young people, but never on her. I think that would have traumatized her."

Counsel

In spite of the huge amount of information available in the form of books, articles, and lectures, unless you catch your loved one's schizophrenia in its earliest stages, you may find yourself pressed with larger-than-life situations that require greater training than you can acquire in a few days. Even if you are a speed-reader who can absorb a lot of information each day, it takes much time to translate information into practical terms and to apply it to your individual case. In these situations, the advice of others is especially important.

In fact, seeking advice in general is wise—it widens our perspective and helps us to see things that we may not have noticed or considered. Besides *doctors*, there are several *support groups* that work hard to assist the mentally ill and their families and that offer helpful advice. The National Alliance on Mental Illness (NAMI), the largest of these organizations in the United States, also provides phone assistance. I called once and received a valuable recommendation to read Amador's book. One of the strengths of NAMI lies in its support groups. Even if the groups I personally attended were somewhat disorganized, it's always helpful to meet others who are experiencing challenges similar to yours.

Some groups provide home visits. The In-Home Outreach Team (IHOT) assigned a special team to our family, visited my son and the rest of us separately, and offered prompt phone or email assistance (see pp. 107, 133, 139, 164). You may be able to find something comparable in your area. Of course, your experience might be different from mine. I have recently discovered that even IHOT has changed some of its policies. You will have to make your own inquiries and see what organization fits your needs.

Due to the urgency of our situation and my limited time and energy, I found it useful to make a list of questions and then consult experts in the field who were well prepared to answer. This may take some research in order to find qualified professionals who have experience with schizophrenia, as well as some money to pay for the visits, but it is well worth the price. Such professionals are in fact able to provide a foundation on which to start building a greater knowledge of this illness and of the best ways to respond, helping you to take better advantage of the books and programs that are widely available.

Christians have also the benefit of receiving advice and support from other church members—especially pastors and elders who have the responsibility of caring for their congregation and have often acquired some experience with mental illness. It's important, however, to remember that pastors and elders have been trained to help people in spiritual matters and may not understand important medical dimensions of the case, just as a doctor may not understand important spiritual or pastoral dimensions. Receiving both types of advice and applying them to your situation, while taking into consideration your personal knowledge of your loved one, puts you in a stronger position to make a wise decision.

Another advantage of having a supportive community is that others may be able to intervene when our emotions run wild. Jody works in a school as an educational assistant and has received competent training in dealing with children who exhibit behavioral issues. When they are in crisis, she can act professionally. But things have sometimes been different at home with her own children, when "all the emotions come bubbling up before the wisdom and training." Most mothers can identify with this.

"I did pray for wisdom and patience and love," Jody told me, "but when Matt was having a psychotic episode and chaos reigned, I reacted from pure emotion and not with my head. There are so many emotions involved when you are with someone having a psychotic episode. Matt was so unreasonable, and I was frightened like he was—and often angry, because I would think, *If he would just listen and get some help—at least take his medicine!* It would be so frustrating."

At times like these, it's useful to reach out to friends and family members who can give more dispassionate advice and even—if they live close enough—come by and ease other aspects of our load.

Prayer

All the while, keep praying for wisdom, even if it seems elusive. God has promised to give it with no strings attached (see James 1:5).[2] I have sometimes felt discouraged by the next verse in James ("Let him ask in faith, with no doubting")—until I was reminded that faith is always a gift of God, not something that we muster up by our own efforts, and it's always based on what God has already done in history. This realization turned the rest of the verse into a balm. By God's grace, I didn't *have* to be "like a wave of the sea that is driven and tossed by the wind" (v. 6), which is exactly

2. See translation given by Steven M. Baugh in "James 1:2–8" (morning devotion, Westminster Seminary California, Escondido, CA, September 24, 2009), available online at http://wscal.edu/resource-center/james-1_2-8.

how I felt most of the time. In Christ, my emotions don't have the last word.

Given the intricacies of the mental health system, coupled with the ordinary complexities of our sinful world, wisdom may seem absent in spite of our prayers. When my son was alive, I rarely knew what to do. When he refused to take medications, I felt like I was waiting for a train wreck to happen. I found myself even wishing for the train wreck to arrive, just so I could move from a state of constant danger to a resolution. Of course, that's not the answer. As a wise friend explained to me, the best thing is to lay open our hearts to God, admit that we don't know how to resolve the situation, and pray that in his providence he would direct events so that our children can get help without hurting themselves in the process.

With that in mind, I kept praying my bumbling prayers, trusting that God would, by his Spirit, decipher the cry of my soul (see Rom. 8:26). As the Heidelberg Catechism teaches, "It is even more sure that God listens to my prayer than that I really desire what I pray for."[3] God's answer was not always what I wanted to hear, but I knew it was according to his will, and he always supplied me with sufficient comfort and strength.

Prayer is one of the great privileges that Christ has purchased for us with his blood—it gives us the ability to go to our Creator and call him Father, and it is in itself a comfort in the midst of all the thorns and thistles that have filled our lives since Adam's sin. In fact, Christ is constantly interceding for us in heaven, even when we forget (or are too lazy)

3. Heidelberg Catechism, answer 129. Translation © 2011, Faith Alive Christian Resources, Christian Reformed Church in North America. Available at https://www.crcna.org/welcome/beliefs/confessions/heidelberg-catechism.

to pray. He will never leave us or forsake us (see Deut. 31:6; Heb. 13:5; see also Matt. 28:20).

The Tough Nature of Love

Love is tough. I am not just talking about "tough love"—a popular expression in today's parenting vocabulary (which I discuss later). Love is tough in every way. It's self-sacrificial and often hurts. The list of love's attributes in 1 Corinthians 13 is enough to prove this point, and caring for someone with mental illness will often put them to the test. It will test our patience, our kindness, and our ability to refrain from insisting on our own way and becoming "irritable or resentful." It will test our capacity to bear all things, believe all things, hope all things, and endure all things. It will take sacrifice, compassion, and courage.

Sacrifice

From the moment we conceive a child, we sign up for self-sacrifice. We are ready to sacrifice our sleep, our time, our comfort, our hobbies, our looks, and much more. As the child grows and becomes independent, however, we are often eager to claim some of our lives back.

Schizophrenia gets in the way of our plans. It typically starts in the teenage years and blooms in early adulthood, when parents (especially in North America) are ready to push their children out of the nest. They may have been planning their child's admission to a good college, or their own early retirement. Instead, they end up trading it all to coexist with a stranger—even an alien at times—someone who is puzzling, often distant, and sometimes scary.

It is then that God calls us to the task, as he does whenever someone is in need. "Keep your life full of good things," Amy says, "but let them all be droppable so that when your ill loved one needs extra time in any way, you can cheerfully attend to him or her. In other words, minimize deadlines, projects with very stressful days, etc. Yes, you will fall behind in your personal goals, but God calls us to give up our lives for each other."

I have always been impressed by John Newton, the famous English pastor who fought the slave trade and authored the famous hymn "Amazing Grace." In one instance, when his friend William Cowper, the renowned poet who lived next door to him, was overtaken by a sudden psychotic attack in the middle of the night, Newton rushed to his side. Over the next few days, he kept visiting him at all hours. When Cowper asked to move in with the Newtons, the couple didn't hesitate, and they kept him with them for thirteen months, until he was well enough to leave.

Newton gave a partial description of the attack, which included Cowper's urge to "sacrifice" his life.

> The first temptation the enemy assaulted him with was to offer up himself as Abraham [offered] his son. He verily thought he ought to do it. We were obliged to watch with him night and day. I, my dear wife and Mrs. Unwin with whom he lived left him not an hour for seven years. He was also tempted to think butcher's meat was human flesh, therefore he would not take it. We found it very difficult to provide any sustenance he would take.[4]

4. John Newton, "Mr. Newton's Account of Mr. Cowper in a Funeral Sermon" (address given at St. Mary Woolnoth, London, May 1800), available

Cowper described a later relapse into illness in vivid terms:

> I was suddenly reduced from my wonted rate of under-standing to an almost childish imbecility. I did not indeed lose my senses, but I lost the power to exercise them. I could return a rational answer even to a difficult question, but a question was necessary, or I never spoke at all. This state of mind was accompanied, as I suppose it to be in most instances of the kind, with misapprehension of things and persons that made me a very untractable patient. I believed that everybody hated me, and that Mrs. Unwin hated me most of all; was convinced that all my food was poisoned, together with ten thousand megrims of the same.[5]

Living with a person who was seized by delusions and paranoia posed a challenge for Mrs. Unwin, as well as for John and Polly Newton, but they readily embraced it. "I have now devoted myself and time as much as possible to attend on Mr. Cowper," Newton wrote a few days after his friend's attack. "We walked today and probably shall daily. I shall now have little leisure but for such things as indispensably require attention."[6]

After Newton moved to London, the care of Cowper

---

online at http://www.johnnewton.org/Groups/251893/The_John_Newton/new_menus/Sermons/Exodus/Exodus.aspx.

5. William Cowper to Lady Hesketh, January 16, 1786, in Anna B. McMahan, ed., *The Best Letters of William Cowper* (Chicago 1893), 179.

6. John Newton, diary entry, January 5, 1773, quoted in Jonathan Aitken, *John Newton: From Disgrace to Amazing Grace* (Wheaton, IL: Crossway, 2007), 219.

fell entirely on Mrs. Unwin, who, according to Cowper, took on her task with joy.

> At the same time that I was convinced of Mrs. Unwin's aversion to me, I could endure no other companion. The whole management of me consequently devolved upon her, and a terrible task she had; she performed it, however, with a cheerfulness hardly ever equalled on such an occasion; and I have often heard her say that if ever she praised God in her life, it was when she found that she was to have all the labor. She performed it accordingly, but, as I hinted once before, very much to the hurt of her own constitution.[7]

In spite of the obvious hardship involved, many people (including Newton's recent biographer, Jonathan Aitken) believe that Mrs. Unwin's and the Newtons' care was a significant factor in preventing Cowper from committing suicide.[8]

Compassion and Courage

Love and courage go hand in hand. In fact, the Bible sees fear and love as opposites: "God gave us a spirit not of fear but of power and love and self-control," Paul wrote (2 Tim. 1:7). In my opinion, compassion is the aspect of love that requires the most courage.

The word *compassion* comes from the Latin words *con* and *patire*, meaning "co-suffering." It requires entering into someone's pain in a way that is uncomfortable and

7. McMahan, *Best Letters of William Cowper*, 180.
8. See Aitken, *John Newton*, 222.

distressing. In some ways, the pain that we feel for others can even be more unsettling and agonizing than our own, because it's even more beyond our control. As a famous saying (which is attributed to the medieval Jewish poet Yehuda Ha-Levi) goes, "'Tis a fearful thing to love what death can touch." It's all the more fearful when death looms uncomfortably near—when our loved one's unpredictable behavior makes us look at each moment together as our last.

For most of us, the natural response is to turn our eyes. When I told my doctor that my son was dead, he grimaced and turned his head, visibly expressing what most of us feel inside. But the advice given to artists by Japanese film director Akira Kurosawa (frequently quoted as "Never avert your eyes") can often apply to caregivers. In our sanitized and highly distracted world, it's often easy to escape other people's pain, even when it's close to us. We justify it with the need to "preserve our sanity."

While it's true that constantly focusing on someone's pain can be depressing and damaging for everyone involved, and while it's important to take some time away from the constant battle, the Bible encourages us to sincerely "weep with those who weep" (Rom. 12:15). The actual word that the Greek New Testament uses for compassion means "to be moved from the bowels." It's a call to feel deeply. Jesus did this (see Matt. 9:36; 20:34). So did the Good Samaritan and the Prodigal Son's father (Luke 10:33–34 and 15:20 use the same Greek word).

A passage from the book *The Little Prince* has impressed me since I was a child. In the story, a prince from outer space meets a fox who begs the prince to tame him. When he leaves, the fox has to face inevitable pain.

"It is your own fault," the little prince said. "I never wanted to do you any harm; but you insisted that I tame you . . ."

"Yes, of course," the fox said.

"But you're going to weep!" said the little prince.

"Yes, of course," the fox said.

"Then you get nothing out of it!"

"I get something," the fox said, "because of the color of the wheat."[9]

To the fox, the color of the wheat fields is the color of the prince's hair—a color that will always have a special meaning for him. To the fox, this was worth the pain. In asking the prince to tame him, the fox allowed himself to become attached and vulnerable.

Love hurts, but it's worth the pain—and not just because of poetic memories, as in the case of the fox, but because it's what we do. It's our calling as Christians and, actually, as human beings. We were created, in the image of God, to be loving as he is loving. The pain results from man's fall into sin, but love must persist regardless. And we do "get something" as partakers and imitators of the love of God.

Even writing this book is painful. To do it, I had to enlist the help of other aching people, asking them to reopen their tender wounds in order to recall their experiences. Their response has been encouraging. "Do all that is in your heart," Jody replied, quoting 1 Samuel 14:7. "Do as you wish. Behold, I am with you heart and soul." That was

9. *The Little Prince*, by Antoine de Saint-Exupéry, p. 61. Copyright © 1943 by Houghton Mifflin Harcourt Publishing Company, renewed 1971 by Consuelo de Saint-Exupery. English translation copyright © 2000 by Richard Howard. Reprinted by permission of Houghton Mifflin Harcourt Publishing Company. All Rights reserved.

the response of Jonathan's armor bearer when he was called to a desperate mission.

The Bible never calls us to escape, to keep a stiff upper lip, or to pull ourselves up by our bootstraps. It calls us to feel other people's pain—even to feel it in our bowels—and to weep with them, while we draw courage and strength from God and keep our eyes on what he has done and has promised to do. That's what the biblical psalmists did over and over.

Forgiveness

Love includes forgiveness, which will be needed repeatedly on both sides. Relatives of people with schizophrenia have come to forgive the unforgivable. A mother told me that she forgave her son, and is still trying to help him, even after he ran away from home several times and threw her down the stairs, causing her to be hospitalized. Another family learned to forgive a young man who killed a relative in a moment of temporary psychosis.

On a regular basis, parents and relatives need to ask for forgiveness countless times, because they are treading unknown ground and will inevitably make lots of mistakes. Asking for forgiveness can be difficult—especially for parents, who may fear losing respect or authority.

When I was in Indonesia, speaking about Christian parenting, I inadvertently shocked the audience by suggesting that parents should ask their children to forgive them when they have sinned. It was a surprising statement because it was contrary to their culture. "Parents and superiors usually show some degree of uneasiness when they are shown to be wrong," my friend Cia Ming told me, "but then they will just brush it aside, changing to another subject."

The Bible gives us a beautiful balance, telling children to obey and respect their parents (see Eph. 6:1) while also teaching that "all have sinned" (Rom. 3:23) and that "none is righteous, no, not one" (Rom. 3:10). At church, our children hear these lessons repeatedly in sermons and Sunday school and join their parents in united, public confessions of sin (as is typical of Lutheran, Reformed, Anglican, and Roman Catholic churches) and in singing songs of repentance. In this context, humbly admitting the sins we commit toward them and asking for forgiveness comes naturally and breaks down barriers, while the very act of forgiving eases tensions.

Asking for forgiveness may also encourage honesty, which is particularly important if families want to learn how to truly help each other. "It just seems to me extremely important for a family to quickly see, in themselves, ways in which they are either helping or hurting the situation," said Dave.

When Love Is Absent

Some parents, exhausted from caring for a loved one with schizophrenia, feel as though all their love for the person is gone. "What to do in those cases?" someone asked me. It's not an unusual feeling. At times, frustrated or hurt by my son's responses, I felt like taking a plane somewhere and washing my hands of him altogether.

Much love and compassion can be restored when we understand what our loved ones have to endure. Reading books and articles written by people with schizophrenia who can express their situation is very useful. When I compared my own mental and spiritual struggles with those of my son, who was often unable to distinguish truth from reality and had to battle not only his thoughts but actual audible voices, I could only feel empathy and even admiration for his endurance, even if I didn't agree with his choices or behavior. This empathy helped me to talk to him in love.

Sometimes love is there but is simply crushed and overwhelmed by the torrent of worrisome and painful situations our loved ones seem bent on pouring on us every day. At those times, it's useful for us to step back for as long as we need. Our loved ones probably don't realize they are hurting us. In my experience, reacting to upsetting words or actions doesn't bear good fruit. Take some time off to assess the situation and choose your battles. When you talk to your loved one later, focus on his or her distress and on your desire to help and support him or her.

It's also important to redefine the word *love*, which is too often equated with a feeling. Without denying feelings, biblical love focuses on commitment and action. That's the only way 1 Corinthians 13:8 makes any sense as a commandment in this fallen world: "Love never ends." Such a description cannot possibly apply to feelings, which are fleeting and unstable.

When Thomas Cranmer and others wrote, in the marital formula of the Book of Common Prayer, "Will you love . . . in sickness and in health . . . as long as you both shall live?" they were not talking about *feelings* of love. Sadly, many people today give up on their marriages when their feelings of love are gone. Conversely, couples who have been married for decades usually agree that their marriage is based on true love, not on feelings.

Ultimately, however, it's important to remember that we are just as weak and prone to sin as our loved ones are, and that it's only by God's providential wisdom that our minds are able to make better judgments than theirs are most of the time. This basic sinful nature is often expressed in our desire for retaliation when someone hurts us—especially someone who is very close to us, someone we have been trying to help, someone we have vowed to love until we die.

"The spirit indeed is willing, but the flesh is weak," Jesus said to his disciples, who couldn't even stay awake for an hour in his time of greatest anguish. He preceded these words with a remedy: "Watch and pray that you may not enter into temptation" (Mark 14:38).

Prayer forces us to realize that we can't muster up feelings of love in ourselves—especially not after our loved ones have repeatedly mistreated, abused, and accused us. When Jesus told his disciples to forgive a person who offends them "seven times in the day," their stunned response was an admission of lack: "Increase our faith!" (Luke 17:4, 5).

I have often found comfort in Margaret Clarkson's hymn "So Send I You."

So send I you to labor unrewarded,
To serve unpaid, unloved, unsought, unknown,
To bear rebuke, to suffer scorn and scoffing—
So send I you to toil for Me alone.

. . . .
"As the Father sent me, so send I you."[10]

Jesus himself suffered humiliation, abuse, and expressions of cruel hatred at the hands of those he had come to save, but he did much more than just leave us an example. He took on himself all our sins, including our lack of love,

10. Margaret Clarkson, "So Send I You," Copyright © 1963 New Spring Publishing Inc. (ASCAP) (adm. at CapitolCMGPublishing.com) / Word Music Publishing (ASCAP) All rights reserved. Used by permission.

and paid the penalty in full. He then clothed us with his righteousness, freeing us from the power of sin and enabling us to embrace love in spite of any feeling that points us to the contrary.

It's with this thought that Margaret Clarkson could later add new lines to her song, emphasizing God's strength.

So send I you—my strength to know in weakness,
My joy in grief, my perfect peace in pain,
To prove My power, My grace, My promised presence—
So send I you, eternal fruit to gain.[11]

On Their Own

While a family environment is considered the best for people with schizophrenia, they may need or want to move out on their own or to a facility. When appropriate, this could be a good opportunity for them to learn to live independently.

Gaining Autonomy

A friend in Italy who lives with schizophrenia feels quite comfortable working as a custodian in a convent of nuns who live a quiet life. This way, he doesn't have to have uncomfortable social interactions. His sister visits him every week, shops for him, and makes sure that his needs are met.

Others have integrated more fully into society. Elyn Saks, who was told her schizophrenia was so debilitating that she could never hold a job, has been teaching for years at the University of Southern California Gould Law School and is happily married.

11. Clarkson, "So Send I You."

Not everyone is ready to live independently, however. Jody says that things didn't go well after Matt moved out. Embarrassed about a twitch he developed as a side effect of his medicine, he eventually quit taking it and started to drink again. As a result, he started two fires in his apartment, was evicted, totaled his truck, and was charged with impaired driving. Even if Jody and her husband visited him daily, they could not supervise Matt as well as they had when he was at home, nor could they be fully aware of any escalating problems. Once again, the decision of helping a loved one to live independently requires much wisdom and prayer.

A Time to Be Firm

The common meaning of "tough love" indicates an action that might hurt someone with the intention of helping them in the long run, and there might be a time to apply it, even if the outcome is never certain.

In *Far from the Tree*, Andrew Solomon tells the story of a woman who asked her adult son (who lived with schizophrenia and resided alone on a family property) to move back home, see a doctor regularly, and take medications, threatening to evict him from the separate property if he didn't. She was terrified that he would refuse her deal and end up homeless, so she found a private eye to follow him around if that happened. "A private eye to shadow someone with a paranoid delusion that he was being tracked by the FBI," she quipped. Thankfully, the outcome was positive. "He screamed how he hated me. Forty-eight hours later he moved home."[12]

12. Andrew Solomon, *Far from the Tree: Parents, Children, and the Search for Identity* (New York: Scribner, 2012), 299.

We made a similar deal with Jonathan, though only after he had been in the hospital for a while, and it worked. We also used this type of "tough love" when we kept him in the hospital until the doctors released him instead of taking him back as soon as he wished (see p. 72).

Later, when he resumed marijuana usage, some people suggested that we give him an ultimatum and throw him out if he didn't comply, but at that time both we and his psychiatrist believed we could help him much more by keeping him at home and persuading him to gradually stop.

Jody and her husband faced the same dilemma. "We tried to use tough love and insisted that Matt not live with us unless he took his meds, but when he started camping in the woods near our house and painting the inside of his tent black so that no one could see inside it, we just couldn't do it. Besides, he just kept coming back. Home and his family were his only sense of safety."

Firmness is definitely appropriate at times, especially when a loved one is manipulating the family (often by inducing guilt) in pursuit of a destructive behavior or addiction, or when he or she abuses others and places the family in danger. Some parents I met had to move away without giving their loved one their new address. They left only one way to contact them (usually a phone number).

Each case has to be judged on its own merits, using wisdom and prayer and acting in true love. This love will of course seek the benefit of the sufferer, but it may need to take other people into consideration. There may be children in the home who are frightened or have been threatened. The caregivers may have health issues that prevent them from giving proper care.

In any case, if we decide to apply this type of "tough

love," we have to be ready to deal with the consequences. Our child may rebel and hate us, at least in words, and the temptation to go back on our word will be strong. It might be helpful to write down the steps we are intending to take and to review them when our determination wavers. While we stand firm, we can empathize with our loved one's anger and sorrow and can work toward finding better solutions.

Nothing is set in stone, and the well-being of our loved one is more important than our adherence to a plan. If we realize that we have erred, we can change course and ask for forgiveness—without promising that we will never do it again. We don't know the future, and what may be a poor decision in one situation may prove to be the best one later.

The dilemma is particularly difficult when the person with schizophrenia is a spouse. Life becomes unpredictable and has to be lived one day at a time. "There are some things you just can't plan or prepare for mentally, and it's impossible to know how they are going to affect you or your family," a friend recently told me. "Sometimes dreaming or thinking ahead is painfully uncertain. Looking back, I just don't know how it was all worked through, and I can just thank the Lord for his grace and strength."

While I have heard of several couples who have weathered the storm (as the couple does in the movie *A Beautiful Mind*), the divorce rate in marriages in which one person lives with any mental illness is high. One couple that I know has taken repeated breaks and sought short, temporary separations to allow each member of the family to regain strength and reevaluate the situation with plenty of counsel.

Once again, these issues require wisdom and discernment. Much depends on the person's willingness to receive treatment, on the actual or potential danger he or she poses toward other family members, and on the mental and physical condition of the other spouse. As with every other aspect of care, what's expedient in one case might be inappropriate in another.

These are all serious matters, but we have the comfort of knowing that God is faithful in leading his children and that our wrong decisions cannot thwart his plans. "For those who love God all things work together for good, for those who are called according to his purpose" (Rom. 8:28).

A United Front

Wisdom, humility, and organization are always required in making parental care a united effort. This is particularly difficult during challenging times. Specifically, dealing with schizophrenia could be compared to a war zone in which personal concerns are dropped in order to maintain unity.

Through speaking to parents of people with schizophrenia, I have encountered different situations. Sometimes one parent is absent or in denial because the pain is too difficult to take or process. Other times parents try to work together but have more difficulty managing disagreements than they would in other situations. For example, if a wife disagrees with her husband's purchase of an expensive new gadget, she can try to dissuade him; but in the end she can let go and trust that God will provide. It's only money. When it comes to a child's serious illness, which is possibly a matter of life and death, it's harder to let go of a pressing conviction.

"Mental illness can be a family circumstance that tests the husband-wife relationship in a manner not unlike chronic illness of any kind," says Rev. Stephen Donovan, pastor of congregational life at Escondido United Reformed

Church, who has had much experience dealing with cases of mental illness.

A pastor with an autistic son told me that his wife does most of the research, so he has learned to listen carefully to her advice and to fight his instinctive desire to take charge and "fix things." The same arrangement can work well with a child who lives with schizophrenia.

Ideally, it's best if husband and wife can work as a couple and attend informational meetings or appointments with the psychiatrist together, so that they can be on the same page and discuss unified methods and goals. "My husband was pretty involved, and we could talk together after an appointment and apply what we learned to our situation," Jody said. "It helped us as a couple to understand Matt and support him together. None of it was easy. There were times when one of us felt alone, and we had our disagreements, but it was good to have each other and to pray together."

In my case, my husband was a great help in distracting me from my over-involvement by taking me out and reminding me that we could talk about other things and enjoy life without feelings of guilt or anxiety.

A united parental front is obviously important. My husband and I agreed on a signal that either of us could use when we were talking together with our son, in order to alert the other that something should be said or done differently (or, when in doubt, that the conversation should be dropped for the time being).

More than ever, spouses have to consider each other's feelings and reactions. Like most men I know, my husband interprets many of my comments as a call to action and gets frustrated if the solution is out of his reach. "What do you want me to do?" is a typical response. Usually I don't want him to do anything. I just want him to empathize or to feel the way I do. In reality, while empathy is always a virtue, a situation is actually best approached through different eyes and different sets of emotions, so I am learning to appreciate both his views and his responses.

Likewise, I found that it's very important to be clear and precise in our communication. When I reported our son's words or behavior to my husband, I had to be as accurate, precise, and thorough as if I had been reporting them to a psychiatrist. It's easy to exaggerate or to emphasize one word or action, especially when we are agitated or distressed.

I also learned to specify whether I had already talked to our son about the issues I was describing. For example, if I said in frustration, "He didn't take his meds," without adding, "I have talked to him about it, so you don't have to," my husband assumed I was asking him to act and talked to Jonathan right after I did, potentially aggravating the situation. Writing things down and rereading them once or twice helped me to collect my thoughts.

It's always important for us to share our honest opinions with our spouses, even if we think they will disagree. My husband was well aware of the seriousness of the situation and was ready to take my concerns seriously, as I was his, but at times we had to verbally reaffirm this—especially if our responses were not as quick as the other expected.

In urgent matters, most health professionals encourage relatives of people who are at risk to err on the side of caution. If time allowed and we had different opinions on a matter, we took time to think about it, do some research, and then discuss it again. Neither of us wanted to be solely responsible for an action that might make a difference between life or death.

In spite of this, we often had to act independently and on the spot, and we made plenty of mistakes. We also had emotional outbursts and arguments that we deeply regretted, but I found that God was always gracious to grant forgiveness on everyone's part and to give us the courage to try again—admitting our sins to him and to each other and clinging to his unfailing faithfulness.

14

Don't Burn Out

Which of you by being anxious can add a sin-gle hour to his span of life? (Matt. 6:27)

"I do remember feeling *battered*," writes Jay Neuge-boren, "feeling an enormous fatigue, a deep desire to be away from it all, from everything and everyone I knew—along with an insatiable hunger for some peace and quiet: for a few days—a few moments!—that might be free of rage and guilt, of exhaustion, frustration, madness, doubt, and family."[1]

At meetings of the National Alliance on Mental Illness, I heard other parents express the same feelings, the same desire to escape it all, because the burden of caring for a gravely ill person can be crushing. I usually had the oppo-site reaction. I found some moments of peace and quiet—especially at church, where my mind was regularly redirected to the only realities that make sense—but my problem was that I was *attracted* to the trouble at hand, as a magnet is

---

1. Jay Neugeboren, *Imagining Robert: My Brother, Madness and Survival; A Memoir* (1997; repr., New Brunswick, NJ: Rutgers University Press, 2003), 184.

attracted to iron. I wanted to be there, in mind if not in body, as if I were the only one who could shield my son—as if my thoughts, prayers, and actions were indispensable to his protection.

Jody agrees. "I did feel like I had to be there all the time. And Matt made me feel like I had to be there all the time. But I felt relieved when he was in the hospital for a while and we could sleep and lose some of the tension. I also feared bringing him home, where I was the one responsible.

"There is a lot of talk about self-care in the family support circles," she continues. "They often use the analogy that you have to put your own air mask on in a plane that is crashing before you can look after someone else. But sometimes Matt's illness just sucked me in, like a big vortex, and there was no way of getting out of it. I just wanted him fixed—healed. It hurt so much to watch him that it didn't matter how many baths I took or how many movies we watched, or if I went out for dinner or away for the weekend. It took up my whole life. He was always on my mind."

Relatives are caught in this tug-of-war between the need to rest and the urge to be involved. The latter usually wins, unless exhaustion takes over. To find a balance, we need to learn when it's time to let go, rest, and ask for help.

Letting Go

Letting go of our loved ones is never easy, whether they move away from home or they think or behave in a way that we don't understand or approve. A letter from John Newton to his adopted daughter Betsy reveals that he had these sorts of apprehensions. She was fifteen years old, attending boarding school in a nearby city, and Newton was plagued by common parental anxieties—especially since her letters to him were short and measured. He feared the unknown thoughts of her heart. "If you could freely open your mind to me," he said, "you might inform me of something I should be glad to know, or you might propose to me some things which now and then trouble your thoughts, and thereby give me an opportunity of attempting to relieve, encourage, or direct you."[2] Most parents share this desire to enter into their children's minds.

Newton also feared the world that his daughter was just beginning to explore. "Sometimes when I consider what a world you are growing up into, and what snares and dangers young people are exposed to with little experience to help them, I have some painful feelings for you," he wrote.[3]

He gave an interesting example, which is strongly related to his experience as a seaman.

The other day I was at Depford, and saw a ship launched: she slipped easily into the water; the people on board shouted; the ship looked clean and gay, she was fresh painted and her colours flying. But I looked at her with a sort of pity:—"Poor ship," I thought, "you are now in port and in safety; but ere long you must go to sea. Who can tell what storms you may meet with hereafter, and to what hazards you may be exposed; how weather-beaten you may be before you return to port again, or whether you may return at all." Then my thoughts turned from the ship to my child. It seemed an emblem of your present state;

2. John Newton to Elizabeth Newton, October 15, 1782, in *The Works of the Rev. John Newton* (New Haven, 1824), 4:397.

3. Newton, 397.

you are now, as it were, in a safe harbour; but by and by you must launch out into the world, which may well be compared to a tempestuous sea. I could even now almost weep at the resemblance; but I take courage; my hopes are greater than my fears. I know there is an infallible Pilot, who has the winds and the waves at his command. There is hardly a day passes in which I do not entreat him to take charge of you. Under his care I know you will be safe; he can guide you unhurt amidst the storms, and rocks, and dangers, by which you might otherwise suffer, and bring you at last to the haven of eternal rest.[4]

Fear causes people to cleave more tightly to each other. "Matt and I were attached, so to speak, at the hip," Jody said. "I felt I was his sense of safety. And the attachment went both ways. I could feel his hurt even when he didn't express it verbally. I was always tuned in to his feelings and could read his face. I could feel his hurt in my heart. You would expect that a child who created so much hardship would make you grow apart, but I don't think that is the case. I think his suffering and my fear of losing him made me cling all the tighter."

Even in these most difficult and complicated cases, however, there comes a time to let go and trust the "infallible Pilot." "It's one of my biggest struggles," Jody said. "As a woman and caretaker, I like to take charge—to be in control. It works well when God seems to be answering all our prayers—but what if the Lord has totally different plans from mine, and something happens that makes no sense?"

4. Newton, 397.

God's Sovereignty

In his memoir, David Sheff, an author whose son struggled with meth addiction, explains how he came to the painful realization that all his anxiety over his son's well-being could not in itself prevent the potential fatal consequences of the boy's behavior. He was left with the "soul-shaking" awareness that parents don't ultimately decide their children's fate.[5]

To an audience that was just as consumed by worry as we are today, Jesus asked a related question: "Which of you by being anxious can add a single hour to his span of life?" (Matt. 6:27). No one. While I often obsessively searched my son's room for drugs, dangerous objects, or telltale writings, I missed the belts he had hidden in his drawers. In the meantime, God preserved his life through a destructive car accident, a medication overdose, and a fire—all without my intervention.

This realization is truly soul-shaking and can propel us in different directions. Ideally, it should drive us to Christ, in whom God's sovereignty becomes a heartening thought. Today, however, the biblical idea of a God who is sovereign over all and who directs every event in history is not popular. In our society we reject anything that sounds even remotely absolutist—even the absolute rule of the God who created all things and has a right to dispose of them as he deems best.

The reason why even well-meaning words of comfort, such as "God loves your son more than you do," don't always produce the intended consolation is that we don't always

5. David Sheff, *Beautiful Boy: A Father's Journey through His Son's Addiction* (New York: Mariner Books, 2009), 15.

know this God—or we forget who he is. And honestly, if another human being took one of my children from me with the excuse that he loved him more than I do, I would charge like a mama bear.

It's only when we realize who God is in Christ that we can not only accept his sovereignty over all but welcome it with joy and relief. And this realization comes when we understand the Bible as the unified story of a loving God who is redeeming a rebellious human race. God is not just an abstract sum of his attributes. He's a God who acts in history, and his acts constitute an integral part of his revelation of himself as an omnipotent, omniscient, all-just, all-loving, all-good, and all-wise God. No one will ever know our loved ones like he does, and no one will ever love them more than Christ, who has died on the cross for them.

Hanging on to one or two Bible verses without understanding how they fit in to both their immediate context and the greater framework of God's overarching story can bring temporary comfort, but this may not last under the barrage of doubts and fears that traumatic situations generate. It's often said that the time to develop a sound theological understanding is before the storm, but it's *never* too late. I recommend finding a good church that holds on to the historical Protestant confessions and preaches the unadulterated gospel.

The idea of God's sovereignty is taught throughout Scripture. God is the sovereign Creator who fashioned everything in his wisdom. To Job, who spent days defending his innocence and questioning God's fairness, God gave a simple reminder of his transcendence: "Where were you when I laid the foundation of the earth? Tell me, if you have understanding. Who determined its measurements—surely you know!" (Job 38:4–5; see also the rest of Job 38–41; Isa. 40:12–28; Rom. 11:33–35). As finite human beings, we don't have the capacity to understand God's plans and purposes. They are beyond us, and most probably it would not be good for us to know them. We can only reply, with Job, "Behold, I am of small account; what shall I answer you? I lay my hand on my mouth" (Job 40:4).

And God is not only all-knowing but also active in the world, arranging each event according to his wise and loving plans. The book of Jonah is probably one of the clearest examples, in which God hurls a great wind upon the sea (see 1:4), appoints "a great fish to swallow up Jonah" (1:17), causes the fish to vomit out the prophet (see 2:10), appoints a plant to grow miraculously and then appoints a worm to destroy it (see 4:6–7)—all as part of his plan to save a penitent people and teach Jonah compassion.

Jesus summed up this divine intervention in a poignant example: "Are not two sparrows sold for a penny? And not one of them will fall to the ground apart from your Father. But even the hairs of your head are all numbered" (Matt. 10:29–30). Once again, God's sovereignty plays out in a context of comfort and love for his people. "Fear not, therefore," Jesus continued; "you are of more value than many sparrows" (v. 31).

The Heidelberg Catechism highlights this communion of God's power and love when it explains,

> The eternal Father of our Lord Jesus Christ, who of nothing made heaven and earth, with all that in them is, who likewise upholds and governs the same by His eternal counsel and providence, is for the sake of Christ His Son my God and my Father; in whom I so trust, as to have no

doubt that He will provide me with all things necessary for body and soul; and further, that whatever evil He sends upon me[6] in this vale of tears He will turn to my good; *for He is able to do it, being Almighty God, and willing also, being a faithful Father.*[7]

Finding a Balance

Over-involvement can be destructive. As Warner points out, "the relapse rate is higher for people with schizophrenia who live with critical or over-involved relatives."[8] It is also accompanied by many problems. When our loved one becomes our whole life, to the neglect of ourselves, our duties, and other people in our family, the situation is detrimental to everyone's well-being. Worry can consume us and become addictive. It imprisons us in a small and confusing universe of pain and of frantic attempts to ease that pain, distorting facts and magnifying problems.

David Sheff's memoir as the father of a young man struggling with addiction is filled with warnings to parents of the dangers of becoming obsessed over their children's problems. Fear, he explains, leads people to become unusually controlling to the point of losing their identity.

Despite this danger, we can't swing to the opposite extreme and switch into a passive mode, with the excuse that we are "letting God."[9] As in everything, we need to find a balance. Just as we can allow our very "bowels" to be

---

6. In the original German, "auch alles übel" (though everything be evil).

7. Heidelberg Catechism, answer 26, emphasis added. See also Isa. 40:10-11.

8. Richard Warner, *The Environment of Schizophrenia: Innovations in Practice, Policy and Communications* (London: Brunner-Routledge, 2000), 30.

9. In reality, we don't have to "let God" do anything. He doesn't need our permission to act. At least not the God described in the Bible.

moved to compassion without sinking into despair, we can be involved in our loved ones' lives without being consumed by this involvement. It's difficult, but it's possible, by God's power and wisdom.

John Newton gives a good example of this balance. Four years before his death, Betsy, then thirty-two, became affected by some form of mental illness. "She is always under the immediate apprehension of death," he wrote, "which is very terrible in her state of despondency. I seldom leave her but she says I shall find her a corpse on my return."[10]

Newton's pain was so intense that his friend William Bull wrote, "He is almost overwhelmed with this most awful affliction. I never saw a man so cut up. He is almost broken-hearted."[11]

Newton did something about it. He pursued ordinary means of healing, taking Betsy to a doctor who was also his friend. Eventually Betsy had to be placed in a mental hospital where she was not allowed visitors, but Newton walked to the building at a certain time every morning and waved in the direction of her window. Since by that time his eyesight was very poor, he would ask a friend or servant to tell him if Betsy waved back. "Do you see a white handkerchief being waved to and fro?" he would say. If his friend said yes, he would go home happy.[12]

While he entrusted Betsy to medical professionals, he didn't lose sight of who really controlled all things—including

10. John Newton to Mr. and Mrs. Coffin, May 8, 1801, in *Letters by the Rev. John Newton of Olney and St. Mary Woolnoth*, ed. Josiah Bull (London, 1869), 396.

11. Bull, 398n.

12. See Josiah Bull, ed., *John Newton of Olney and St. Mary Woolnoth: An Autobiography and Narrative* (London, 1868), 350.

this sickness. "I believe only the help of him who made heaven and earth, and who raises the dead, can effectually relieve us," he said. "I aim to commit her into his faithful hands, and I trust He will help me to abide by the surrender I have made, of myself and my all, to him."[13]

It was not easy. "I feel too often the workings of unbelief and self-will," he said. What gave him faith and strength was the memory of what the Lord had already done for him. "My life has been a series of wonders, mercies, supports and deliverances, in which I can myself (though I cannot prove it to others) perceive the hand of my Lord, no less clearly than in the miracles He wrought by Moses in Egypt, and at the Red Sea."[14]

This is what the psalmists in the Bible did repeatedly. They based their praises to God on what he had already done for Israel. They remembered how he had kept his promises, and from that they drew faith that he would continue to fulfill them. Today we can look back to an even clearer history of redemption in Christ.

Newton had to keep a similar balance of involvement and trust during the illness of his friend William Cowper, which he described as "mysterious" and "a very great trial to me." To a friend, he wrote, "I hope I am learning (though I am a slow scholar) to silence all vain reasonings and unbelieving complaints with the consideration of the Lord's sovereignty, wisdom and love."[15]

13. Bull, *Letters*, 396.
14. Bull, 396.
15. John Newton to Samuel Brewer, August 1773, in Bull, *John Newton*, 198.

Learning to Rest

Resting is difficult, because trusting is difficult. We want to be in charge. That's why the gospel is so counterintuitive and alien to us. By living a perfect life and dying in the place of sinners, Jesus met the requirements of God's justice and reconciled us to God. This is a wonderful truth—but it's also so inconceivable that Christians have deviated from it countless times throughout history, unable to believe that God requires nothing else of us for our redemption.

One of the best illustrations of our natural resistance against simple trust in Christ is the story of a man who fell off a cliff and managed to save himself by grabbing a hanging branch. Both the branch and his arm were too weak to maintain that position for long, so he desperately cried, "Help! Can anyone help?" From heaven, the voice of God boomed, "I'll save you. Just trust me and let go of the branch." After a brief reflection, the man cried again, "Can anyone *else* help?"

The Bible encourages us time and again to trust in God and rest in him. In Matthew 11:28–30, Jesus invites us to

> come to me, all who labor and are heavy laden, and I will give you rest. Take my yoke upon you, and learn from me, for I am gentle and lowly in heart, and you will find rest for your souls. For my yoke is easy, and my burden is light.

To reinforce the importance of rest, God even instituted a weekly pause, kept it, and commanded us to keep it.

The Sabbath

Even in non-religious circles, keeping the Sabbath as a weekly day of rest is making a comeback as an antidote to our frenzied lifestyles. In "Bring Back the Sabbath," *New York Times* columnist Judith Shulevitz describes it as a cultural phenomenon—a day of "organized nonproductivity" that is "counterintuitive" but actually essential in a hyperactive age when most people don't know how to rest.[16] For *Vogue* contributor Ariel Okin, it's a time to disconnect and take a pause.[17] Author and former emergency room physician Matthew Sleeth made the Sabbath a cornerstone of his manual, *24/6: A Prescription for a Healthier, Happier Life.*[18]

They are obviously correct. No one can dismiss the physical and mental benefits of taking a weekly pause from constant, regular activity. For a Christian, however, there are better reasons to keep the Sabbath than a purely utilitarian advantage: God has instituted it from creation for our good and his glory (see Gen. 2:2–3; Ex. 20:11), and will realize it in full in the end (see Heb. 4:11). It's a gift—a time to recognize that our activities are pointless without God (see Ex. 16:22–30; Ps. 127).

This day of rest is not a day of passivity, however. The Puritans called it a "market-day for the soul." The Sabbath is a day to focus on God's overarching promise: "You shall be my people, and I will be your God" (Jer. 30:22; see also Song 6:3), and to draw comfort from it (see Isa. 40:1–2). It's a day to remember and receive: to remember who God is, what he has done in history, and what he has promised to do; to

16. Judith Shulevitz, "Bring Back the Sabbath," *New York Times Magazine,* March 2, 2003, https://www.nytimes.com/2003/03/02/magazine/bring-back -the-sabbath.html.

17. See Ariel Okin, "How to Host a Shabbat Dinner and Why You Should— Even if You Aren't Celebrating," *Vogue,* March 9, 2017, https://www.vogue.com /article/how-to-host-friday-shabbat-dinner.

18. Matthew Sleeth, *24/6: A Prescription for a Healthier, Happier Life* (Carol Stream, IL: Tyndale House, 2012).

receive his announcement of grace; and to acknowledge that we don't know where we are going unless we understand why Jesus walked to Calvary. It's also a day to focus on the everlasting Sabbath that is to come—the land of eternal rest from illness, pain, anxiety, and our own frantic labors.

We do this best by regularly attending a good local church that faithfully preaches the gospel, because our private time of Bible reading was never meant to be a substitute for the external preaching of God's Word (see Rom. 10:14–17).

Ordinary Tasks

Schizophrenia is such a staggering illness, and one so clearly out of our control, that my efforts to bridle, contain, or even understand it often seemed like chasing the wind, and I found comfort in doing the daily, ordinary tasks we all have to face. Except during catastrophic events, beds still have to be made, dishes have to be washed, meals have to be prepared, bills have to be paid, and cars have to be maintained. If there are other people in your family, they need your love and support more than ever.

Apart from their immediate utilitarian purpose, these tasks provide order in a jumbled life. For a Christian, they can be acts of faith and courage that propel us out of our Gollum caves of gloominess, self-commiseration, and fixation on our problems, weariness, and fears into a world that still needs us, where we perform the obvious duties God has appointed for us to do, in love for others and grateful obedience to God. They can help us to get things into perspective and to distinguish what we can do from what only God can do.

At the same time, our ordinary tasks can be highly

beneficial to our loved ones. Psychiatrists believe that an orderly environment and a structured lifestyle have a positive effect on schizophrenia. The reasons are evident. People with schizophrenia have enough disorganization in their own minds without also having a chaotic environment around them.

Be Real

"We don't have to pretend that every day with Jesus is sweeter than the day before," said Dr. W. Robert Godfrey, former president of Westminster Seminary California, in a morning devotion. "There is some truth in that, but some days are better than others."

Living with schizophrenia is stressful enough without trying to keep a constant positive outlook or stiff upper lip. We may never achieve the composure of doctors who see our loved ones for a few minutes every month—and we don't always have to. Families are communities in which we learn to accept each other and our imperfections, and our loved ones understand that, as long as we make every effort to listen and are willing to apologize and change. "Parents should be as 'human' as possible to their children, so that their children may feel as comfortable as they can," Britton said.

Even the apostle Paul, who wrote, "Do not be anxious about anything" (Phil. 4:6), fretted and worried when his disciple Titus didn't meet him at Troas as they had agreed. At that time of no computers and no phones, he had no way to find out what had happened. "My spirit was not at rest," he confessed (2 Cor. 2:13). It was not a double standard. His exhortations, inspired by the Spirit, were still valid, but Paul, like every human being, was a learner as well as a teacher, and his moments of weakness are recorded in the Bible for our encouragement.

We don't need to be heroes. The only hero who is "sure," "fast," and "larger than life," as in the popular song by Bonnie Tyler,[19] is Christ. The sooner we realize that we are not our loved ones' saviors and can't provide an answer to all their needs, the easier both our lives and theirs will be. We will be able to relax and persevere on our course, because we will not be leaning on our own strength.

"Perseverance means getting real about who we are and what we are and going again and again and again to the grace of God—the free favor of God for us that was earned for us by Jesus Christ," Dr. Robert Scott Clark said in a recent sermon.[20]

There is, of course, a balance, and we don't need to "let it all out." Self-restraint is important, especially around people who are paranoid or particularly sensitive to emotional outbursts. But we need to stop trying to create a hyper-sanitized environment in which the "sane" people are always poised, detached, ever smiling, and too often condescending.

We especially don't need to pretend in our prayers to God. We shouldn't be afraid to express our frustrations and doubts. The biblical psalmists weren't. They asked God why he was sending affliction and how long it would last. At one point, David, frustrated by the persistence of his enemies, asked God, "Why do you hold back your hand, your right

19. Bonnie Tyler, vocalist, "Holding Out for a Hero," by Jim Steinman and Dean Pitchford, recorded 1984, track 4 on *Footloose: Original Soundtrack of the Paramount Motion Picture*, Columbia, 1984.

20. Scott Clark, "Even the Holiest" (sermon, Christ United Reformed Church, Santee, CA, May 6, 2018), available online at http://www.christurc.org/sermons/2018/5/6/even-the-holiest.

hand? Take it from the fold of your garment and destroy them!" (Ps. 74:11). As W. Robert Godfrey points out in his devotional speech, in today's language we would say, "Get your hands out of your pockets!" It's a bluntness that many of us hesitate to employ in our prayers.

The Psalms cover a large spectrum of emotions, including joy, pain, grief, frustration, and fear—something that the church has always appreciated. That is why, in the past, most Protestant churches sang the Psalms exclusively, as divinely inspired prayers to God. Even the saddest psalm in the Bible (Psalm 88) can be a true encouragement to the Christian because it's real and honest, and because even from the deepest pain—a pain we can easily recognize—it cries out to a God who is always there, as silent and perplexing as he may sometimes seem.[21]

It's a relief to know that, while God welcomes our questions, he doesn't require that we discover the reason for his actions. I used to rack my brain with such questions until I realized that the Bible never says, "Find out why God is afflicting you." Instead it encourages us to pour out our questions to God and to rest in the knowledge that his ways are not our ways and his timeframe is often different from ours.

Besides, this type of anxious inquiry can lead us on

---

21. The Psalms are much deeper than some of today's songs of persistent triumph, which repeat commitments or slogans as if a victorious attitude could be achieved by reiteration. Dr. Godfrey says, "Part of the sadness of contemporary Protestant religion in America is the pretense that we all can be happy and have a wonderful life all the time. It's a lie, and if you try to sell people a lie, the great danger is that ultimately they will turn against the whole thing" (W. Robert Godfrey, "The Word in Preaching" [sermon, Tenth Presbyterian Church, Philadelphia, PA, October 28, 2007], available online at https://www.tenth.org/resource-library /sermons/the-word-in-preaching).

a dangerous course. "While we are asking God why, we are busy coming up with reasons of our own—and ways maybe to punish ourselves, in order to somehow absolve ourselves of our sin, as if that could work," says Jody. In fact, our conclusions are often wrong, because our natural minds are quick to condemn and slow to accept God's unfathomable grace.

Dealing with Guilt

Like worry, remorse can consume our days, driving us on a useless quest to undo what has been done and robbing us of the peace of mind we need in order to properly deal with present circumstances. Some of this remorse is unjustified—for example, when parents feel responsible for their child's schizophrenia, as if common parental mistakes could have caused it (a notion that was quite popular a few decades ago). E. Fuller Torrey, research psychiatrist and founder of the Treatment Advocacy Center, finds this notion unwarranted. "Any parent who has raised a child knows that parents are not powerful enough to cause a disease like schizophrenia simply by favoring one child over another or giving the child inconsistent messages."[22]

Even if today this blame ascription is mostly gone, many parents still feel responsible for their children's illness, maybe because it is the only explanation that seems to make sense. Andrew Solomon gives an interesting interpretation: "The attribution of responsibility to parents is often a function of ignorance, but it also reflects our anxious belief that

---

22. E. Fuller Torrey, *Surviving Schizophrenia: A Manual for Families, Patients, and Providers*, 5th ed. (New York: Harper Collins, 2006), 152.

we control our own destinies."[23] Once again, it brings us back to an acceptance of God's sovereignty and providence.

At times, feelings of guilt and remorse *are* justified—not in relation to the *cause* of schizophrenia but regarding decisions we have made or actions we have taken that might have affected its course or hurt our loved ones. Some of these actions may be actual sins, in which case feelings of guilt are appropriate, as they drive us to seek forgiveness. Often we mourn our lack of wisdom, which seems like a constant obstruction as we struggle to learn how to navigate the uncertain paths of this life. In any case, we can rest in the fact that forgiveness has been granted to us on the cross once and for all.

My friend Jody is probably experiencing the greatest remorse of any parent I know. Her son Matt eventually died, shot by the police who she had called for help. "When Matt held a knife to me that night, I was definitely frightened; but the other thing that went through my mind was, *Finally they will believe that he is a danger to himself and others and will finally take him back to the hospital*," she said. "We were told to lock the door and call them if Matt came back. So we did—but when it comes to the 'what ifs,' this is the big one. Matt was sitting on the step smoking a cigarette. What if I had taken a cup of coffee out and sat down with him on the step—just told him I wasn't trying to get rid of him, that I loved him? He might be alive today."

What to do in a tragic case like this? "Should I throw myself on the floor in a heap of guilt?" Jody asked. "I feel like it at times. I locked the door and didn't let him come into

23. Andrew Solomon, *Far from the Tree: Parents, Children, and the Search for Identity* (New York: Scribner, 2012), 22.

the house. There are so many what ifs. What if we had just opened the door? What if I hadn't said so many cruel things because I was impatient? All the mean, impatient things I had ever said to Matt came in waves like a giant flood of guilt. I felt as if I had murdered him myself.

"Sometimes I tell myself that I did the best I could under the circumstances and that I loved Matt and he knew it, and other times it hits me like a brick wall and I could fall on the ground and weep forever."

This reminds me of David's reaction after Absalom's death, when he repeated, "O my son Absalom, my son, my son Absalom! Would I had died instead of you, O Absalom, my son, my son!" (2 Sam. 18:33). He felt that he deserved to die in the place of his son. He was very conscious of his sins, specifically in his dealings with Absalom. If only he had done something when Ammon raped Tamar instead of letting Absalom take matters into his own hands (see 2 Sam. 13)! If only he had truly reconciled with Absalom and confessed his own sins, instead of keeping him at a distance (see 2 Sam. 14)!

"What can I do with all this guilt?" Jody continued. "I could make excuses for it, or deny it—or I can confess it. 1 John 1:9 tells us, 'If we confess our sins, he is faithful and just to forgive us our sins and to cleanse us from all unrighteousness.'"

David knew that. In Psalm 32, he explained how confessing his sin brought immense relief to the torment of keeping his guilt brewing inside. But it was not simply a psychological relief. "I said, 'I will confess my transgressions to the LORD,'" David wrote, "and you forgave the iniquity of my sin" (v. 5). There is *real* forgiveness, because Christ has taken all of our sins on himself on Calvary. In fact, he has even taken sins that we have never confessed because we have not noticed them. We are completely covered.

We have here an enormous advantage over non-believers, because the phrase "turn a new leaf" is for us much more than a positive attitude of mind. We are resting on firm scriptural promises, knowing that, as certainly as Christ rose from the dead (as proved by many eye-witnesses and an empty tomb), so certainly "the steadfast love of the LORD never ceases; his mercies never come to an end; they are new every morning" (Lam. 3:22–23), because his faithfulness to us and our children is much greater than we can conceive.

Whether the guilt is justified or not, we cannot go back in time and undo what has been done. I could write a long list of regrets at the end of my son's story. Even if well-meaning people have comforted me by saying I have done all I could, I know very well that I could have done more and could have caused him less pain. But brooding over my faults is pointless, and I have lived long enough to know that I can't find relief in my own commitments or in futile attempts to make atonement.

I can only confess my sins and accept God's bountiful forgiveness through Christ's atonement, knowing that

> He does not deal with us according to our sins,
>> nor repay us according to our iniquities.
> For as high as the heavens are above the earth,
>> so great is his steadfast love toward those who fear him;
> as far as the east is from the west,
>> so far does he remove our transgressions from us.
> As a father shows compassion to his children,
>> so the LORD shows compassion to those who fear him.

For he knows our frame;
he remembers that we are dust. (Ps. 103:10–14)

Only this certainty can give true peace to my guilt-stricken heart and impart the strength I need to face my present situation. Even if my actions have caused some damage, God is much greater than that, and he "will restore . . . the years that the swarming locust has eaten" (Joel 2:25).

As the prophet Samuel told his guilt-stricken people, "Do not be afraid; you have done all this evil. Yet do not turn aside from following the Lord, but serve the Lord with all your heart. . . . For the Lord will not forsake his people, for his great name's sake" (1 Sam. 12:20, 22). In other words, as my pastor said in a sermon on this passage, "Get back on the bike and pedal!" God's forgiveness is sure because it's based on his faithfulness to his promises, which can never be shaken, and not on our own weak promises or commitments.

"The way out of the situation that we have to own up to now is by saying, 'Lord, by your grace and your gospel, strengthen me to do what you command me to do and what I ought to do and to assume the responsibilities that I should' —and go forward. The Lord has an amazing way of bringing blessing out of something that was so evil or foolish to begin with."[24]

24. Michael Brown, "The Lord Will Not Forsake His People" (sermon, Christ United Reformed Church, Santee, CA, February 15, 2015), available online at http://www.christurc.org/sermons/2015/2/16/the-lord-will-not-forsake-his-people.

15

Communicating the Gospel

Come to me, all who labor and are heavy laden.
(Matt. 11:28)

"Give him the gospel" was a common refrain I heard from other Christians while my son was with us. Sometimes I wondered how to do it. Jonathan was raised in a Christian family, and from a young age he attended a Reformed church where the gospel had primacy and was clearly explained for what it is—the good news of Christ's life, death, and resurrection for our salvation. Still, we all need to hear the gospel on a regular basis, because it's so alien and implausible to our natural minds that even when we rationally assent to it, we continue to reject it in practical ways.

What Is the Gospel?

The gospel is a simple announcement. Michael Horton compares it to a declaration of victory in a war—a pronouncement that Christ has done for us what we could never do and has met the greatest need that all human beings share: the need to be reconciled with a God whose perfect justice naturally demands a punishment for our constant rebellion. And it's even more than that. It's a message that accomplishes what it pronounces. It is "the power of God for salvation" (Rom. 1:16).

In spite of the ways the word *gospel* has been misinterpreted and misused, the Christian gospel is *not a form of therapy*. It was not given as a message for us to post on our fridge or to repeat during a meditation session to convince us that we are loved, to give us self-esteem, or to impart a sense of meaning to our lives. It's not the Christian way to meet our felt needs.

It's also not something to try out a few times to see whether it may "work." It will *not* work, because it was never meant to work in this pragmatic, therapeutic way. You can't go to church and listen to a few sermons, as gospel-filled as they may be, and expect to be free from all your problems. The gospel has tremendous power, but it works in ways that are counterintuitive, mysterious, and even imperceptible, transforming us into conformity to the image of Christ—a Christ who, in this life, was more anguished than we could ever know.

As an announcement, the gospel is also *not something we "do" or "live"* (even if we can say that we live *in light* of the gospel). It's something we hear and receive—and something that transforms our lives in a way that rules and regulations never could. It's a balm for the soul, freeing us from our futile efforts to gain acceptance with God through our own merits.

"The gospel helps me because it's not an imperative," says Britton. "It's not telling me I have to change in order to be accepted by God." God accepts us, in Christ, because of what Christ has done by taking the punishment for our sins and giving us his righteousness.

The Dangers of You-Can-Do-It Preaching

Some time ago I read an article by Steve Neumann, a man who lived with depression and had become frustrated with his efforts to "will" himself to health—efforts he attributed to a religious background that emphasized the power of his own efforts and his ability to "choose" not to be depressed. "The implication of that thinking," he wrote, "is that if I couldn't make myself not be depressed, then it was a defect of will, a character flaw. Needless to say, it didn't work," Neumann continued, "and a new element was added to my profound feelings of sadness, anxiety, and meaninglessness—a sense of shame."[1] Ultimately, some therapies helped Neumann to overcome his depression. In the meantime, he had come to the conclusion that Christianity is wrong—especially about the existence of a soul.

The notion that human beings have within themselves the power, activated by their will, to obey Scripture, resist temptation, and be acceptable to God is as old as the early church and has been attacked by Paul, the apostles, and the church fathers—including, famously, fourth-century theologian Augustine of Hippo, in his controversy with the monk Pelagius. It has continued throughout history and is emphasized today by so-called "health and wealth" (or "prosperity") preachers. These men and women teach that God wants all Christians to have health and wealth. They just need to "positively confess their faith" and then "name and claim" the healing and riches that they want. Consequently, a lack of health and wealth is seen as a sign of deficiency of faith and/or a result of disobedience.

1. Steve Neumann, "Mental Illness and the Belief in a Soul with Free Will," Patheos, June 12, 2015, http://www.patheos.com/blogs/newchimera/2015/06/mental-illness-and-the-belief-in-a-soul-with-free-will/.

Apart from being unbiblical and denied by countless examples of godly Christians throughout history who persevered through suffering and poverty, this teaching creates a false reality and false hopes, which are often crushed. And the mentality that mental health can be achieved by a leap of faith or by strength of character can have other devastating consequences besides. For one thing, it can feed the grandiose delusions of power that are already common in many people with schizophrenia and can enhance their denial of being ill or needing necessary medications. It can also deprive them of support, if those around them follow the same theology.

"My nephew suffered from mental illness and had discipline issues since he was a very small child," my friend Tammy told me. "He had problems focusing and dealing with his emotions. Several years ago, he discussed with me the voices he heard, and I urged him to get help. Unfortunately, our background included many years at a church where mental illness was considered sin."

Tammy was hesitant to talk to her church leadership because she had seen many similar concerns being dismissed. When she finally did, the reaction was the same. "Maybe I'm wrong here," she explained, "but to me teaching that mental illness is simply a manifestation of sin is as bad as teaching someone to withhold medication because God will heal people."

Eventually, Tammy's nephew ended up in prison, where he was murdered by another inmate. "I can't help but wonder what his life may have been like had he been treated properly for mental illness—but I will never know," she said. "He came to faith in Christ not long before his death, which gives our family some comfort."

Americans are brought up with an ideology of independence and self-service, which is reinforced by a plethora of "You can do it" messages—the good old story of the self-made man, picture books promising children that they can be anything they want to be, and ads that encourage potential customers to have it their way.

In this context, talks of a suffering Christ who promises a cross (see Matt. 16:24–25) and a yoke (see Matt. 11:29) among the world's hatred (see Mark 13:13) and persecution (see John 15:20) seem terribly gloomy and pessimistic. To the contrary, they are bracingly realistic, allowing us to take a clear look at our limitations, at the instability of our bodies and minds, and at the transience and fragility of our lives. They are also comforting and encouraging, because Christ's "yoke is easy," his "burden is light," and his cross is a refuge where a "gentle and lowly" Savior gives true rest to our souls (Matt. 11:29–30), promising a glory to which "the sufferings of this present time are not worth comparing" (Rom. 8:18).

Sermons that affirm the sinfulness of human nature and the miseries of this world, while pointing to the bigger picture, the realities to come, and the triune God who still works his irrepressible redemption plan in both history and the human heart, are much more useful to a suffering soul than denials of present pain or encouragements to find and harness one's spiritual power . . . encouragements that will lead hearers to try hard to suppress the subtle fear that the healing may not come—and that it will be their fault.

Do Talks of Sin Ever Hurt?

Some critics, who are mostly unfamiliar with the biblical narrative, have accused Christians of exacerbating the dark thoughts of people with mental illness by mentioning sin and

God's anger against it. A psychiatrist once warned Jody that her husband's preaching might be detrimental for her son because it might make him feel guilty. Similar accusations were leveled against John Newton, blaming his preaching as a cause or aggravation of William Cowper's depression.

Undeniably, much insistence on God's law and our disobedience to it can lead to discouragement and even depression—but the answer is not to edit or reinterpret the Bible in order to obliterate those teachings, which *are* part of reality. The answer is balancing those necessary teachings with a strong emphasis on the gospel—the good news of the solution that God has mercifully provided in Christ.

William Jay, an author who knew both Newton and Cowper, defended the preacher:

> Some have thought the divine was hurtful to the poet. How mistaken were they! He was the very man, of all others, I should have chosen for him. He was not rigid in his creed. His views of the Gospel were most free and encouraging. He had the tenderest disposition; and always judiciously regarded his friend's depression and despondency as a physical effect, for the removal of which he prayed, but never reasoned or argued with him concerning it.[2]

While it's true that some preachers today preach the law as an imperative ("Do this and you will live") without announcing the gospel ("Christ has done it for you"), there are many others who, like Newton, communicate the gospel in a "free and encouraging" manner.

---

2. George Redford and John Angell James, eds., *The Autobiography of the Rev. William Jay*, 3rd ed. (London, 1855), 276.

Rev. Zach Keele, pastor of Escondido Orthodox Presbyterian Church, who has encountered several cases of schizophrenia and other mental illness in his congregation, has seen firsthand the healing power of the gospel in people's souls. "Very often, people with mental illness have deep issues with anxiety and fear," he explains. "They feel preyed upon by their own minds. They are also often plagued by guilt, so they mostly need to hear about the free grace of Jesus Christ and the tenderness of the gospel. Legalism is a primary danger for a pastor. We shouldn't be judgmental."

In the words of sixteenth-century Reformer Juan de Valdés, the gospel has the task of "healing the wounds inflicted by the law, preaching grace, peace, and remission of sins, calming and pacifying consciences, imparting the spirit that allows us to keep what the law shows about God's will and to fight, conquer, and crush the enemies of our souls."[3]

If your church is not giving primacy to the gospel, find one that does. It's much more important than the appeal of the church's songs, the warmth of its members, or the abundance of its programs.

The External Gospel

According to Martin Luther, the efficacy of the preached gospel is partially due to the fact that it's an external declaration. It comes from outside us, invading the darkness of our minds, proclaiming a message that is contrary to our natural reason, and demanding our attention. "Stick to God's external word, and listen to it," he told his Wittenberg

---

3. Juan Valdés, *Alfabeto Cristiano: Dialogo con Giulia Gonzaga* (Bari, Italy: Giuseppe Laterza & Figli, 1938), 22.

congregation in 1531. "It tells you that God is your gracious Father. This is how the Father draws you."[4]

This external nature of the gospel is particularly important for people for schizophrenia who are besieged by an overwhelming succession of contradictory internal voices (which they often perceive as external). Instead of relying on inner feelings to sort out reality from fantasy, they can place their trust in the Word of a transcendent God. "Reality has to be grounded in something outside of us," Britton explained. "Nothing in our will can help, because our will is not completely free. All things were created good, but everything is now affected by sin—including our decisions and desires. My hope is grounded in the gospel."

As well as by preaching, the gospel is also conveyed by the sacrament of the Lord's Supper—another external means that regularly reminds us of what God has done in Christ. Of course, it's not only a reminder, because the Holy Spirit also uses it to unite us to Christ and strengthen our faith; but every time we taste the bread and wine in our mouths, we also hear the gospel proclamation, "This is my body, which is given for you.... This cup that is poured out for you is the new covenant in my blood" (Luke 22:19–20).

Yet even though it is important for your loved ones to hear these external proclamations, bringing them to church can be challenging. John Newton faced a similar problem with William Cowper, who chose a solitary life after his psychotic attack and kept close to home for years. This reclusion continued on Sundays, when he preferred to keep to his "calm and usually contented routine of reading, writing

---

4. Jaroslav Pelikan and Daniel E. Poellot, eds., *Luther's Works*, vol. 23, *Sermons on the Gospel of St. John: Chapters 6–8* (1959; repr., St. Louis: Concordia, 2007), 93.

poetry, gardening, and enjoying the company of an extensive menagerie of pets, headed by a trio of tame hares. . . . Newton was baffled by his friend's decision to cut himself off from worshiping and serving God but recognized that it was a side effect of the mental illness."[5]

Rev. Keele agrees with this assessment. "Part of these individuals' anxiety stems from being around other people. We should find ways to help them to attend worship, but we also need to be longsuffering."

Some churches have a separate room where people can listen to the sermon without being surrounded by others, or there may be a section in the back next to the exit where a person can feel free to leave if needed. It's also important for the other church members to be sensitive and friendly but not overbearing.

If none of these approaches will work, then listening to recorded sermons (while normally not a substitute for church attendance) is better than no preaching at all for people who are homebound.

The Gospel at Home

If you have already established a regular routine of family devotions and/or prayer in your home, these can be wonderful opportunities for your family to remind one another of God's promises. Family memorization of Scripture or a catechism is also an excellent habit to keep up, as it reinforces important gospel truths in the memory. If you have not developed these habits before, you can always start now.

---

5. Jonathan Aitken, *John Newton: From Disgrace to Amazing Grace* (Wheaton, IL: Crossway, 2007), 221.

Beginning this routine during this phase of life might present difficulties. When my kids were young, it was easier to get them all together around the table at the same time each day. Schizophrenia, however, normally occurs in the late teens or early adulthood, when new daily schedules might have already caused family habits that allow opportunities for this sort of togetherness to be interrupted or seriously disrupted.

Still, eating at least one meal together as a family (however small the family might have become) is a healthy practice that fits well into the medical recommendation of establishing a daily routine for people with schizophrenia.

It doesn't have to take long. From a spiritual point of view, even reading a short psalm and praying together for a couple of minutes before a meal can have a greater impact than many people realize, because God's Word is efficient, no matter how much of it is read (see Isa. 55:11; Heb. 4:12). Besides, this daily practice establishes a habit of prayer and daily recognition of God's primacy in our lives, and it leaves the door open for other days when there will be more time for reading, prayer, discussion, and celebrations of God's love, forgiveness, protection, and strength.

Your family can also decide to start a memory project, whether everyone participates in it or not. Catechisms are excellent memorization tools, because they were created for that purpose. For example, while a single verse might be remembered out of context, a catechism question and answer is formulated in such a way that it summarizes a biblical truth clearly and coherently. Heidelberg Catechism question and answer 1 is an outstanding encapsulation of the gospel.

Memorization is also valuable because it imprints God's promises into the mind—promises that can often still be remembered when other mental functions are impaired. There are countless testimonies of Alzheimer's patients who have forgotten both the people around them and the events of their lives but can still quote or sing a comforting psalm. The same is true with other mental illnesses.

However, these moments of devotion and prayer must never become new occasions to nag or "preach a prayer." For example, if you have been reminding your loved one for some time of the importance of attending church, reading a passage that reinforces your point will be easily recognized for what it is: a way to manipulate his or her feelings. And if your loved one is living with paranoid schizophrenia, anything that feels like manipulation may aggravate his or her fears.

One way to avoid this problem is to read through the Bible, following some type of reading program or going chapter by chapter until you are done. That way, if you happen to read a psalm on the beauty of God's temple, it will be because it's the next in line. Your feelings of concern that your loved one is not attending church are best left for a private conversation, at an appropriate time, when you can honestly and openly share your apprehensions as a concerned parent. Again, ask God for wisdom on how best to do this.

While the law without the gospel is only bad news, there *is* a place and time for it. Britton agrees that it plays an important role in his life. "Even though I have mental illness, Jeremiah 17:9 tells me of a worse, incurable sickness[6]— incurable without the gospel. There is no gospel where there

---

6. "The heart is deceitful above all things, and desperately sick; who can understand it?"

is no sin; there is no sin where there is no law. That's why I
need the proper uses of the law and gospel. I need to know
my dire state so that I can live to God and my neighbor."

I was often blunt with my son about scriptural injunctions regarding church attendance and drug abuse. I tried,
however, to present the law in conjunction with the gospel,
which is the only thing that both motivates and enables us to
keep the law. God's commandments are given for our good
and "are not burdensome" (1 John 5:3). I was careful not
to exasperate Jonathan's already heightened sense of guilt,
and I emphasized instead the delight of obeying God out of
gratitude and the freedom from sin that we enjoy in Christ.

So in the case of church attendance, I tried to point to
the joy and power that come from hearing Christ's voice in
church and to the grace that God imparts through his Word
and sacraments. If my son still refused to come, I related the
sermon to him as soon as I came home.

Christ gives us a good example of being both direct and
gentle, while also personalizing his mode of teaching for
the needs and character of his audience. He had infinite
patience with his disciples, who often seemed annoyingly
slow to understand. "A bruised reed he will not break, and a
faintly burning wick he will not quench" (Isa. 42:3).

The goal is to heal, not to crush—to draw near, not to
alienate. Your loved one should know that he or she can
always come to you for mending, encouragement, understanding, and support with finding solutions and moving
forward on this pilgrim way. The pain that I felt whenever
my son tried to exclude me from his struggles gave particular meaning to God's repeated calls, "Come to me, all who
labor and are heavy laden" (Matt. 11:28); "Come, everyone
who thirsts, come to the waters; and he who has no money,

come, buy and eat!" (Isa. 55:1); "The Spirit and the Bride say, 'Come.' And let the one who hears say, 'Come'" (Rev. 22:17). It's also important to be generous with forgiveness. If you have been hurt so much that forgiving seems impossible, think of Christ and his free gift of forgiveness to those who have hurt him and abused him and continue to do so—us included. Your forgiveness to your loved one will reflect God's forgiveness.

Sanctification—We're All in It Together

In a home setting, the gospel is best shared when we remember that we are all weary, stumbling pilgrims traveling together to our heavenly destination. We are all in equal standing with God, all created in his image, all marred by sin, and all redeemed by Christ. This very realization brings us together and helps us to encourage one another with humility and compassion as we recognize that we have all the same struggles—even if some of them are more intensified by mental illness.

This realization is not always easy. I often reacted in anger and frustration, doubting the work of the Holy Spirit in my son's heart and keeping my eyes on his failures instead of on Christ, who is far more tender, longsuffering, and gracious than I could even attempt to be. That's why the proclamation of the gospel, along with constant reminders of its power, has been as helpful to me as it was to Jonathan.

Our sanctification, or the process by which God makes us conformed to Christ, is gradually accomplished by the Holy Spirit according to God's timetable, and it might take longer than we think. In fact, it usually does, because we are by nature impatient.

In a letter to a friend, John Newton warned against

people who tried to make their own experience the measuring stick for the experience of others and who expected everyone to grow at the same speed and in the same way.

We say such a building is a house, not only when it is tiled, painted and furnished, but while the walls are yet unfinished, while it is encumbered with rubbish and surrounded with scaffolds, which though not a part of the edifice (but are designed in time to be removed) are helpful for carrying it on. We speak of a field of wheat not only in harvest but in spring, and say "It is day," when the light is gradually increasing, though the sun be not risen. . . . It is true there are unsound convictions, and impressions which are not abiding, but the Lord's labourers should weed with a gentle and cautious hand, lest in their attempts to pull up the tares, they should pluck up the wheat also.

It would be well if both preachers and people would keep more closely to what the Scripture teaches of the nature, marks, and growth of a work of grace instead of following each other in a track (like sheep) confining the Holy Spirit to a system, imposing at first the experience and sentiments of others as a rule to themselves, and afterward dogmatically laying down the path in which they themselves have been led, as absolutely necessary to be trodden by others.

There is a vast variety of the methods by which the Lord brings home souls to himself, in which he considers (though system-preachers do not) the different circumstances, situations, temperament, etc. of different persons. To lay down rules precisely to which all must conform, and to treat all enquiring souls in the same way, is as wrong as it would be in a physician to attempt to cure all his patients who may have the same general disorder (a fever for instance) with one and the same prescription. A skillful man would probably find so many differences in their cases, that he would not treat any two of them exactly alike.[7]

It's especially so in the case of schizophrenia, when reactions might appear "strange" to our eyes. Yet we don't know what's happening in the heart. Progress is often unseen. Only God knows how it proceeds. We can just take comfort in the assurance that "it is God who works in [us], both to will and to work for his good pleasure" (Phil. 2:13) and that "he who began a good work in [us] will bring it to completion at the day of Jesus Christ" (Phil. 1:6).

What Medications Can't Do

While medications seem necessary in most cases of schizophrenia, there are limitations on what they can do—especially for Christians, who have different needs and sensibilities than nonbelievers do. Our perception of sin is stronger and our spiritual battles more frequent because we are aware of our rebellion against God and its biblical consequences. With mental illness, these sensibilities are often magnified and, in the case of schizophrenia, distorted.

Medications are valuable, providential tools to clear the mind of cluttering, disturbing, and dangerous psychotic thoughts, and therapy can help to manage confusing perceptions, but both these tools are powerless in the face of man's greatest problem—sin and enmity with a sovereign God.

This is particularly true when tragic events expose the

---

7. Grant Gordon, ed., *Wise Counsel: John Newton's Letters to John Ryland Jr.* (Edinburgh, UK: Banner of Truth Trust, 2011), 120–21.

horror of our sinful nature in shocking and mystifying ways. Struggling to live with depression and occasional psychosis, Dave attacked and killed a close relative without realizing what he was doing. "At that time, everything to me was meaningless and hostile; everyone was an enemy," he said. "Mid-attack I slightly snapped out of it for a moment as I saw a glimpse of reality—what I was doing and to whom. I called the police instead of killing myself. It was too late."

What do we do when our minds betray us, causing us to lose our power to assess the reality around us and control our responses? This happened to my son in smaller ways. Once, after church, he got into his brother's car and drove home. It was obviously not the correct way to act. And, what's more, we had asked him not to drive for a while, due to a recent accident. When I asked him about his action, I realized he was sincerely puzzled. He really didn't understand that he had done it. This is where the illness can become extremely dangerous.

But what do we do when the illness leads to tragedy, destroying a home and devastating mind and soul with feelings of guilt? "I went into shock for about six months," Dave explained. He was sent to youth prison without a trial, because his family wanted him to be treated, not punished.

"I was on every medication imaginable," he continued, "talked with countless doctors and psychiatrists, and went through every 'program' they had. My immediate family was supportive this entire time. That only did so much, though; and it was two chaplains who, in the end, helped me the most. There I became a Christian. The meds and programs did help me, but they could not keep me from killing myself due to guilt (I was quite often thrown into suicide watch rooms). Over the course of years, I slowly became a little better and sought the forgiveness of my family I had harmed."

Today Dave stands amazed at the forgiveness of God and his family. "I shouldn't be free," he says. "I should not be of a somewhat sound mind. I don't deserve a 'normal life'— yet here I am. Next month I am going to a family reunion, and it boggles me that I will be there and that they *want* me to be there."

He is still wracked with guilt, which may never completely go away in this life. He still sorely misses the person he took from this world ("the person I loved most") and watches with pain the gaping void in his family. But he also marvels at God's mercy as expressed in the gospel—a story of redemption and victory over all sin, which is as real as and more lasting than any foul action we commit in this world. No medication or therapy can ever provide this assurance.

Make Room for Joy

One pitfall of caring for people with a serious illness like schizophrenia is to see them only as patients. It's an attitude that they often notice before we do. They notice when we start suspiciously watching their every move or rushing to their side to help them, suddenly treating them with an increased amount of care as if they were about to break. And they resist it. No one wants to be classified primarily as a mental patient. William Cowper once wrote to his cousin, Lady Hesketh, "I write thus to you that you may not think me a forlorn and wretched creature."[8]

8. William Cowper to Lady Hesketh, July 1, 1765, in *The Best Letters of William Cowper*, ed. Anna B. McMahan (Chicago, 1893), 21.

As difficult and persistent as their condition may be, people with schizophrenia are much more than simple mental patients. They are interesting and valuable individuals made in the image of God, and we can genuinely enjoy our time with them if we can move beyond the fears, concerns, and preconceptions that limit our minds. In a *Time* magazine article, author and artist Myriam Gurba described the experience of enjoying her uncle Henry's company. Whenever his words shifted into what she called "the poetry of schizophrenia," strangers normally turned away, thinking that he was crazy. But Gurba had come to learn that his apparently incoherent communication could be understood through sincere love, which is "founded on expansive curiosity."[9]

Our fears keep us focused on ourselves, even when they are expressed as unselfish concern. Gurba's final assessment is quite accurate: it's easy to perceive others as a danger, but it's much more difficult (and yet "more loving and real"[10]) to understand how they might feel threatened, too, and to open our hearts to meet their need for safety and understanding.

Similarly, it's easy to limit our conversations with our loved ones to medications, doctors' schedules, symptoms, relief from symptoms, therapies, training programs, or (for Christians) church attendance, Bible reading, and whatnot—and to completely lose sight of the people in front of us. Who are they now? What are they thinking or dreaming?

My son kept a very keen sense of humor. I often joked with him, and he laughed heartily (a small comfort for an amateur joke-teller). He also noticed details more keenly

9. Myriam Gurba, "Behind My Uncle's Schizophrenia," *Time*, September 2, 2014, http://time.com/3259382/schizophrenia/.
10. Gurba, "Behind My Uncle's Schizophrenia."

than ever before. We talked about the plants in our yard, the ripples in the water, the movement of the wind through the leaves. We remembered fun moments from his childhood or discussed books that we read. Once we started, he often talked for a while about his thoughts.

According to a study, "Experiencing the person only as a patient tends to increase the staff's hopeless feelings about her."[11] This is also true of relatives. This perception is depressing and detrimental for everyone involved.

Enjoying our loved ones' company brings us back to the issue of trust. We can enjoy the present because we trust God for the future. Granted, the Christian life is full of suffering and involves sacrifices, but the Bible talks of a "joy that is inexpressible and filled with glory" (1 Peter 1:8). Peter founds it on the fact that God,

> according to his great mercy . . . has caused us to be born again to a living hope through the resurrection of Jesus Christ from the dead, to an inheritance that is imperishable, undefiled, and unfading, kept in heaven for you, who by God's power are being guarded through faith for a salvation ready to be revealed in the last time. (1 Peter 1:3–5)

This long sentence includes every major reason to rejoice even in a context of suffering.

The Bible gives us many exhortations to rejoice. As in many other cases, seen in the context of God's grace, these are really a *permission* to rejoice—an invitation to let go of our persistent grief and worry and to enjoy the fruits that

---

11. Robert Buckhout et al, eds., *Toward Social Change: A Handbook for Those Who Will* (New York: Harper & Row, 1971), 352.

the Spirit is producing in our lives, which include joy (see Gal. 5:22).

Sometimes we hesitate to be joyful because we feel that we don't deserve to feel joy or that joy distracts us from pressing issues that we need to resolve. We act as if a constant state of mourning were more appropriate to our situation. We share the grieving William Wordsworth's feelings of guilt for letting a joy that's as "impatient as the wind" surprise us "even for the least division of an hour."[12]

But that's because we look at only one aspect of our condition. Yes, we are in a "vale of tears," as some have expressed it. And yes, we often walk "through the valley of the shadow of death" (Ps. 23:4)—but the Shepherd who is with us with his comforting rod and staff is also our loving Bridegroom, who has manifested his love to us so that our "joy may be full" (John 15:11) and who will be with us "always, to the end of the age" (Matt. 28:20).

While the biblical Psalms are evidence that there is a place in our lives and prayers for mourning and grief, when the Lord surprises us with joy and grants our souls, as William Cowper wrote, "a season of clear shining to cheer it after rain,"[13] the best response is to embrace it with gratitude and faith.

A Time to Keep Silence

There is also "a time to keep silence" (Eccl. 3:7). We can learn from Job's friends, who, when they first saw him, "sat

---

12. William Wordsworth, poem XXXII, in *Poems by William Wordsworth: Including Lyrical Ballads, and the Miscellaneous Pieces of the Author* (London, 1815), 2:190.

13. William Cowper, "Sometimes a Light Surprises," 1779.

with him on the ground seven days and seven nights, and no one spoke a word to him, for they saw that his suffering was very great" (Job 2:13). That was probably the wisest thing they could do, because once they started to speak, they went down a slippery slope of self-righteousness and presumption.

In a letter to his adopted daughter Betsy, when she was still young, Newton admitted that his chief desire was for her to know and love the Lord, but that he didn't want to overdo "upon this subject." Christian parents often have a tendency to harp incessantly on matters of faith, as if a multitude of words could change people's minds. "I know that I cannot make you truly religious," Newton said, "nor can you make yourself so. It is the Lord's work, and I am daily praying him to bless you indeed. But he has a time."[14]

While we can't "be the gospel" or "live the gospel"—which is an account of Jesus's life, death, and resurrection, not ours—our own lives should be consistent with what we profess about his. The Reformers believed that efforts to live in conformity to Christ, though they are in themselves unable to save, can soften people's hearts and prepare them for the gospel. This is expressed in the Heidelberg Catechism, which lists, as one of the reasons to do good works, that we "by our godly walk may win others also to Christ."[15]

Sometimes we will do well to say with Shakespeare's Cordelia, in *King Lear*, "Love and be silent." Or, as my friend Jody often reminds herself, "Shut up and pray."

---

14. John Newton to Elizabeth Newton, October 17, 1781, in *The Works of the Rev. John Newton* (New Haven, 1824), 4:390.

15. Heidelberg Catechism, answer 86.

16

Advocacy: Fighting for Those Who Can't

As you did it to one of the least of these
my brothers, you did it to me.
(Matt. 25:40)

In my first National Alliance on Mental Illness (NAMI) meeting, advocacy was described as the last stage that caregivers enter after dealing with the initial crisis and learning to cope. In reality, the present situation in both society and the medical system forces a caregiver to become an advocate from the start. As fancy as the word may seem, it includes many things you are probably already doing for your loved one.

Sometimes advocacy means standing up against a faulty medical system. Just last week, Jody took some letters from friends to the CEO of the mental health department in their local hospital. "My friends are frustrated," she said. "The hospital is not taking seriously what they, as parents, are saying. They are often told that there is nothing wrong with their child—that he is just being manipulative and should be kicked out of the house. No further follow-up is offered."

Jody describes advocacy for people with schizophrenia as "a lonely job." In some ways, it seems like a losing battle from the start. "The person you are advocating for doesn't want your help, and the people you are trying to get help from start to wonder if you are the one who is really mentally unstable."

Still, someone has to do it, because the cases of abuse and neglect of people with schizophrenia are numerous and serious and are often met with indifference both from the general public and, paradoxically, from those who are living with the illness and are simply struggling to determine what is real and not real.

My son initially reacted to his hospitalization with anger, which was exacerbated by his confused state of mind that frustrated him and let him down. He was furious at the police for forcibly taking him to a hospital and at us for allowing him to stay there. Later, he gave up the fight and took whatever came his way, seemingly unperturbed (although I don't know what he really felt inside).

I was left to fight single-handedly for him, for services that, as Andrew Solomon explains well, "are seldom available to anyone who does not have the wherewithal to battle agencies"—meaning that they need "education, time, and money."[1]

Mental health patients have been abused and dismissed in more ways than one. We used to lock them up in asylums. Pressed by popular outrage, President John Kennedy signed a bill in the 1960s to close down as many asylums as

1. Andrew Solomon, *Far from the Tree: Parents, Children, and the Search for Identity* (New York: Scribner, 2012), 177.

possible, which were allegedly "replaced by therapeutic centers."[2] Other countries, such as England and Italy, followed suit one or two decades later.

In reality, adequate therapeutic centers have remained scarce and underfunded. All those patients had to go somewhere, but the political motivation to close malfunctioning facilities was not met by an equal urge to provide sufficient care.

Jody's friends have a long list of complaints, starting with dirty waiting rooms that are patrolled by a security guard, where patients have to sit for more than four hours with no medical support. Then, after a frustrating wait, they "are often sent home because there are no beds," Jody says. "Some are admitted and sent home the next day, even after a suicide attempt. In one case, nurses gave no encouragement to shower or change clothes."

Indifference and abuse can have tragic consequences, as Elyn Saks points out. Once, she came close to dying when doctors at an emergency department gave little notice to her threatening symptoms. "Once the ER learned I had a mental illness and was on antipsychotic medication," she said, "the diagnosis was written in stone: I was 'just' having an episode."[3] She was sent home.

A friend who had taken her to the ER practically jumped up and down, insisting that she had seen Saks during a

---

2. John F. Kennedy, "Remarks Upon Signing Bill for the Construction of Mental Retardation Facilities and Community Mental Health Centers" (spoken address given in the Cabinet Room at the White House, Washington, D.C., October 31, 1963), available online at http://www.presidency.ucsb.edu /ws/index.php?pid=9506

3. Elyn R. Saks, *The Center Cannot Hold: My Journey through Madness* (New York: Hyperion, 2007), 232.

psychotic episode and that this was very different. The tests came back positive for a type of brain hemorrhage with a 50 percent mortality rate, and Saks was readmitted and treated. "Stigma against mental illness is a scourge with many faces," she explained, "and the medical community wears a number of those faces."[4]

The Grim Picture

The inadequacy of mental health programs and facilities in the United States has prompted some pejorative expressions like "Revolving Door Syndrome" (the patients' tendency to discontinue care, only to relapse and be readmitted again) or "Greyhound Therapy" (the practice of giving difficult cases a Greyhound bus ticket out of town). As outrageous as the latter procedure sounds, it is still ongoing in some states.

Whether they are prematurely released or shipped out of town, many patients end up in the streets with no medical care. Of these, a large number eventually land in jail, mostly for "small transgressions that are inevitable for people impervious to social reality," says Andrew Solomon. There, these people "are dealt with not by doctors, but by police officers—and then prison guards and other criminals."[5]

According to a background paper from the Office of Research and Public Affairs of the Treatment Advocacy Center, "Serious mental illness has become so prevalent in the US corrections system that jails and prisons are now

4. Saks, 232.
5. Solomon, *Far from the Tree*, 342.

commonly called 'the new asylums.' In point of fact, the Los Angeles County Jail, Chicago's Cook County Jail, or the New York's Riker's Island Jail Complex each hold more mentally ill inmates than any remaining psychiatric hospital in the United States. Overall . . . approximately 383,000 individuals with severe psychiatric disease were behind bars in the United States in 2014 or nearly 10 times the number of patients remaining in the nation's state hospitals."[6] The report goes on to explain how the practice of incarcerating people with mental illness generates a high cost in both tax money and lives.

NAMI estimates that a total of two million people with mental illness are taken to jail each year and pins some of the blame on the fact that, "in a mental health crisis, people are more likely to encounter police than get medical help."[7]

Calling the police in a mental health emergency is common practice. In this context, Jody's experience of losing a son is scarcely unique. According to a *Washington Post* analysis, in the first half of 2015, people who were killed by police during a mental or emotional crisis amounted to 25 percent of the total number of fatal police shootings.

Some of these shootings were absolutely horrific. *The Atlantic* reports two back-to-back deaths in Seattle: "A 30-year-old pregnant woman shot in front of her children, and a 20-year-old man killed right before his high-school graduation during what appeared to be his first psychotic

---

6. Treatment Advocacy Center, *Serious Mental Illness (SMI) Prevalence in Jails and Prisons*, September 2016, http://www.treatmentadvocacycenter.org /storage/documents/backgrounders/smi-in-jails-and-prisons.pdf, p. 1.

7. "Jailing People With Mental Illness," National Alliance on Mental Illness, accessed September 6, 2018, https://www.nami.org/Learn-More/Public-Policy /Jailing-People-with-Mental-Illness.

episode, with a pen in his hand police mistook for a knife."[8] Both newspapers blame the officers' lack of training.

"How do the people making those decisions determine what is a danger to oneself or someone else?" Jody told me. "We both know how quickly that can change. If it is all about safety, that doesn't seem right to me. One time we called the police when Matt was sleeping in the storage part of our basement, on the cement with a blanket, because he was afraid. They came and talked to him. It was two in the morning. They determined that he wasn't in any danger and that neither were we. Before they left, they told us they didn't want to be bothered in the middle of the night for such trivial reasons."

Some Remedies

Many cities or states have remedied this situation by creating specialized units, which are variously called Psychiatric Emergency Response Teams (PERT), Psychiatric Mobile Response Teams (PMRT), Mental Health Response Teams (MHRT), Community Service Officers (CSO), or Crisis Intervention Teams (CIT). Just remember that, while they are qualified, some of these teams may not be as gentle as you are hoping. Handcuffs are standard, even when the person in crisis is compliant. In my son's case, they added pepper-spray, which was traumatic for our whole family. Also remember that they are typically very busy and that their response might take time if your situation is not

8. Norm Ornstein and Steve Leifman, "How Mental-Health Training for Police Can Save Lives—and Taxpayer Dollars," *The Atlantic*, August 11, 2017, https://www.theatlantic.com/politics/archive/2017/08/how-mental -health-training-for-police-can-save-livesand-taxpayer-dollars/536520/.

considered a true emergency. In my case, it took three days, after repeated calls on my part.

These teams are, however, more specifically trained than other police officers, and they often exhibit a great deal of wisdom and compassion. An example of the operations of the Memphis CIT in particular has been captured in a PBS video clip (with transcripts), which gives a good model to follow for anyone who may be dealing with a mentally ill person at a time of crisis.[9]

According to NAMI, today CITs are present in nearly three thousand communities around the country. If your city doesn't have one of these teams, you can partner with NAMI to advocate for a change.[10]

You can also ask your psychiatrist for other emergency numbers to call. Organizations like NAMI provide phone consultations, but the volunteers who answer the phone are generally limited in what they can say. They can, however, refer you to these valuable units or to one of the many independent programs that are thankfully springing up throughout the country.

Christian Advocates in the Public Sphere

When it comes to advocating for a specific group or defending civil justice in the public sphere, Christians often

---

9. See "How Memphis Has Changed the Way Police Respond to Mental Health Crises," PBS News Hour, Nov 7, 2015, https://www.pbs.org/news hour/show/memphis-changed-way-police-respond-mental-health-crises. See also http://www.citinternational.org/.

10. "Crisis Intervention Team (CIT) Programs," National Alliance on Mental Illness, accessed September 6, 2018, https://www.nami.org/Get-Involved /Law-Enforcement-and-Mental-Health.

take one of three extremes: they absent themselves from the battle, make it a religious crusade, or join the fight but forget who they are in Christ.

Justice to the Weak

The Bible is full of injunctions for championing the cause of those who can't defend themselves. "Give justice to the weak and the fatherless," says God in a psalm of Asaph; "maintain the right of the afflicted and the destitute. Rescue the weak and the needy; deliver them from the hand of the wicked" (Ps. 82:3–4).

The prophet Isaiah told the nation of Israel what kind of fast is pleasant to the Lord: "To loose the bonds of wickedness, to undo the straps of the yoke, to let the oppressed go free . . . to share your bread with the hungry and bring the homeless poor into your house; when you see the naked, to cover him, and not to hide yourself from your own flesh" (Isa. 58:6–7; see also Isa. 1:17; Deut. 14:29). To the apostle James, these duties are the essence of a "religion that is pure and undefiled" (James 1:27). Moreover, Jesus told his hearers that, ultimately, the good works done for strangers and prisoners, or for those who are hungry, thirsty, and naked, are done to him (see Matt. 25:31–46).

Many Christians in history have taken up these challenges in the public sphere. In the context of a Roman Empire in which (in spite of a few philosophers' injunctions) charity was given to enhance one's reputation and the sick were often left to fend for themselves, Christians such as Basil of Caesarea built hospitals and leprosariums.

Others fought for civil liberties and justice without turning issues into religious crusades or confusing the roles of church and state. William Wilberforce and his protracted and successful campaign for the abolition of slavery in England is one of the best-known examples. In his case, he was in the perfect position to advance this cause, and he did so relentlessly, even when his ideas were shut down.

His friend John Newton was not in a position of political power, but he encouraged Wilberforce and helped him as he could: by supporting him in discouraging times, by giving his testimony in court, and by publishing a book that revealed the cruelty of the slave trade.

You may have some of these opportunities yourself. If not, there are many other venues. NAMI, the Treatment Advocacy Center, the Bazelon Center for Mental Health Law, the Saks Institute for Mental Health, and many similar groups are valuable sources of information that provide many suggestions for how people can become involved in creating awareness, changing laws, and increasing the availability of care for people with mental illness. Even if you don't agree with their political views, they will help you to stay abreast of needs and problems and to make informed decisions.

The need is widespread and the possibilities unlimited. For example, *Walking Man*, a 2014 documentary, tells the story of a father and son—both diagnosed with bipolar disorder—who walked two hundred miles across Missouri after three high school students committed suicide within seven weeks. Their statewide mission of bringing awareness to high school students forced them to express their feelings and struggles for the first time—both to strangers and to each other.

Jody is actively working in her city. "I am part of a group called Families for Families," she said. "I am also on the board of Lanark Leeds and Grenville Addictions and

Mental Health service (LLGAMH), join the Silver Ribbon campaign in the spring, and hold a program called 'Soul Socks' at Christmas." Soul Socks, a collection of socks for area food banks and shelters, is a program she created to honor Matt's memory. The idea came from her recollection of a Christmas day when "Matt pulled off his old socks and put on a new pair. He looked at his feet and said, 'There is nothing nicer than a new pair of socks.'"

Given that one third of the homeless are diagnosed with mental illness (and that many more probably live with it but are undiagnosed), her efforts certainly also benefit this significant part of our population.

"Sometimes I feel sad and I wonder if I should drop it all and try to just put it all behind me," Jody said. "But if I can do some good, if I can see someone get the help they need, if I can change someone's mind about people with mental health issues, if I can give of myself even in small ways and reach out to people who are like Matt, then I feel like he is still part of my life and that by loving them I am still loving him."

She can already see some tangible fruits from her efforts. "Many changes are taking place in the mental health care system in Brockville and the surrounding area as a result of the thirty-seven recommendations that stemmed from the inquest that took place after Matt's shooting."

Much of what you can do is related to your talents and opportunities. If you are a writer, write articles or stories. If you are a blogger, consider pointing out dangerous perceptions of mental illness in our society. If you are part of a book club, suggest including a helpful book on mental illness. Most of all, continue to educate yourself, and your passion and conviction will eventually spread to others. In fact, if people know you are interested in providing education on mental illness and promoting safe treatment for those who are living with it, the response might surprise you, opening further doors.

Remembering Who We Are in Christ

While it's true that Christians and non-Christians can fight side by side for the same social justice issues, it's important for Christians to remember who they are in Christ and to speak humbly and lovingly, promoting peace, as the Bible instructs us to do.

This is certainly not easy. In this fallen world, all social relationships are corrupted, and it's quite common to have to deal with other sinners who are as combative, hard-headed, antagonistic, and proud as we can be. On top of these common problems, the prevailing disrespect for the mentally ill and the countless obstacles their advocates have to cross are frustrating, disheartening, and infuriating.

If we know ourselves well enough to fear that breaking sinful habits such as "enmity, strife, jealousy, fits of anger" (Gal. 5:21) is a losing battle, the apostle Paul takes us back to the cross, reminding us that "those who belong to Christ Jesus have [already] crucified the flesh with its passions and desires" and that "Christ has [already] set us free," allowing us to "stand firm" without having to "submit again to a yoke of slavery" (Gal. 5:24, 1). All those qualities that seem so out of reach—"love, joy, peace, patience, kindness, goodness, faithfulness, gentleness, self-control"—are in reality the "fruit of the spirit," which we simply need to pick and enjoy.

Excuses come easy. I blame my argumentative nature on my Italian heritage (as the movie *My Cousin Vinny* seems to confirm). But that's just what it is: an excuse. I find it helpful to remember that the person I am talking to is also made in God's image, has probably been trained to follow a protocol, and might be having a rough day. I also try to check my motivation. I tend to push harder when I want to prove myself right, which makes me lose sight of my initial goal of finding efficient ways to resolve a problem.

An instructional video from Samaritan Ministries, a healthcare ministry that helps members to share medical costs, gives a good balance. "Be patient and gracious as you represent Christ to your provider, but also remember that you are making a reasonable request, and they should be able to give you what you need."[11]

As sad as it sounds, some people still respect men more than women. This is wrong—but in this battle for the welfare of our loved ones, personal rights can take second place. If you have the impression that a health professional respects your husband (or another male relative) more than you, take him along.

It also helps to look professional. "After our daughter had a medication change that potentially endangered her life," Amy said, "my husband and I went to see the psychiatrist together. We had called her earlier, saying we did not blame her and that we respected her judgment. But it was obvious that we were quite concerned and wanted to take more responsibility ourselves.

"If you are both calm, dress in 'power clothing' (my husband dresses in a suit and tie for these occasions), and yet

---

11. The direct source of this quote is an instructional video from Samaritan Ministries to its members—but you can learn more about this ministry, and read more advice about navigating the medical industry, on their website at https://www.samaritanministries.org/.

manage to show medical professionals you respect and value them, you will increase your influence and their willingness to cooperate with you."

Barring urgent cases—which are all too frequent when we deal with schizophrenia—I also found that writing is often the best way to communicate my concerns, as long as I can take the time to measure my words, let them rest, and ask others to give me feedback before I send them. Even when direct, face-to-face communication is more appropriate or required, I like to write down what I have to say and go through the same editing process first.

Keeping a journal of your loved one's progress (and setbacks), including any details that you are concerned about, is also a useful tool, and most psychiatrists and therapists greatly appreciate this window into your daily life—one that they are not usually able to access. You can send these journals even if your loved one has not given you permission to hear from the practitioner, because you are giving and not receiving information.

Overall, "parents should try to be poised and composed in the presence of the practitioners," Britton explains. "I've seen parents get very angry at doctors, which inhibited treatment, causing their kid to have a lot more distrust."

I am guilty of fits of anger. In spite of its inclusion in the historical list of "seven deadly sins," anger is deceiving because it appears so right at times—especially when no one seems to share the urgency that we feel—and plenty of movies and shows, as well as social media, reinforce this conviction. In reality, while "righteous indignation" and firm protest are appropriate at times, especially when we are standing up for the oppressed, anger can become addictive.

Once again, the sovereignty of God is a source of great

comfort and peace. If I can stall my anger long enough to catch my breath, I usually remember that God is still in control and that the hearts of kings (and physicians) are in the hand of the Lord, who "turns [them] wherever he will" (Prov. 21:1). In the words of Maltbie D. Babcock, a Presbyterian pastor who lived with depression, "This is my Father's world, O let me ne'er forget that though the wrong seems oft so strong, God is the Ruler yet."[12]

Christian Advocates in Daily Encounters

We can advocate for mental illness in our daily encounters just by being there for those who are living with it and by cultivating an attitude of respect for each human being as one who is made in the image of God.

Not Just Sticks and Stones

For example, we can make a difference by watching our language—avoiding words like *psycho* or *schizo* and educating others when we have an opportunity to do so in a meek and humble manner. Even common phrases like "Have you gone insane?" or "Are you crazy?" can be hurtful when said to a person who may be struggling with an actual mental disorder, and they only contribute to the prevailing stigma. I have found it best to just avoid them altogether. I also suggest avoiding the words *schizophrenia* or *schizophrenic* to indicate a split personality. This is not the correct usage, and it can cause confusion in a person who is affected by the true illness.

The same love and respect can be manifested in our

---

12. Maltbie D. Babcock, "This Is My Father's World," 1901.

attitude toward the homeless. It's easy to judge them for having made the wrong choices in life, but how much do we know about each individual's story? Many live with a serious mental illness and are unable to keep a job or lead a normal life without someone's help and support. We can't help everyone who crosses our path, and it's true that many of these people are not willing to seek treatment, but we still owe them respect, compassion, prayer, and—when possible—tangible assistance.

These expressions of tangible love are easier if we remember our own frailties and how easy it would be for any of us to suddenly become underprivileged, marginalized, and needy. Our minds, our bodies, and our finances are all tenuous commodities that can give way any time.

"People with mental illness are often like lepers in our society," Jody said. "Sometimes they are made fun of, or they are feared, or they are blamed for their illness. Often we hear things like 'He did drugs. It's his own fault,' or 'She should smarten up and quit feeling sorry for herself.' If someone falls off a tree and breaks a leg, do we walk away and say, 'It's your own fault. You shouldn't have climbed the tree'?"

"People didn't understand, and they judged us," said Beverly, whose son has been diagnosed with bipolar disorder and anxiety and is on the autism spectrum. His parents suspect schizoaffective disorder. "When he was young, he suffered from ADHD and was always bouncing around," she said. Regrettably, the church didn't respond with compassion. "'Did your kid need any more sugar?' many people said."

Jody remembers similar remarks. "We felt bad enough and were already blaming ourselves for Matt's illness. Statements like 'You need to get that kid out of your house,' 'He needs to join the army,' or 'He needs to be converted' might have been well intentioned, but they were not really helpful or encouraging. Neither was blaming the person with the illness ('He is not a Christian' or 'He is rebellious') instead of seizing the opportunity to show love. After Matt died, someone said to my husband, 'Well, he was a lot of trouble anyway, wasn't he?'"

Many of these are just off-the-cuff remarks. I am guilty of similar things. Sometimes it seems that the popular saying "Sticks and stones may break my bones, but words can never hurt me" has become a convenient motto. In reality, words hurt deeply. In fact, the emotional pain caused by words can last longer than physical pain. As Christians, we should be especially careful in our speech, which is supposed to reflect our new nature in Christ and bring glory to God.

The Bible is full of instructions on the importance of watching our language, particularly in the books of Proverbs and James. Proverbs tells us that "death and life are in the power of the tongue" (18:21) and that "rash words are like sword thrusts, but the tongue of the wise brings healing" (12:18). James is realistic about the power of the tongue, stating that it's "a restless evil, full of deadly poison" and that "no human being can tame" it (3:8–9).

Even when they are flippant, the hurtful words that come out of our mouths are a constant reminder that we, even as Christians, are still polluted by sin and unable to keep our tongues perfectly tamed in this life. That doesn't that mean we shouldn't try, by God's grace and the power of his Spirit, as we remember how hypocritical we are when "with [the tongue] we bless our Lord and Father, and with it we curse people who are made in the likeness of God" (James 3:9).

Christian Advocates in the Church

According to a 2014 report by the Canadian Mental Health Association, "recovery from mental health problems is improved through social networks and community connections. The extent to which people with common mental health conditions report a strong sense of belonging to their local communities reflects one component of support for recovery."[13] This is not an uncommon recommendation, and many groups have been formed to create this sense of community. For Christians, it seems only natural that the church should provide such a place.

All the Lonely People

Mental illness is much more real and present than we often recognize. The smiling person sitting in the pew next to us might be affected in deeper ways than we realize. I was never much aware of it before my son's diagnosis. I knew that one young man in our church had schizophrenia, but I never researched the details involving his condition. Later, after I started to share my experience and trials, many people opened their hearts and I discovered many similar cases in my own congregation—if not from actual members, then from their close relatives.

This silence is understandable. "People with schizophrenia—people like me—read the papers and watch the evening news," Elyn Saks said. "We see how the illness is portrayed and how a friend-in-the-making is likely to perceive us, once they hear the truth. We move forward with

13. Quoted in Lydia Monk, "6 Tips for Improving Mental Health Individually and Collectively," Crisis and Trauma Resource Institute, accessed September 6, 2018, https://blog.ctrinstitute.com/6-tips-for-improving-mental-health/.

great caution because we must. We'd have to be . . . well, crazy to do otherwise."[14]

This reticence to speak, however, isolates people even more, reinforcing the common perception that others can't understand. "I live in my world compared to other people," Britton told me. "My reality is kind of strange. I feel like I'm in a strange place, even if I am in a familiar place. I still struggle. I feel like there's no way out—no other option. I have to live in this world—a world which is not pleasant. I feel isolated and alienated. I feel there is nothing I can do."

Unfortunately, this same vicious cycle of silence and loneliness is present also in our churches. "One of the things I have found in pastoral ministry is that there is such a stigma attached to mental illness that often times people do not seek help from their pastor or church," Todd Pruitt, lead pastor at Covenant Presbyterian Church in Harrisonburg, Virginia, told me. "As a pastor, I normally do not hear of such problems until things have reached a crisis point."

There may be other reasons, besides the common fear of being stigmatized, for some people's reluctance to share a mental condition with a pastor. "Certainly, people are not obligated to share their problems or diagnoses with me," Pruitt continued, "but I fear that the hesitancy is due to fear that a pastor and/or church will not sympathize properly with their struggle. My guess is that they have heard their pastor or another preacher lament the number of people who take medications rather than 'trusting God.' Perhaps they have heard a pastor misapply Philippians to mean that all experiences of anxiety or depression are inherently sinful."

While pastors today "are better informed than they used

---

14. Saks, *The Center Cannot Hold*, 290.

to be about mental illness," Pruitt wonders if they still "struggle to understand that mental illness is as much an illness as is diabetes or cancer and often requires medical treatment." Given the respect that most Christians hold for their pastors, this lack of understanding can cause much pain.

Pastors should also be careful not to confuse their role as ministers of the gospel with the role of a physician and should refrain from giving advice on medical issues such as therapy and medications (just as psychiatrists and psychologists should avoid giving advice on theological matters). When Christians are trying to make a medical decision, a pastor can encourage them to pray for wisdom as they research their options.

The Heidelberg Catechism asks, "Is it then enough that we do not kill our neighbor in any such way?" "No," it replies, "for in condemning envy, hatred, and anger, God requires us to love our neighbor as ourselves, to show patience, peace, meekness, mercy and kindness towards him, and, so far as we have power, to prevent his hurt; also to do good even unto our enemies."[15]

I was especially impressed by that injunction "to prevent his hurt." It seems particularly relevant when we care for people with schizophrenia, who are often abused by others or end up harming themselves. How can the church protect them? A good starting point is to listen, learn, and care.

Michael E. Emlet, a counselor and faculty member at the Christian Counseling and Educational Foundation, wrote, "A diagnosis waves a yellow caution flag that says, 'Slow down! Be quick to listen and slow to speak! Take the time to discern the complexity of this person's struggle as a

---

15. Heidelberg Catechism, question and answer 107.

sufferer and sinner before God.'" [16] Since, however, a person's diagnosis is often hidden from both pastors and fellow church members, slowing down and taking time to listen is a good suggestion in any case. We never know what depths of suffering another person has reached.

Be a Friend

"If people avoid others who live with schizophrenia or other mental illness, it's not because they are mean," says Rev. Stephen Donovan. "They just don't know what to say or do, so they don't do anything."

Some years ago, I wrote an article about the problems that deaf people face in the church. A young woman who is deaf told me of her obstacles when she tries to talk to hearing people. As soon as they realize she is deaf, they often look surprised, say "Sorry," and walk away. It's actually a very understandable response, which I have probably given myself in similar situations. The key, however, is to realize that there is something inherently wrong in avoiding a person who is different from us, simply because we don't know how to react. This realization should motivate us to do something about it—to get informed and try again.

In Donovan's experience, those who are willing to share their problems with others and who have at least one or two meaningful friendships make the greatest progress. "I encourage them to find someone," he says. "Those who are entrusted with that knowledge have been respectful and understanding."

It's a challenge that few people dare to undertake. "By

16. Michael R. Emlet, *Descriptions and Prescriptions: A Biblical Perspective on Psychiatric Diagnoses and Medications* (Greensboro, NC: New Growth Press, 2017), 46.

nature, if we can't fix a problem, we'd rather avoid it," he continued. "It's especially challenging for caretakers, who end up living their lives while trying to live another life at the same time—but many are able to do it by God's grace. Most people, however, don't grow in that maturity until the Lord puts them in a box. I've witnessed some people growing in that regard."

If you are honored with trust by a person with schizophrenia, it's important to know that you don't always need a strategy. You can just sit next to him or her and be available and friendly. The most meaningful conversations I had with my son started when I sat next to him in silence. There is a difference between the awkward silence of a person who would rather be somewhere else and the silence of someone who is sincerely concerned and present.

Ben, who has been a friend to a person with schizophrenia for years, remembers how he had to learn to help him when needed. "I think what drew him to trust me was that I often did not try to prove that he was wrong in his suspicions. Empathizing with him, and trying to re-narrate the events he told me, usually went a long way over time. I would tell him that perhaps it was true that he is being watched—but why should that be a bother? That is not the same thing as being controlled.

"I know that may not sound very effective," he continued, "but it was really thinking on my toes to find ways that would dissociate his account from his fear. I found repeatedly that many of his beliefs were based on a fear and anxiety that were not always tied to anything in particular. He often constructed a narrative that made sense of that fear and gave it an object (there were times when it was a normal object of fear, but he would project beyond that).

"When I could bear with him, his anxiety usually dropped and he would forget about the object of his fear. Bearing with him often meant listening to him talk for a long time and, instead of responding directly, just asking if he wanted ice cream."

There are of course times when true friendship requires vigilance and protection. For example, if someone starts talking about harming himself or committing suicide, a caregiver or someone else who is close to the person should be alerted. In certain settings, such as a school campus, you can alert someplace like a health center. In the meantime, a peaceful attitude can do much to defuse the situation. "I recall that he had several suicidal thoughts as well," said Ben. "The fact that I remained calm when he felt that way may have calmed him down."

If the situation doesn't seem urgent, a simple encouragement to seek help might be sufficient. Ask the person if he or she has anyone else to talk to, if he or she has enough professional support, and if there is anything you can do. You can also direct the person to a helpline. Don't be afraid to address the subject. As I learned later, it isn't dangerous to ask questions about someone's suicidal thoughts. On the contrary, letting the person know you are there might provide him or her comfort and might help you to assess the situation. In an urgent situation, stay there and call for help.

Supporting the Family

Families of people with schizophrenia can feel equally lonely, cautious, or forced behind a veil of silence out of respect for their loved ones' wishes.

"My experience is that serious mental illness is far more difficult for individuals and families to navigate than a cancer diagnosis," Todd Pruitt said. "When someone reveals that he has cancer, the church is typically mobilized. Prayers are offered openly. The sufferer gives regular updates about symptoms and treatments. But not so with mental illness. The individual and his family feel a sense of shame, which adds profound pain and loneliness to the struggle."

Conversely, church members may feel unprepared to talk to a family of people with schizophrenia. "I believe my most difficult challenges in pastoral care are those connected to helping people with chronic mental illness and their families navigate this difficult situation," he continued. "What is the right thing to say to the family whose loved one is living with depression or schizophrenia? And so, while we all may possess the knowledge that something should be done to alleviate the situation, no one dares to bring it up until a hospitalization or suicide attempt."

Don't worry if you don't know what to say. Be friendly and available. Your shoulder might just be the one they need to cry on. "Just having others is better than being alone, even if none of us knows what to do," Dave said. If you have had a similar experience, you will of course have specific words of comfort (see 2 Cor. 1:4). Knowing that we are not alone in our struggles goes a long way. But Paul urges us to have empathy even if we have never been in another person's shoes: "Remember those who are in prison, *as though* in prison with them" (Heb. 13:3). Just speak honestly and avoid empty clichés. Simply talking about your own struggles might help others to do the same.

You may offer to pray for them and give them your number in case they want to talk—but unless you have an established connection with them, they may never do so. In that case, send them messages from time to time, ask how they are doing, and bring them some comfort food. Especially in times of heavy stress—when their loved one is hospitalized or is increasing the level of stress in the family—offer to help with their chores. My friend Dianna swept my floor or did the dishes every time she came over. It was a little humbling for me, but I never stopped her.

And, families, do talk to your pastor—no matter how busy he seems to be. Pastors are always busy, but shepherding their sheep is their job. When I told my pastor about my hesitations to talk to him, he sent me a comforting answer: "I am your pastor, and that is what I am here for. Yes, I receive a lot of emails, FB messages, and other correspondence during the week, and it can be difficult to get to all of them with equal concern. But anything that is of a pastoral nature gets top priority. While you should always feel at liberty to bring your questions to others, you should always feel free to continue bringing them to me, Simonetta. The truth is that I would be heartbroken if you didn't."

17

Recovery from Schizophrenia in the "Already / Not Yet"

Now I know in part; then I shall know fully,
even as I have been fully known.
(1 Cor. 13:12)

In his book *Christ and Time*, New Testament professor Oscar Cullmann compared our condition as redeemed sinners who are traveling to our final destination to the situation of the Europeans after D-day.[1] Technically, the victory had been won. In reality, the eighteen-month mop-up campaign was still filled with blood, pain, and suffering. Likewise, Christ has already won the decisive battle, but the complete cease-fire is still to come. We are at peace with God but not with sin. In God's eyes, we are already made righteous through Christ, but the reality of our sinful nature stares back at us whenever we dare look within. We are, as Martin Luther put it, righteous and sinners at the same time. We are simultaneously renewed and sinful.

1. See Oscar Cullmann, *Christ and Time: The Primitive Christian Conception of Time and History*, trans. Floyd V. Filson (London: SCM Press, 1951), 84.

In other words, Cullmann says, we live in the overlap of two ages: this present evil age and the age to come—in a state of constant tension "between the decisive 'already fulfilled' and the 'not yet completed.'"[2] It's a tension that seems evident in the book of Revelation, in which Jesus appears as the ruling conqueror while his saints on earth are still struggling against evil and looking for the new heaven and new earth. This tension can be frightening and confusing unless we are constantly reminded of who we are in Christ, where we are headed, and what is really happening behind the scenes.

In approaching this difficult task of assessing visible and invisible realities, Christians have often swung toward one of two extremes: either an under-realized eschatology that emphasizes the "not yet" at the expense of the "already" or an over-realized eschatology that does the opposite. When living with serious mental illnesses like schizophrenia, those who emphasize the "not yet" may focus on the disease as an inevitable consequence of sin that must be endured with patience, while those who emphasize the "already" challenge themselves and others to recognize that God works in the here-and-now and that resurrection power already flows through our veins. When harmonized and properly applied, these two tendencies are complementary and biblical.

Remember the "Not Yet"

The tendency to emphasize the "already" at the expense of the "not yet" may generate excessive optimism and unrealistic expectations—a way of thinking that has often been

---

2. Oscar Cullmann, *Salvation in History* (London: SCM Press, 1967), 172.

described as a "theology of glory," which carries the intrinsic idea that illness, poverty, and suffering can be overcome here and now by virtue of our faith. This emphasis often leads to a criticizing of sufferers for their lack of faith or a questioning of their obedience to God, as Job's counselors did. It was also the attitude of the apostle Paul's critics, especially in Corinth, where the church was enticed by those who Paul called "super-apostles" (2 Cor. 11:5)—the first-century version of prosperity gospel preachers.

This extreme can have terrible consequences. A friend of mine who went blind through Stickler Syndrome told me how the people at her church became discouraged when their prayers didn't restore her sight. One pastor even left the ministry partially for this reason. "I was left with the impression that prayer was a tool to manipulate God," she said. Thankfully, her faith is still strong in spite of her disability.

My friend Dave has had time to reflect on this problem. "A friendly and zealous Pentecostal person tells you," he says, "while you are dealing with illness, that prayer and carrying an anointed cloth will heal you. You are not healed. A fervent non-denominational fundamentalist may tell you that you have sin in your life not being dealt with, that all this is a consequence of your sin, and that you should seek God and his law if you are to be 'whole.' You do not become 'whole.' Pretty much any advice one wants one can find, and there are steps to follow leading to supposed success or healing.

"Any and all options exist for the ill individual; they are there on the table to be picked up; and, in the end, none of them will suffice. Something is wrong. Something is off. Something is broken. The ill individual knows this better than anyone, if and when brief moments of clarity are to be had."

These steps and options, however, always require

willpower and a commitment that often fades, leaving room for discouragement. The biblical psalms of praise and victory are balanced with psalms of anguish and cries to God of utter dejection, maintaining the Bible's realistic view of human life.

Weakness and Patience

The apostle Paul was not afraid to portray repeated images of personal weakness in the face of the Corinthian critics who compared him negatively to the "super-apostles." He could rejoice, knowing that God's "power is made perfect in weakness" (2 Cor. 12:9). Once, after confessing the derailment of a mission due to his personal anxiety, he burst into a cry of gratitude to God "who in Christ always leads us in triumphal procession" (2 Cor. 2:14)—an image of a victor leading his prisoners to death.[3] The image is comforting only to those who know the excruciating pain of a difficult battle against sin and the confusion it generates. We are blundering sheep who often fail, but thank God that Christ is leading us to die to ourselves and to live in him.

We have a natural tendency to claim victory for the Christian in the here and now, which is why many translators have tried to soften this image of slaves following Christ to death. But accepting our weakness and limitations, along with God's loving guidance, is important for us if we want to "run with endurance the race that is set before us" (Heb. 12:1), with all the obstacles, setbacks, and pains it includes. And patience is paramount when we are dealing with mental illness.

---

3. See Scott J. Hafemann, *2 Corinthians*, The NIV Application Commentary (Grand Rapids: Zondervan, 2000), 107.

"Coming alongside someone with a mental health issue takes a very committed, patient person or group of people," Rev. Keele told me. "Most mental health issues are not something that can be cured in six weeks or less; they are kind of unpredictable and a bit of a roller-coaster ride." Besides, "while family involvement improves the lives of schizophrenics, it does not transform them into who they might have been without the illness. We can do everything we can and still not make it manageable." We have to be prepared for that.

"I still can't tell the difference between reality and the world of my dreams," Britton admitted. "I still feel isolated and alienated. It feels like certain things never get solved."

Patience is a hard lesson to learn. "The urge to think we can fix things is often very destructive, but it's a strong urge because it means we're not helpless," Philip Cary, author of *Good News for Anxious Christians*, told me in a recent discussion of this topic. "And often that's just a lie. You can work very hard, exhausted, day in and day out, and still find that you can't fix what's making you suffer. You just have to keep suffering with problems you can't fix. That's one of the most important ways we take up a cross.

"Christian hope means you can keep carrying that cross even when you don't see any end to this but death," he continued. "The only real hope has to be a hope for the defeat of death itself. And that means, in the near term, that trust in the sovereignty of God really is essential. I cannot fix this, I can't guarantee it won't end badly, and I cannot defeat death if that's where it ends. But there is One who defeats death, and therefore I can keep going with the suffering that love entails."

The Bible makes it clear that our patience must be

long-term. Ultimately, we are not waiting for temporary relief from our struggles. We are "waiting for our blessed hope, the appearing of the glory of our great God and Savior Jesus Christ" (Titus 2:13), when we will end this earthly exile, with all its suffering and pain, and enter into his everlasting city. It's not a pie in the sky. It's a certainty, and its constant presence in our thoughts shapes the way we live daily (see Matt. 6:21).

Waiting is especially hard in a culture in which, on the one hand, we are used to receiving instant gratification and, on the other hand, are bombarded with promises that are rarely fulfilled. Long-term waiting is possible only when we remember who God is (he is a God who "comes with might" but also gently tends "his flock like a shepherd" [Isa. 40:10–11]), his track record throughout time, and his unfailing promises.

Remember the "Already"

I often gravitate toward an under-realized view of God's promises. I know that his kingdom will one day come in all its fullness and that there will be no more illness, evil, or fear, but I tend to forget the "already." In reality, this "vale of tears," as the Puritans called our age, is not simply filled with defeat and disappointment. Not only has Christ already won the decisive victory over death, hell, and sin, but he is sitting at the right hand of God, daily interceding for us and operating in history as powerfully as he did in the pages of the Bible. Besides, his Spirit lives and works in our hearts daily in ways that are imperceptible but real, transforming us into the image of Christ—as unrecognizable as this work sometimes seems.

In the context of schizophrenia, lack of appreciation for the "already" can aggravate the pessimism that has traditionally plagued both caregivers and professionals. In fact, the psychiatric community is still divided in its expectations of recovery from this illness, although it is gradually moving from a largely pessimistic view to an acceptance of hope and of the possibility of recovery.

I saw signs of improvement during the short eighteen months of treatment that my son received for schizophrenia, even if I focused too much on the backward falls. Just the fact that he could admit he was sick and could recognize that the voices he heard were not real was a major step forward. Through cognitive behavioral therapy, he learned to develop some techniques for keeping those voices at bay. He was planning to go back to school and was filling countless pages with mathematical equations, showing that he still had exceptional abilities in that field.

People with schizophrenia should not be seen simply as gravely ill individuals in need of love and attention. They are equally capable of giving love and attention. In fact, they may want and need to do so. My son was looking forward to being an usher at church, but I had to talk to a deacon and assure him that he was capable. Once I suggested that Britton could assist me in teaching Sunday school (when he was at our church), because his theological knowledge was impressive and sound. Opportunities should be there if individuals want to take them.

The greatest consolation for me as a Christian, however, has been to see my son grow in God's grace, which is properly the Spirit's work in this "already/not-yet" age. It's interesting to see that Paul's prayers for the churches were not filled with the typical requests we see today (for healing, finances, and so on). He prayed that the Christians' "love may abound more and more, with knowledge and all discernment," that they "may approve what is excellent, and so be pure and blameless for the day of Christ, filled with the fruit of righteousness that comes through Jesus Christ" (Phil. 1:9–11), and that they would have "the eyes of [their] hearts enlightened" and "know what is the hope to which he has called [them], what are the riches of his glorious inheritance in the saints, and what is the immeasurable greatness of his power toward us who believe [. . .] not only *in this age* but *also in the one to come*" (Eph. 1:18–19, 21).

Things Are Not What They Seem

Pessimism largely stems from staring at a negative situation without admitting other scenarios. Christians have an advantage, because they have promises and glimpses of unseen realities.

It's a lesson that the young servant of the prophet Elisha learned when he woke up to find a formidable Syrian army surrounding his city. He knew what this meant. Syrian soldiers were bloodthirsty, destroying and plundering without mercy. He ran instinctively to Elisha, who seemed incongruously unperturbed. "Do not be afraid," the prophet said, "for those who are with us are more than those who are with them" (2 Kings 6:16).

If the young servant was anything like me, he may have dismissed this as theological rhetoric. Yes, yes; I know, the Lord is on our side—but really, "what shall we do?" (v. 15). Our heads are about to become Syrian trophies! At any rate, he must have looked unconvinced, prompting Elisha to pray, "O LORD, please open his eyes that he may see" (v. 17). And there it was. "The LORD opened the eyes of the young man, and he saw, and behold, the mountain was full of horses and chariots of fire all around Elisha" (v. 17).

It's the same lesson the apostle Paul learned while he was traveling in Asia Minor. "For we were so utterly burdened beyond our strength that we despaired of life itself," he said. "Indeed, we felt that we had received the sentence of death" (2 Cor. 1:8–9). In spite of this, he didn't give up hope.

> We are afflicted in every way, but not crushed; perplexed, but not driven to despair; persecuted, but not forsaken; struck down, but not destroyed. . . . So we do not lose heart. Though our outer self is wasting away, our inner self is being renewed day by day. For this light momentary affliction is preparing for us an eternal weight of glory beyond all comparison, as we look not to the things that are seen but to the things that are unseen. For the things that are seen are transient, but the things that are unseen are eternal. (2 Cor. 4:8–9, 16–18)

Understanding the unseen realities makes our prayer all the more relevant, as we realize that "we do not wrestle against flesh and blood, but against the rulers, against the authorities, against the cosmic powers over this present darkness, against the spiritual forces of evil in the heavenly places" (Eph. 6:12). Exodus 17:8–13 gives a great image of this reality, encouraging us to fix our eyes, in the course of a fierce battle, not on the armies and their leaders but on Moses and his raised hands on the nearby hill. God is at war for us through his Son.

The whole book of Revelation is filled with examples of invisible realities and their contradiction with what is visible. Dennis Johnson describes it well in the introduction to his book, *Triumph of the Lamb*: "One of the key themes of the book is that things are not what they seem. The church in Smyrna appears poor but is rich, and it is opposed by those who claim to be Jews but are Satan's synagogue (Rev. 2:9). Sardis has a reputation for life but is dead (3:1). Laodicea thinks itself rich and self-sufficient, but this church is destitute and naked (3:17). The beast seems invincible, able to conquer the saints by slaying them (11:7; 13:7); their faithfulness even to death, however, proves to be their victory over the dragon that empowered the beast (12:11)."[4]

The whole Bible teaches that our limited experience doesn't have the final word in establishing what is real. From its start, it exposes the devil's lie to our first parents and the illusions of man-made idols, gives object lessons through the signs and shadows of the Old Testament, provides glimpses of heaven through Christ's miracles and descriptions of kingdom realities in his parables, and constantly exhorts us to look beyond the constricted kingdom of self in order to get a sense of the much bigger story of God redeeming a people for himself in Christ and of who we and our loved ones are in this context.

The wise recommendations for caregivers to take time off and recharge are extremely limited, temporal, and sometimes impossible to achieve unless they are accompanied by a supernatural opening of our vision. Finding rest and even joy in our situation is possible only when we remember that we are Christ's adopted children, his beloved bride, the sheep of his pasture, his chosen people to whom he is united forever by virtue of a sacred and unbreakable covenant.

4. Dennis E. Johnson, *Triumph of the Lamb: A Commentary on Revelation* (Phillipsburg, NJ: P&R Publishing, 2001), 9.

God with Us

The greatest invisible and comforting reality is the sustaining presence of God, who is with us in Christ in every moment of life. In fact, God's answer to a wide array of bewildering emotions in his people has often been the same: "Fear not; I am with you." It's the answer that he gave to Jacob in the face of a frightful and uncertain future away from home, to Moses in the face of the alarming prospect of returning to a people who had threatened to kill him, to the prophets in the face of their challenging mission to bring a message of warning, and to the people of Israel in the face of their daunting and weary task of fortifying a broken-down city. It's also the last message that Jesus (whose name is also Emmanuel—"God with us") left to his disciples: "I am with you always, to the end of the age" (Matt. 28:20).

God's constant assurance of his presence with us in the face of all our trials reminds us of his sufficiency. He didn't tell Moses, "You can do it; I believe in you." He didn't always promise his people that he would deliver them from their troubles, even if he usually did. He knew that their greatest comfort was simply his presence, because "If God is for us, who can be against us?" (Rom. 8:31). In fact, if he is not with us, we lose every reason to exist, as Moses emphatically explained when God wanted to draw back and send his people to the promised land with only an angel as their guide: "If your presence will not go with me, do not bring us up from here" (Ex. 33:15). In other words, "Leave us in the desert to die. All your promises of victory and prosperity mean nothing without your presence."

An under-realized eschatology tends to ignore this tangible and essential involvement of God in our daily lives, relegating him to a remote space and disregarding the significance of his presence and the accompanying power, strength, and joy that he supplies even now through his Spirit, regardless of our condition. It overlooks the fact that God will sustain us to the end, as he has promised (see 1 Cor. 1:8), simply because he is faithful to his word.

One Day at a Time

Only by being conscious of the concerned presence of God in my life, in the here and now, am I ever able to "take one day at a time"—a piece of advice that is often given to both people with schizophrenia and their caregivers, and especially to those who live in unpredictable and perplexing situations.

"I don't know what the future holds, but I know who holds the future" is certainly a comforting thought—but at times of great impatience, when God truly seems to be sitting with his hands in his pocket (see Ps. 74:11), it's even more comforting to realize how much the triune God is doing in the present, in ways that are often hidden from our eyes, and how much he has done in the past, as we read in the pages of the Bible. Even the simple fact that I still believe is a miracle and a demonstration of God's power, because only God can keep my wandering heart faithful. Theologically speaking, God's kingdom is not yet *consummated* (as is obvious in our suffering), but it has been *inaugurated*, which is clear from the very fact that we are still persevering in the faith. As Scott J. Hafemann, Professor of New Testament at Gordon-Conwell Theological Seminary, wrote, "It is endurance *in the midst of* adversity, not immediate, miraculous deliverance *from* it, that most profoundly reveals the power of God."[5]

5. Scott J. Hafemann, *Paul's Message and Ministry in Covenant Perspective:*

Every day we draw closer to the time of Christ's return, when minds and bodies will be restored. The gap between the "already" and the "not yet" is getting closer. Whenever I wake up with this realization, I find fresh courage. But it's not just a distant hope. Jesus has promised that he would not leave us orphans (see John 14:18). I recognized his intercession and the work of his Spirit every time my son grasped the Scriptures for comfort. Even in the bleakest days, I could look back to every miracle of healing performed by Christ and his apostles, which pointed to that final day.

"Not only is Christ in heaven directing this warfare," Michael Horton wrote, "but he has also sent his Spirit into our hearts to lead the ground campaign. . . . What we need most in times of spiritual and physical trials are not more imperatives (our plans for our victory), but to be reminded again of the triumphant indicatives (God's plan for victory, achieved for us in Christ)."[6]

A Proper Balance

"A proper eschatology will teach us to expect change because of the reality of Christ's work for us and in us by his Spirit," Michael Horton wrote, "but it will also teach us to expect some disappointment and failure—not because we have lost but precisely because we do now belong to Christ and are therefore struggling with indwelling sin."[7]

Selected Essays (Eugene, OR: Cascade Books, 2015), 139. Used by permission of Wipf and Stock Publishers. www.wipfandstock.com

6. Michael Horton, *Too Good to Be True: Finding Hope in a World of Hype* (Grand Rapids: Zondervan, 2006), 147.

7. Michael Horton, *A Better Way: Rediscovering the Drama of God-Centered Worship* (Grand Rapids: Baker Books, 2003), 132.

We all live in a tension between the "already" and the "not yet"—a tension that the apostle Paul underscores in his letter to the Romans. For a mentally ill person, that tension is highlighted, as Dave describes: "You are severely depressed, and there seems to be no hope. You are then highly energetic, and anything seems possible. The inner state of an ill individual can easily find resources that reinforce this condition in perpetuity, especially via the internet. The world is more than happy to entertain both your pessimism and your triumphalism. Entire industries are built around them." The only answer is to hold on to a solid and unmovable anchor, which Dave found in the unchanging gospel.

"That anchor will be there amidst all the confusing internal voices," Dave continued, "and amidst all the confusing—sometimes helpful, and sometimes not helpful—treatments one may seek. Hopefully things will get better. Hopefully treatments of an ordinary variety will help. No matter what, that anchor needs to be there and sought. Come all treatments and opinions and all things ordinary, that anchor needs to be reinforced. Seek help—seek all help, within bounds, as long as that anchor is there. We do not know what will help, but many others have been through this. Take their advice into account, as long as you are able and as long as it is within Scriptural bounds."

Dave speaks from personal experience. "Once I had the gospel, I could move forward. Everything else was and is secondary. From there I sought help. All forms. Some did help; others did not; but I always had a goal—an anchor despite everything. I listened. I watched. I opened doors when I heard knocking, and sometimes doors were opened for me when I did not hear knocking. How this works is beyond me. Does that mean you are instantly healed? Does that mean you are all of a sudden sitting next to Jesus in your right mind, like the demoniac? Probably not—but possibly, as well. I know of cases representing both possibilities, but all of them are unclear as to how it happened. It is beyond our understanding. But in the meantime, in the here and now and amidst the trials of daily life, I keep my eyes on the cross and seek ordinary means with an eye open to the extraordinary."

And for those who mourn the fact that, besides being ill, their loved ones have not professed to believe in Christ, a proper eschatology helps to remember that God is still active today and still performing the greatest miracle of all—the conversion of stony hearts to hearts of flesh that are supernaturally ready and willing to love God and enjoy him forever (see Ezek. 36:26). "With man this is impossible, but with God all things are possible" (Matt. 19:26). As long as our loved ones are alive, there is no reason to give up hope. We can always intercede for them and repeat the good news of the gospel of Christ, who said, "Take heart; I have overcome the world" (John 16:33).

Conclusion

While most people would not classify Jonathan's experience as a success story, the fact that his and our faith survived the ordeal is a testimony to God's grace.

If you feel lonely or misunderstood in your experience or are in the thick of the battle, I hope this book has been helpful. Rereading it during the editing process has been of encouragement to me, as I was going through some of the same situations and was reminded of what gave me strength in the past.

Discussions with other people who have shared similar stories, as well as new personal experiences—this time with more positive encounters and more hopeful prospects—have convinced me that schizophrenia is a generic label and that each case is unique. Recovery—usually through proper medical care and family support—is possible, as many people with schizophrenia can attest, even if their lives might be more challenging than others. And while the mental health system is in need of a serious overhaul, many of those who work in it have sincere love and care for their patients.

Keep hoping and praying. Whatever the outcome, we have a good and powerful God, who "has done [and does] all things well" (Mark 7:37).

Acknowledgments

A list of acknowledgments of all the people who have encouraged me, advised me, and assisted me with this book would take pages. The first person to thank is Patricia Anders, who suggested this project soon after my son died. It has taken me a long time to even come to grips with the idea and with the thought that this book could be helpful to others. I also want to thank my pastor, Michael Brown, who has encouraged me to remember that this book will be an opportunity for me not only to minister to others but also to "share in suffering for the gospel by the power of God" (2 Tim. 1:8).

Rev. Michael Brown, Dr. Michael Horton, Britton Garleb, Brooke Ventura, Rev. Jonathan Cruse, Troy Howell, Rev. Nicholas Davis, Timothy Massaro, Farrah Lennon, Jody Roke, Rev. Zach Keele, Rev. Stephen Donovan, Ellie Charter, and Noah Collins are only some of the many people who have read this manuscript, either partially or entirely, and have offered suggestions and comments. There are many others who have chosen to remain anonymous for the sake of their loved ones.

A special thanks to Dr. Steven Ornish, MD, past

president of the San Diego Psychiatric Society, for his advice on my chapter about doctors and medications ("The Medical Dilemma"), and to Dr. Elyn Saks, associate dean and Orrin B. Evans Professor of Law, Psychology, and Psychiatry and the Behavioral Sciences at the University of Southern California in Los Angeles, for patiently answering my questions in a phone interview.

I thank P&R Publishing, particularly Kristi James and Amanda Martin, for picking up this project and coaching me through the editing process in a timely and caring manner.

A great thanks, of course, goes to my husband and children, who have encouraged me to persist and who never failed to believe that this book would be valuable and uplifting for many who are passing through similar challenges along this earthly, pilgrim way.

Selected Books and Resources

This list includes only some of the books and resources that I have found particularly useful. There are many more out there. Some of these books and websites provide longer lists of their own.

Books

Amador, Xavier. *I Am Not Sick, I Don't Need Help!: How to Help Someone with Mental Illness Accept Treatment.* 10th anniversary ed. New York: Vida Press, 2007. [An excellent book on the common problem of anosognosia (a refusal to acknowledge one's illness and to take necessary medications)].

Bloem, Steve, and Robyn Bloem. *Broken Minds: Hope for Healing When You Feel Like You're "Losing It."* Grand Rapids, MI: Kregel, 2005. [A memoir of a pastor and his struggle with depression. It includes helpful sections and insights on mental illness in general, useful advice from the author's wife, and interesting quotations from Puritan authors.]

Campbell, Bebe Moore. *Sometimes My Mommy Gets Angry.* New York: G. P. Putnam's Sons, 2003. [An interesting and compassionate book for children whose parents are struggling with mental illness. It isn't meant to provide a wide range of coping strategies. For Christians, the conclusion that, in spite of everything, the girl "can find sunshine in her mind" is insufficient and misleading; but parents can use the book as a starting point for honest discussion about a distressing situation and to direct the child to Christ.]

Emlet, Michael R. *Descriptions and Prescriptions: A Biblical Perspective on Psychiatric Diagnoses and Medications.* Greensboro, NC: New Growth Press, 2017. [A short book on mental illness from a Christian (mostly pastoral) perspective.]

Jaffe, DJ. *Insane Consequences: How the Mental Health Industry Fails the Mentally Ill.* Amherst, NY: Prometheus Books, 2017. [A clear, well-researched, and up-to-date source of information on serious mental illness and the US mental health system. Includes practical suggestions.]

Jones, Steven, and Peter Hayward. *Coping with Schizophrenia: A Guide for Patients, Families and Caregivers.* Oxford: Oneworld Publications, 2005. [A positive and helpful guide both for people living with schizophrenia and for their caregivers. Well written and well organized.]

Mueser, Kim T., and Susan Gingerich. *The Complete Family Guide to Schizophrenia: Helping Your Loved One Get the Most Out of Life.* New York: Guilford, 2006. [Its information on medication is somewhat outdated, but the rest of the book includes useful suggestions on how to help a loved one and how to deal with various aspects of his or her illness].

Saks, Elyn R. *The Center Cannot Hold: My Journey through Madness.* New York: Hyperion, 2007. [This book contains the best description of schizophrenia and its environment from the point of view of a person who has overcome many of its challenges.]

Sederer, Lloyd I. *The Family Guide to Mental Health Care.* New York: W.W. Norton & Company, 2013. [Helpful and compassionate, this book includes many good suggestions for families of people who live with mental illness in general. The interesting and well-organized list of resources at the end of this book is a good starting point for learning more about mental illness.]

Shusterman, Neal. *Challenger Deep*. New York: HarperTeen, 2015. [Written as a diary, this book describes the arduous and perplexing experience of a young man who lives with a serious mental illness. While the characters are fictional, the story is based on the struggle of the author's son and its effect on his family. The book ends on a hopeful note. Written for young adults, it is equally valuable for older readers. It provides readers the comfort of knowing that others have walked the same path and have found some form of healing. It's also a good way to introduce serious mental illness to others who might feel puzzled and confused.]

Simpson, Amy. *Troubled Minds: Mental Illness and the Church's Mission*. Downers Grove, IL: InterVarsity Press, 2013. [A comprehensive book on the church's response to mental illness. It includes a good list of Christian books and websites at the end.]

Steel, Craig, ed. *CBT for Schizophrenia: Evidence-Based Interventions and Future Directions*. Hoboken: Wiley-Blackwell, 2013. [A helpful and informative resource on the value of cognitive behavioral therapy for schizophrenia. Its language is academic, but it is well worth the read, as it uncovers very important details, provides practical tools, and facilitates communication with professionals.]

Weaver, Mary Wenger. *Mommy Stayed in Bed This Morning: Helping Children Understand Depression*. Scottdale, PA: Herald Press, 2002. [This book is similar to Bebe Moore Campbell's book; plus, it adds the scenario of hospitalization and the benefits of an understanding and supportive church community. It is meant to help children understand depression, but it can be adapted to include other mental illnesses. It can provide Christians with a starting point for a discussion of God's sovereignty, providence, love, and overarching plan of salvation.]

Websites

"ASIST Two-day Training." LivingWorks. https://www.livingworks .net/programs/asist/ [Living Works offers this two-day training program for suicide prevention.]

Brain and Behavior Research Foundation. https://www.bbrfoundation .org/ [This website is a great source of information, including useful webinars.]

"Caring for People with Psychosis and Schizophrenia." Future-Learn. https://www.futurelearn.com/courses/caring-psychosis -schizophrenia [This is a four-week course for caregivers. It includes excellent tips, and I found it very useful for anyone who either is starting this journey or has been in this situation for a while. It's free of charge, as long as you finish within four weeks.]

"Help with Schizophrenia." American Psychiatric Association. https:// www.psychiatry.org/patients-families/schizophrenia [This is a useful section of the APA's website on schizophrenia.]

Mad in America. https://www.madinamerica.com/ [This website is committed to serving "as a catalyst for rethinking psychiatric care in the United States (and abroad)," as stated in their mission statement. Its contents are controversial, but they provide a good balance for those who want to evaluate psychiatric practices.]

National Alliance on Mental Illness. https://www.nami.org/ [NAMI is the most commonly recommended mental illness organization. Their website includes much useful information and advice. The usefulness of local chapters and phone services is subjective and varies from place to place and from volunteer to volunteer.]

National Institute of Mental Health. https://www.nimh.nih.gov /health/index.shtml [NIMH's website is useful for understanding mental illness in its various forms and for staying informed on the latest research.]

Schizophrenia International Research Society. https://schizophrenia

researchsociety.org/ [SIRS can keep you abreast with the latest research in this field.]

Treatment Advocacy Center. http://www.treatmentadvocacycenter.org/ [This website contains many useful resources, including a section on how to respond in a crisis ("Get Help") and information on anosognosia. It's also a great site for those who want to get involved in fixing a faulty mental health system.]

Other Resources

Brain Myths Exploded: Lessons from Neuroscience. Season 1, episode 3, "Is Mental Illness Just a Chemical Imbalance?" Featuring Indre Viskontas. Released February 2, 2017, by The Great Courses. https://www.amazon.com/Brain-Myths-Exploded-Lessons -Neuroscience/dp/B07575HP2X [The entire course *Brain Myths Exploded: Lessons from Neuroscience* can be purchased from The Great Courses, but this is episode is specifically about mental illness. It provides a clear overview of the concept of chemical imbalance and how it cannot provide by itself a sufficient explanation for mental illness. In fact, relying solely on this explanation can become an impediment to further research and can foster the misleading idea that curing schizophrenia is as easy as popping a couple of pills.]

Simonetta Carr was born in Italy and has lived and worked in different cultures. She worked first as an elementary school teacher and then as a home-schooling mother for many years. The author of a number of books, including the award-winning series Christian Biographies for Young Readers, she writes a regular column, "Cloud of Witnesses," for the Alliance of Confessing Evangelicals, has contributed to newspapers and magazines around the world, and has translated the works of several authors from English into Italian and vice versa. She lives in San Diego with her family, where she is a member and Sunday school teacher at Christ United Reformed Church.

From P&R and the Biblical Counseling Coalition

DAVID R. DUNHAM

MICHAEL SCOTT GEMBOLA

MEGAN HILL

ELYSE FITZPATRICK

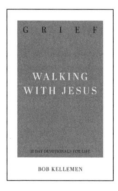

BOB KELLEMEN

DEEPAK REJU

In the 31-Day Devotionals for Life series, biblical counselors and Bible teachers guide you through Scripture passages that speak to specific situations or struggles, helping you to apply God's Word to your life in practical ways day after day.

Devotionals endorsed by Brad Bigney, Kevin Carson, Mark Dever, John Freeman, Gloria Furman, Melissa Kruger, Mark Shaw, Winston Smith, Joni Eareckson Tada, Ed Welch, and more!

Also from P&R Publishing

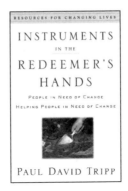

We might be relieved if God placed our sanctification only in the hands of trained professionals, but that is not his plan. Instead, through the ministry of every part of the body, the whole church will mature in Christ.

Paul David Tripp helps us discover where change is needed in our own lives and the lives of others. Following the example of Jesus, Tripp reveals how to get to know people and how to lovingly speak truth to them.

"A wonderful application of the old Gaelic saying, 'God strikes straight blows with crooked sticks.' As inadequate as we are, God is eager to use us to help others change. The more you apply the biblical principles discussed in this book, the more readily you will fit into his mighty hand."

—**Ken Sande**, author of *The Peacemaker: A Biblical Guide to Resolving Personal Conflict*

Also by Simonetta Carr

Olympia Morata (1526–1555) is her father's finest student and a girl far ahead of her time. A quick tongue and a ready pen are her mind's tools to record her vivid thoughts, poetry, songs, and opinions. Appointed tutor to Duchess Renée's children, Olympia looks forward to a bright future—when suddenly, evil rumors threaten to turn her world upside down. In the midst of it all a young doctor comes courting. Will their love survive the danger waiting on the other side of the Alps?

The Chosen Daughters series highlights the lives of ordinary women who by God's grace accomplish extraordinary things.

"Readers will face, with Olympia, the daily dangers and insecurities that accompanied a faithful witness to the truth of the gospel."
—**Starr Meade**, bestselling author of *Training Hearts, Teaching Minds* and *Grandpa's Box*

"With the precision of a scholar and the heart of a storyteller, Simonetta Carr brings to life the story of . . . a daughter of the Italian Reformation."
—**Eric Landry**, executive director of White Horse, Inc., home of *Modern Reformation* and the *White Horse Inn* radio program